WARFARE

A VISUAL
HISTORY

WARFARE

A VISUAL
HISTORY

consultant editor
TIM NEWARK

IVY PRESS

This edition published in the UK in 2016 by
Ivy Press
Ovest House
58 West Street
Brighton
BN1 2RA
United Kingdom
www.quartoknows.com

First published in the UK in 2009

This book was conceived, designed and produced by
Ivy Press
Creative Director: PETER BRIDGEWATER
Publisher: JASON HOOK
Editorial Director: CAROLINE EARLE
Senior Project Editor: JAMES THOMAS
Copy Editors: TOM MUGRIDGE & SIMON SMITH
Art Director: MICHAEL WHITEHEAD
Design: JC LANAWAY
Image Reproduction: LYNDSEY HARWOOD & LES HUNT

British Library Cataloguing-in-Publication Data
A catalogue record for this book is available from
the British Library

ISBN: 978-1-78240-423-1

Printed in China

10 9 8 7 6 5 4 3 2 1

Contents

Introduction

"The ability to gain victory by changing and adapting according to the opponent is called genius"

So wrote the warrior-philosopher Sun Tzu over two thousand years ago in his great work *The Art of War*. Adapting to changing circumstances is indeed a key to military success. In war, victory depends more upon the wit of man, more upon invention and innovation than upon raw strength. That indomitable spirit of overcoming the odds, outwitting an opponent and developing new ideas is the main concern of this book.

What follows is a study of the grammar of warfare, the nuts and bolts of armed conflict, telling the story of how the individual elements of war developed and how they link one with the other. It examines weapons systems, command structures, logistics, organization, communications, recruitment, training, troop types, and the strategy and tactics for their deployment, spanning a period from the earliest known conflicts to the American Civil War. Telecommunications in the form of the telegraph, iron-clad ships, and steam trains to transport men and equipment are just some of the by-products of the industrial revolution that caused the American Civil War to be considered "the first modern war." It also saw the widespread introduction of rifled weapons that shot further and more accurately than anything before, meaning that the carnage was on an unprecedented scale. The progression of warfare to that point of critical mass is a story of constant evolution.

Weapons are developed in an attempt to defeat the latest armor, which itself has evolved to be proof against the weapons of the day. This technological arms race has often been at the forefront of man's scientific discoveries. The ingenuity of military engineers, especially those of the distant past, never fails

to astonish us. In this book we take a close look at many of the most significant (and indeed some of the most surprising) weapons that have been evolved by man. However, weapons systems are only part of the story.

The invention of a weapon leads to the introduction of a new type of troop. He has to be armored appropriately, balancing the level of battlefield risk he will be exposed to with the need for him to be able to operate his weapon effectively, and also factoring in the cost of equipping him. An archer, for instance, is not going to be heavily armored, as it would interfere with his ability to shoot his bow. Moreover, given that battlefield archery depends on mass volume, it would be prohibitively expensive to provide full plate armor for thousands of archers. The advantage of archers is that they are light, mobile troops and can be recruited from the general populace. Knights on the other hand are shock troops whose principal tactic is the impact charge. They need full armored protection, a horse to ride on and spare horses in case their mount is injured. Knights are expensive troops and can only be recruited from the wealthier sections of society who can afford to provide their own equipment. All armies have a mixture of light and heavy troops and, in different circumstances, each has different tactics for success.

Introduction

"Tactics" means the art of deploying troops and equipment in an engagement with the enemy. The great commanders in history have either changed the traditional tactics of their armies or have been able to adapt them in the field to achieve victory. Charting the developments in tactical trends from around the world, our story of military evolution takes us from the chariot warfare of Ancient Egypt and the Near East to the breakthrough of men riding horses into battle and the age of the horse archer. We see how these fluid hit-and-run tactics of the East were in sharp contrast to a tradition of Western fighting that was more concerned with brute strength and head-on engagement, as in the massed pike phalanxes used by Alexander the Great or the massed legions of Rome.

Again, tactical innovation is only one piece of the puzzle. Carl von Clausewitz, an 18th-century Prussian military writer, defined war as "an act of violence

intended to compel our opponent to fulfill our will." Often this will be achieved by winning a series of battles. At other times it will involve a siege of a town or castle (in fact in the history of warfare there have probably been more sieges than there have been battles). Sieges are about controlling the land; they are about *strategic* advantage. Strategy, as distinct from tactics, is a plan to achieve an overall aim, so that by occupying Constantinople, for instance, a power would have military control over the trading routes of both the Dardanelles and the Bosphorus, connecting the Black Sea to the Mediterranean. The means by which a siege is carried out—bombardment with cannon or siege engines, escalade, undermining, starving the occupants by surrounding the walls for months on end—are the *tactics* of the siege. Siege warfare is given a prominent place in the pages that follow.

Numerous factors, including geography, climate, culture, and natural resources, have influenced both the timing and speed of military development around the globe. To reflect this, our narrative is structured both chronologically and by theme. Section one, *The Evolution of Warfare*, forms an overview of how technology and tactics evolved while section two, *Revolutions in Arms and Armor*, focuses in greater detail on the development of weapons.

Although covering an extremely wide range of cultures and epochs, the 19th-century illustrations used throughout the book serve to unify the story. This was an age of pioneering scholarship and although from time to time the Victorian artist exercised his license, he generally had a good eye for fine detail and created wonderfully evocative images. On the few occasions where the original artist has slipped in his interpretation of ancient technology, the writers have pointed out where this is at variance to present-day thinking. It all adds to the interest of this most fascinating of subjects.

THE EVOLUTION
OF WARFARE

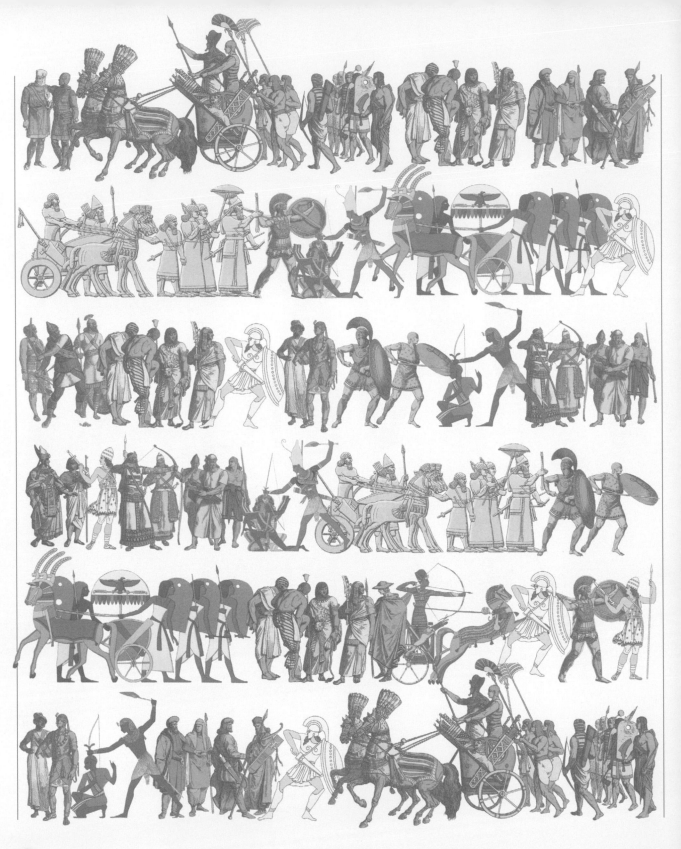

The Ancient Way of War
3000–323 BCE

This chapter considers the evolution of warfare from the dawn of civilization to the death of Alexander the Great, a period spanning nearly three thousand years. However, warfare was already ancient when the first complex civilizations arose *c.* 3000 BCE, so some comments about its origins seem appropriate.

A shadowy prototype of human warfare can be seen among chimpanzees, whose bands carry out lethal raids and ambushes against members of neighboring bands. However, these do not give rise to organized conflicts between entire bands. The human species became capable of a much higher level of organization when it developed the "tribe," a federation of kinship groups united partly by biological ties but also by ethnic markers such as language, customs, symbols, and art styles. Among other animals, cooperative activity is limited to small groups of close kin, but the tribes of mankind are capable of organized conflicts involving hundreds of individuals. Such tribal warfare probably appeared as soon as *Homo sapiens* acquired sufficient cognitive ability to create ethnic markers—at the latest by the Upper Paleolithic, some fifty thousand years ago, when a sudden explosion of the visual arts provides the first certain evidence of advanced cognitive levels. Since then conflict between groups of increasing size has been a standard feature and an important trigger of cultural evolution.

The rise of complex societies did not alter the basic pattern of warfare, but made it possible to mobilize resources far larger than those of tribal societies. Differentiated kinds of soldier appeared: in the late Bronze Age (*c.* 1650 BCE) the horsed chariot introduced mobility; the early Iron Age (*c.* 1000 BCE) brought the first disciplined infantry, the first cavalry, the idea of using different arms in combination, and the first effective siege trains. In the 7th century BCE the Greeks used heavy infantry in shock combat. In the 4th century BCE the Macedonians added heavy cavalry and the first artillery. The army of Alexander fused all this into a military machine that was not essentially improved upon until the gunpowder age.

Ancient Egypt at War, *3000–1000* BCE

The Old and Middle Kingdoms

The history of Egypt was divided in ancient times into thirty dynasties. Modern Egyptologists have divided it into three major periods called the Old Kingdom, the Middle Kingdom, and the New Kingdom, separated by "intermediate periods" when the country broke apart into petty principalities. The Old Kingdom, from the 3rd to the 6th dynasties (2686–2181 BCE), was the age of the pyramids, when the foundations of Egyptian civilization were laid. The First Intermediate Period lasted from 2181 to 2040 BCE. Then the pharaonic system was restored under the Middle Kingdom (11th and 12th dynasties, 2040–1786 BCE). In the Old Kingdom the only standing army was a royal bodyguard. The Middle Kingdom felt need of more serious military organization, and even conducted occasional raids into the Levant.

Shields

The Egyptian shield was made of a cowhide stretched over a wooden frame, usually tapering toward the top (left). It could be slung on a soldier's back to allow him to use his arms, for example in siege work (right).

Nubians

Nubia, or the upper Nile valley, now divided between Egypt and Sudan, was called *Kush* by the Egyptians. Nubia became a united kingdom almost as early as Egypt and produced a distinct Nubian civilization marked by pervasive Egyptian influence. Egyptians had frequent commercial contacts with Nubia, trading for ivory, gold, ostrich plumes, leopard skins, and other African products, and there were frequent military expeditions, probably to control the trade routes. In this image, a king rides in an ox-drawn cart, with pyramids of the distinctive narrow Nubian shape in the background. The king's attendants and a scribe (Nubians wrote in Egyptian hieroglyphics) are also pictured.

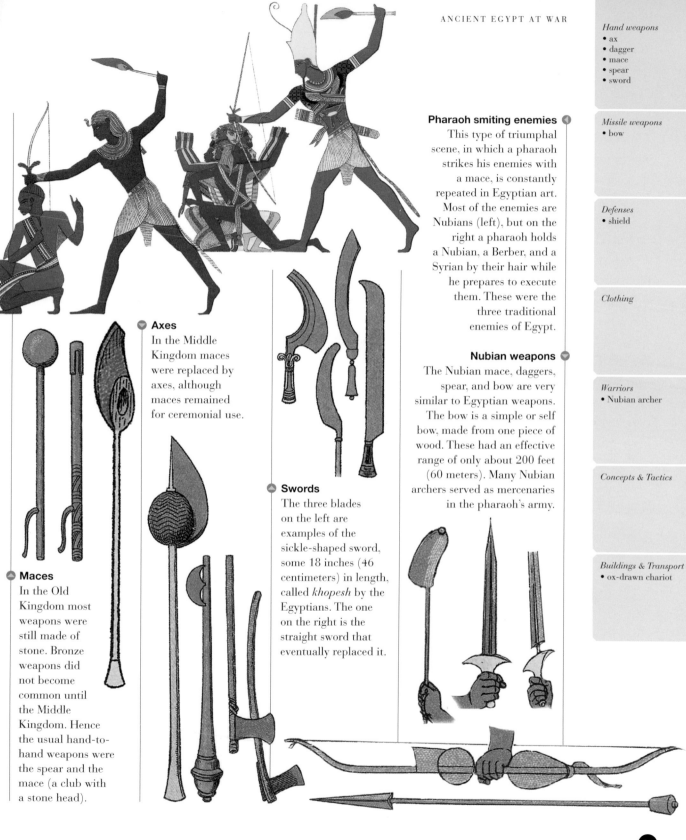

Hand weapons
• ax
• dagger
• mace
• spear
• sword

Missile weapons
• bow

Defenses
• shield

Clothing

Warriors
• Nubian archer

Concepts & Tactics

Buildings & Transport
• ox-drawn chariot

Pharaoh smiting enemies

This type of triumphal scene, in which a pharaoh strikes his enemies with a mace, is constantly repeated in Egyptian art. Most of the enemies are Nubians (left), but on the right a pharaoh holds a Nubian, a Berber, and a Syrian by their hair while he prepares to execute them. These were the three traditional enemies of Egypt.

Nubian weapons

The Nubian mace, daggers, spear, and bow are very similar to Egyptian weapons. The bow is a simple or self bow, made from one piece of wood. These had an effective range of only about 200 feet (60 meters). Many Nubian archers served as mercenaries in the pharaoh's army.

Axes

In the Middle Kingdom maces were replaced by axes, although maces remained for ceremonial use.

Swords

The three blades on the left are examples of the sickle-shaped sword, some 18 inches (46 centimeters) in length, called *khopesh* by the Egyptians. The one on the right is the straight sword that eventually replaced it.

Maces

In the Old Kingdom most weapons were still made of stone. Bronze weapons did not become common until the Middle Kingdom. Hence the usual hand-to-hand weapons were the spear and the mace (a club with a stone head).

15

Ancient Egypt at War

New Kingdom: tactics and technology

During the long Third Intermediate Period the Nile
Delta was occupied by invaders from Asia known to
the Egyptians as "Hyksos." When Egypt was reunited
by the rulers of Thebes in the 16th century BCE, it could
no longer afford its splendid isolation. Egypt became an
imperial power, ruling all of Nubia and much of the
Levant. The New Kingdom (18th–20th dynasties) was
the height of Egyptian power, wealth, and splendor.
There was a large standing army, in which the most
important element was chariotry. The light two-horse
chariot had been invented in Anatolia *c.* 1650 BCE and
was introduced into Egypt by the Hyksos. In the Late
Bronze Age (1550–1069 BCE), something like our idea
of international relations appeared, with several
powers in constant diplomatic contact.

See also
**The Old and
Middle Kingdoms,**
pages 14–15
**Clubs, maces,
and axes,**
pages 286–7

The Pharaoh goes to war

In the Late Bronze Age a unique kind of
warfare was developed in which the only
effective offensive arms consisted of horsed
chariots firing composite bows. Infantry
probably played no part in the action
except to guard camps and city walls.
The group depicted below following the
standards is probably realistic in its loose
formation and heterogenous equipment:
spears, axes, maces, *khopesh* swords, and
simple bows.

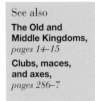

Courtiers of the New Kingdom

The Egyptian state became heavily militarized in the New Kingdom. A new aristocratic warrior class arose and the military elite, especially the commanders of chariots, tended to replace the traditional scribal elite as the pharaoh's chief counselors.

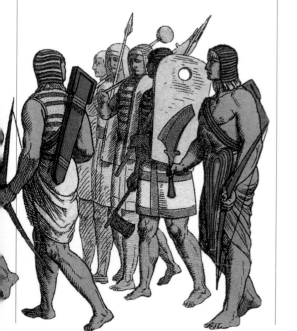

Pharaoh of the New Kingdom

A pharaoh is pictured here with an official. The image of the pharaoh also became heavily militarized. In the Old and Middle Kingdoms pharaohs were portrayed as benign gods in repose. But in the New Kingdom the pharaoh is typically shown as a chariot warrior shooting his bow (*see page 19*).

Ancient Egypt at War

The chariot

The original range of the wild horse was the Eurasian steppe, where it was probably domesticated in the fourth millennium BCE, and was used primarily as a food animal. Wheeled vehicles were invented *c.* 3000 BCE but were heavy wagons drawn by oxen (*see page 14*). The light two-horse chariot was invented in the 17th century BCE, perhaps in Anatolia, and was probably used for hunting, which always remained one of the favorite uses of the chariot in antiquity. By about 1650 BCE chariots were being used for warfare, and made possible the rise of the Hittite kingdom in Anatolia and the invasion of Egypt by the Hyksos. The two major powers of the Late Bronze Age were Egypt and the Hittite kingdom; the Levant was the battleground between them.

Egyptians pursuing Canaanites
The Egyptians always portrayed their enemies, Hittites or Canaanites (Syrians), using spears, not bows, hence many modern scholars have assumed Asians really did use spears from chariots. That would be a physical impossibility; they were surely armed with bows like the Egyptians. Egyptian iconography required enemies to be portrayed as weak and helpless.

Egyptian chariotry
The chariot was simply a mobile platform for archery, capable of speeds up to 10 miles (16 kilometres) per hour. The Egyptian chariot shown here carries two men, one a driver and shield-bearer, the other an archer equipped with a composite bow, which had twice the range of a simple bow (*see page 15*). A quiver and a bowcase hang by the side of the chariot.

See also
Bows,
pages 290–1
Body armor,
pages 302–3

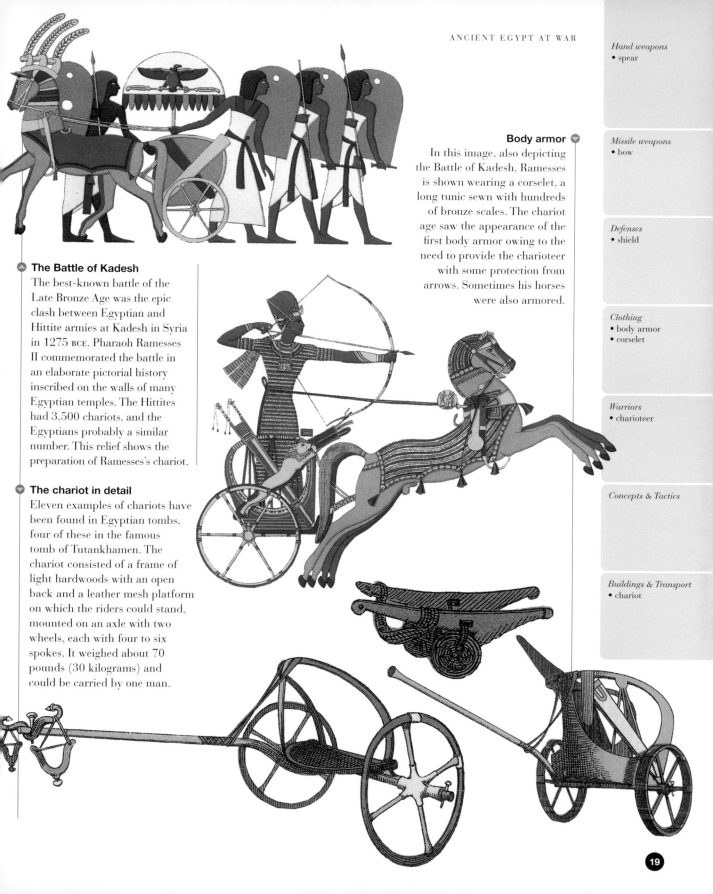

Body armor ○

In this image, also depicting the Battle of Kadesh, Ramesses is shown wearing a corselet, a long tunic sewn with hundreds of bronze scales. The chariot age saw the appearance of the first body armor owing to the need to provide the charioteer with some protection from arrows. Sometimes his horses were also armored.

○ **The Battle of Kadesh**

The best-known battle of the Late Bronze Age was the epic clash between Egyptian and Hittite armies at Kadesh in Syria in 1275 BCE. Pharaoh Ramesses II commemorated the battle in an elaborate pictorial history inscribed on the walls of many Egyptian temples. The Hittites had 3,500 chariots, and the Egyptians probably a similar number. This relief shows the preparation of Ramesses's chariot.

○ **The chariot in detail**

Eleven examples of chariots have been found in Egyptian tombs, four of these in the famous tomb of Tutankhamen. The chariot consisted of a frame of light hardwoods with an open back and a leather mesh platform on which the riders could stand, mounted on an axle with two wheels, each with four to six spokes. It weighed about 70 pounds (30 kilograms) and could be carried by one man.

Assyria, *c.1000–612* BCE

Assyria: tactics and technology

In the Bronze Age, Mesopotamia was divided into many warring city-states. There were occasional attempts to unite the region under one ruler; the first Mesopotamian empire was that of Sargon of Akkad, *c.* 2300 BCE. But none of these empires lasted long. In the Late Bronze Age two great kingdoms arose, Babylonia in the south and Assyria in the north; both, like New Kingdom Egypt and the Hittite kingdom, relied on chariot armies. At the end of the Bronze Age there was a general decline of civilization across the Middle East. The Iron Age, which began *c.* 1000 BCE, brought radical changes in the art of war: disciplined infantry formations appeared for the first time and armies generally became armies of infantry. The empires of the Iron Age acquired unprecedented size and power, and the first of these was the Assyrian empire.

See also
Bows, *pages 290–1*
Siege engines, *pages 294–5*
Shields, *pages 306–7*

Assyrian siegecraft

The most dreaded component of the Assyrian army was its siege train. On the right are two different types of battering rams on wheels. Ramming, escalade with ladders, and sapping (undermining the walls) were used simultaneously in storming fortifications. The siege tower in the rear carried archers who protected the men carrying out this work.

Heavy infantry

The Assyrian heavy infantryman (*kallapu*) was equipped with a spear, large circular shield, conical iron helmet, and cuirass of scale armor; these heavy infantry were recruited from the native Assyrians and formed the backbone of the army. Auxiliaries, recruited largely from Aramaean tribes, were more lightly armed, some with spears and others with bows or slings.

Hunting party

The figures on the left are Assyrian royals with composite bows, preparing for battle or hunting. One wears the Assyrian royal crown, a flat-topped miter. They are accompanied by lightly armed foot soldiers and a zither player.

Assyria

Assyria: tactics and technology

The Assyrian homeland was a 100-mile (160-kilometer) strip along the upper Tigris river containing Assur, the ancient religious capital, and the imperial capital Nimrud. In the Late Bronze Age Assyria had been a great power, controlling all of the northern Mesopotamian plain between the Tigris and the Euphrates. At the start of the Iron Age the kingdom was reduced to the original heartland, but in the 9th century BCE Assyrian power was revived, based on an infantry army. Ashurnasirpal II (reigned 883–859 BCE) restored the previous frontiers and acquired a cordon of client states in northern Syria that stretched to the Mediterranean. Under Tiglath-Pileser III (744–727 BCE) this became the first centralized empire in history, and united Assyria and Babylonia. In the 7th century BCE, Egypt was added to the empire.

The king and his court

A king at the gate of his palace has dismounted from his portable throne, surrounded by courtiers and musicians. The empire was divided into some eighty provinces under governors who were required to report constantly to the court. It was the largest and most complex state that had ever been created, ruling several million people. The total armed forces available may have numbered half a million men.

The mature Assyrian army 750–612 BCE

This palace relief shows heavy infantry (spear and shield), light infantry (bow and sling), and cavalry, some with bows and some with spears. Spearmen and archers seem to have worked in cooperation. It is likely that battles were won mostly by archery, and the spearmen moved in to mop up a defeated enemy.

See also
The chariot,
pages 18–19

Assyrian chariotry

The Assyrian chariot was heavier than the Egyptian, sometimes carrying three men: a driver, an archer, and a shield-bearer.

Riding in pairs

The art of effective riding was developed *c.* 1000 BCE, probably on the Eurasian steppe. The Assyrians adopted the art from nomadic peoples in the 9th century BCE, but at first used riders in pairs, one man holding the reins while the other fired his bow. By *c.* 750 BCE Assyrians had become sufficiently proficient riders that they could dispense with the second rider and the chariot became obsolete for military purposes.

King's chariot

In the 8th century BCE, the Assyrian chariot was replaced by cavalry and continued in use only as a prestige vehicle. Kings are usually portrayed riding in a heavy four-horse, four-man chariot under a parasol.

Hand weapons
• spear

Missile weapons
• bow
• sling

Defenses
• shield

Clothing

Warriors
• archer
• cavalry
• infantry
• spearman

Concepts & Tactics

Buildings & Transport
• chariot

23

Greece at War, *1200–300 BCE*

The Bronze Age to Classical Greece

In the Late Bronze Age, the Greek-speaking world (the lands around the Aegean Sea) was closely tied to the Middle East and its warfare resembled that of Western Asia. At the close of the Bronze Age (*c.* 1200 BCE) came a largely mysterious upheaval when the palaces and citadels around the eastern Mediterranean were nearly all sacked. There followed a dark age of some four centuries, during which city life around the Aegean faded away and the art of writing was lost. When civilization began to revive in the 8th century BCE it was a new type of society, known to us as Classical Greece, unconnected with the Orient and characterized by a novel art of war based on heavy infantry in shock combat.

● Homeric warfare

The earliest written descriptions of Greek warfare are the two long epics attributed to Homer, the *Iliad* and the *Odyssey*, probably composed around the 8th century BCE. They depict the legendary war of the Greeks against Troy, which was supposed to have happened *c.* 1200 BCE, and must have been part of the general crisis that put an end to the Bronze Age world. However, Homer lived four centuries later and knew only confused traditions about the Bronze Age Greeks (also called Mycenaean or Achaean Greeks).

● Heroic combat

This figure from a vase painting shows how the later Greeks visualized the battle scenes in the Homeric poems. The heroes wear heavy armor and carry large round shields and long spears like the later Greek hoplites, but instead of fighting in massed phalanx formations they challenge one another to individual duels.

See also
Assyrian chariotry,
pages 22–3
Body armor,
pages 302–3

Greek chariots

One of the elements of Achaean warfare accurately described in the *Iliad* is the use of chariots—but the poets had forgotten how chariots were actually used. Homer's heroes ride to battle in their chariots but then dismount and fight on foot. It is more probable that Mycenaean chariots were mobile platforms for archery, just like Asian chariots, though the rugged Greek terrain may have placed more importance on fighting on foot.

Amazons

The Greeks believed that on the steppes north of the Black Sea lived a tribe of manless women warriors called Amazons. Greek mythology contains many stories about battles between Amazons and Greek heroes such as Theseus and Hercules. The Amazons in this image are wearing Persian costume.

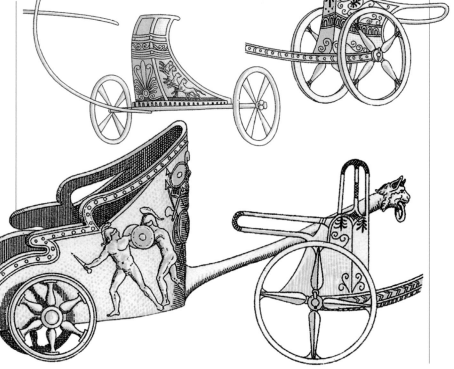

Greece at War

Classical Greece: tactics and technology

In the 7th century BCE, there developed the
peculiar Greek way of war that relied on a type
of heavy-armored infantryman called a hoplite,
organized into a close-packed formation called
a phalanx, usually about eight ranks deep.
The problem with shock weapons had always
been the difficulty of making soldiers come to
close combat, hence the general preference
for missile weapons. The phalanx solved
this problem because the sheer depth of
the formation literally threw the men in the
front ranks onto the spears of the enemy.

Spartan training

Phalanx warfare may
have been invented in
Sparta, whose army was the most feared in
Greece. The peculiar Spartan culture was
highly militaristic and communistic: men lived
in barracks and underwent a fantastically
rigorous training called the *agoge* (upbringing).
When a young man went to war, his mother
gave him his shield and told him to come back
with the shield or on it.

Classical Greek soldiers

Several types of
soldier are shown
here. Cavalry were
recruited from
wealthy citizens who
could afford horses,
and were used mostly
for reconnaissance.
Light infantry were
recruited from poor
citizens and used as
skirmishers. But the
main type of soldier
was the hoplite, who
came from a middling
background and could
afford the armor and
shield. The hoplite at
the top has not yet put
on his bucket-shaped
helmet, which covered
the entire head. A
helmet of the type
called "Corinthian"
is also shown here.

Hoplite armor

The hoplite's body was protected by a bronze cuirass (left). By the 5th century BCE this was generally replaced by a more flexible cuirass of canvas strengthened with metal scales, with strips of canvas hanging from its lower edge to protect the groin (right).

Hoplite helmets

Two common styles of helmet are shown here, called by modern archeologists the "Corinthian" helmet (top), which covered the entire head, and the more open "Attic" type (bottom). The helmets were not particularly associated with Corinth or Attica.

See also
Anatomy of a phalanx, *pages 38–9*
Weapons of reach, *pages 284–5*
Body armor, *pages 302–3*
Helmets, *pages 304–5*
Shields, *pages 306–7*

Hoplite arms

The main offensive weapon was a spear about 8 feet (2.5 meters) long, usually made of cornel wood with an iron head. A short sword, 2 feet (60 centimeters) long, was used only if the spear broke.

Leg protection

Often the hoplite wore metal greaves to guard his lower legs.

Hoplite shields

The big hoplite shield (*hoplon*) with its convex interior, held by an arm band and hand grip, is shown here. Made of wood faced with bronze, it was designed to cover the hoplite from chin to knees, and also the unprotected right side of the man standing to his left, thus presenting a solid wall of shields to the enemy.

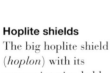

Hand weapons
- spear
- sword

Missile weapons

Defenses
- shield

Clothing
- "Attic" helmet
- "Corinthian" helmet
- cuirass
- greaves

Warriors
- hoplite

Concepts & Tactics
- phalanx

Buildings & Transport

Greece at War

Defending the republic

Greek warfare was characterized by an ideology we can describe as "civic militarism." This was the military aspect of what was later called "republicanism": the belief in a body of self-governing citizens whose primary duty is to defend their republic (Greek *polis*, Latin *res publica*), which in the ancient world meant a small city-state. A free citizenry in arms was considered superior to armies of conscripts or mercenaries because its solidarity and high morale was capable of producing soldiers willing to fight as heavy infantry in close order. A formation of heavy infantry could be used most effectively in the offensive, creating a tendency to settle wars by a single decisive battle. The citizen militia and offensive tactics became the main characteristics of a kind of warfare unique to Western civilization.

Peltasts

In the later 5th century BCE, Greek warfare became more complicated and much more use was made of light infantry (*peltasts*), usually armed with javelins and carrying a light shield. At first they were recruited from Thracian mercenaries, but poor Greek citizens who could not afford armor also served as *peltasts*.

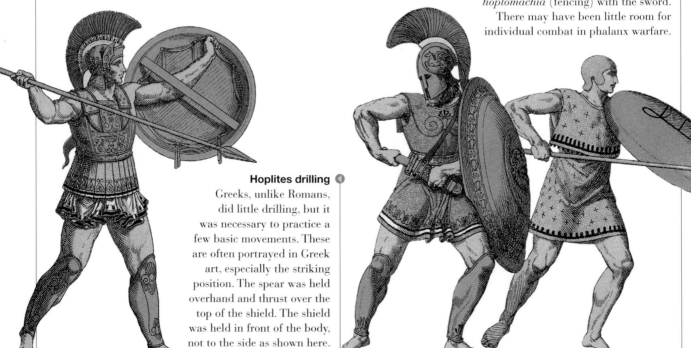

Fencing practice

The hoplite on the left is practicing *hoplomachia* (fencing) with the sword. There may have been little room for individual combat in phalanx warfare.

Hoplites drilling

Greeks, unlike Romans, did little drilling, but it was necessary to practice a few basic movements. These are often portrayed in Greek art, especially the striking position. The spear was held overhand and thrust over the top of the shield. The shield was held in front of the body, not to the side as shown here.

Hoplites in individual combat

In the original style of phalanx warfare, the only tactic was the frontal charge and no soldiers mattered but the hoplites. However, when one phalanx or the other broke there may have been duels between individual hoplites like the one pictured here. The man on the left has lost his spear and drawn his sword.

Siege warfare equipment

Siegecraft played little part in Greek warfare until the 4th century BCE, when Eastern siege tactics were introduced. Greeks invented the catapult (*katapaltes*, "shield-piercer"), the first artillery, *c.* 400 BCE. The earliest catapult, the *gastraphetes* ("belly-shooter") worked like a large crossbow (*1*). In the late 4th century BCE came the torsion catapult, powered by twisted skeins of hair or sinew, firing either darts or stones. Enormous siege towers also came into use (*2*).

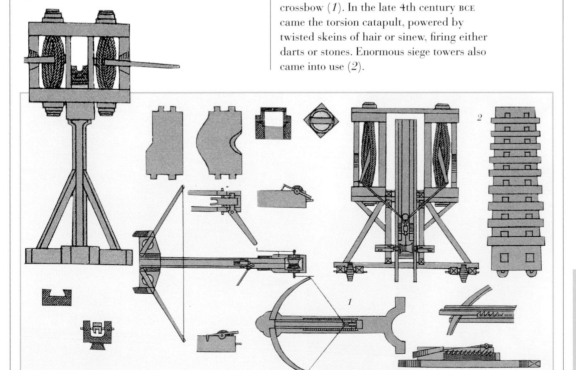

See also
Crossbows,
pages 292–3
Siege engines,
pages 294–5

Hand weapons
• spear
• sword

Missile weapons
• catapult

Defenses
• shield

Clothing

Warriors
• hoplite
• *peltast*

Concepts & Tactics
• civic militarism
• phalanx
• siegecraft

Buildings & Transport

Scythians and Sarmatians, *c. 1000–300 BCE*

Horse nomads of the steppe

Around the 10th century BCE, the invention of the metal bit made possible the art of effective horseback riding. The foot nomads of the Eurasian steppe were converted to an equestrian way of life and became a threat to the settled peoples to the south. The first horse people to emerge into history were the Scythians, a collection of Iranian tribes who inhabited the grasslands north of the Black and Caspian Seas. They were first described by Greek writers in the 5th century BCE. In the 3rd century BCE the Sarmatians, a group of Iranian tribes originally inhabiting Central Asia, migrated westward and replaced the Scythians on the European steppe. All steppe nomads fought entirely on horseback and avoided pitched battle, retreating before organized armies and harassing them with arrows from composite bows.

Artifacts
These images show bronze arrowheads, a pin in the form of a bird and a knife hilt carved with tigers or leopards.

Scythian weapons
A gold decorative plaque features a horseman armed with a long lance. Scythians used two kinds of spears, the lance and a short javelin. Another plaque shows two archers on foot; notice the short Scythian recurved bow, well suited for use on horseback.

Grave goods
Scythian tombs, which dot the steppes of southern Russia and Ukraine, have yielded rich grave goods decorated in the distinctive "animal style" designs of the steppe, which tell us much about the nomads' equipment and way of life. This gold vessel shows two spearmen in conversation.

See also
Bows, *pages 290–1*
Helmets, *pages 304–5*

Scythian warriors
These Scythian warriors are identified by their trousers, boots, and hoods. They are armed with composite bows and carry small shields. The man on the left carries a *gorytos*, a combination bow case and quiver.

Sarmatian helmet and shield

At the top of the picture is a Spangenhelm helmet with cheek pieces and a leather neck guard. Below it is a shield of the type carried by light cavalry.

Cataphract

The Sarmatians mostly fought as light cavalry, but they also developed a type of very heavy cavalry called *kataphraktoi* (Greek for "completely covered"): both horse and rider wore full scale or mail armor, though this is exaggerated in the relief on Trajan's Column, on which this figure is based. Cataphracts were armed with a *kontos*, a spear up to 15 feet (4.5 meters) long. They also carried bows; this rider shoots backwards as he retreats—the famous "Parthian shot" was used by all the steppe riders, not just Parthians. Cataphracts were later incorporated into the Roman army and became the prototype of the medieval knight.

Sarmatian weapons

On the left are a battle ax, carried by heavy cavalry, a sword, and knives.

Sarmatian warriors

The Sarmatians were closely related to the Scythians. They were allies of the Dacians (inhabitants of modern Romania) against Rome, hence some Sarmatians are represented on Trajan's Column commemorating the Dacian Wars of the emperor Trajan (2nd century CE). One of these wears a tunic of scale armor and a conical helmet of the Spangenhelm type, made of metal strips; this would become the most common European helmet of early medieval times. Next to him (far left) stands a warrior in a curious armor known only from Trajan's Column, which appears to be made of leather bands.

Hand weapons
- ax
- knife
- *kontos*
- lance
- sword

Missile weapons
- composite bow
- javelin
- recurved bow

Defenses
- shield

Clothing
- armor
- Spangenhelm helmet

Warriors
- archer
- heavy cavalry (cataphract)
- light cavalry

Concepts & Tactics
- fighting on horseback (Parthian shot)

Buildings & Transport

Persia, *c. 625–334 BCE*

Persia: tactics and technology

The Iranian (Aryan) peoples, whose most important branches were the Medes and the Persians, were originally Central Asian horse nomads who occupied the Iranian plateau early in the last millennium BCE. They retained their skills at horsemanship and archery but soon learned to rule agricultural peoples instead of raiding them. In *c.* 625 BCE the Medes, whose homeland lay in the Zagos mountains of western Iran, put together a vast but probably loosely organized kingdom stretching from eastern Anatolia across Iran. In 550 BCE Cyrus, king of the Persians (inhabitants of Persis in southwestern Iran) overthrew the Median king and within a decade created the largest empire yet, embracing all of Iran, Mesopotamia, and Anatolia. Later rulers of his dynasty, the Achaemenids, added Egypt and parts of India and Central Asia.

▶ **Soldiers of the Persian Empire**
The figure on the left of the picture is an Achaemenid prince, wearing the distinctive hood (*tiara*) of the Persian elite.

▶ **The Immortals**
The two figures on the right of the picture are members of the Immortals, the crack infantry troops of the Persian army, numbering exactly ten thousand. They were divided into ten units, the first of which formed the royal bodyguard. They were armed with both spear and bow but were essentially archers. The Persians relied on archery even more than the Assyrians had done before them.

The Great King of Persia in his court

Cyrus the Great (reigned 559–530 BCE) divided his empire into large provinces called *satrapies*, of which there were, eventually, about twenty. The army was distributed throughout the empire under the command of the *satraps*, who were normally Persians or Iranians. The main capitals were Persepolis in Persis (ceremonial capital), Susa in Elam (winter capital), and Ecbatana in Media (summer capital).

Persians and Medes

In this picture, a Persian noble stands between two Medes. The Persians and Medes were closely related; Greeks often referred to Persians as "Medes." Persians, Medes and to some extent other Iranians made up the ruling elite of the empire, but they ruled the *satrapies* through local elites, using Aramaic as the administrative language. In general they were lightly armored, owing to a reliance on missile weapons.

Persia

Fall of the Persian Empire

The relative ease with which Alexander of Macedon (*see page 36*) conquered the Achaemenid empire has often been taken as evidence of deep structural weaknesses in the Persian empire. But there seems to be no real evidence that the empire was in a state of decay. It had held together for more than two hundred years despite many internal revolts, succession disputes, and frontier problems, and kept its vast territory intact right up to the time of Alexander's invasion in 334 BCE. The most important loss of territory had been the secession of Egypt *c*. 400 BCE; but this loss was not permanent, and Egypt was recovered sixty years later. It should be remembered that it took Alexander twelve years of continuous hard fighting to subdue the entire empire. There are, however, signs of growing military weakness in the late 4th century BCE. The Persian elite seem to have been losing their archery skills, for in the battles with Alexander, the Iranian nobles mostly fought with javelins, a missile weapon far inferior to the composite bow. But the main weakness was the failure to adapt to the new style of warfare developed by the Greeks (*see pages 26–9*).

Bedouin Arab camp ◗
Fully developed nomad pastoralism appeared on the fringes of the great empires in the last millennium BCE, made possible by the spread of riding animals. Pastoral tribes, whether camel nomads like these Bedouins, or horse nomads like the steppe peoples, were not incorporated into the empires but left to be independent, serving the Assyrian and Persian armies as mercenaries using missile weapons.

Hand weapons

Missile weapons
• composite bow
• javelin

Defenses

Clothing

Warriors

Concepts & Tactics

Buildings & Transport
• camel
• horse
• scythed chariot

Scythed chariots

One of the most bizarre features of the Persian army was the use of chariots with scythe-like blades fixed to the wheels. It was the last attempt in the Middle East to use chariots as a serious military weapon, and was probably intended as a psychological tactic to terrify inexperienced infantry. It was rarely used and never very successful, as it was easy to stop the vehicles with missiles.

Battle of Issus, 333 BCE

The Persian empire collapsed with dramatic suddenness when the Greco-Macedonian army of Alexander the Great invaded. In this detail from the Alexander Mosaic found at Pompeii, the last Great King, Darius III, turns to flee from the battle in his chariot.

See also
Alexander the Great,
pages 36–7

Alexander the Great, *336–323 BCE*

A peerless army

The Macedonians, who lived just north of peninsular Greece, were ethnically Greek, but the southern Greeks considered them almost barbarians and affected not to understand their dialect. The kingdom was not so much a state as an unusually anarchic chiefdom that imploded in a succession crisis every generation or so. Alexander the Great's father, King Philip II (reigned 359–336 BCE), turned this backwater into a powerful kingdom with a peerless army. He greatly expanded his force of heavy cavalry, the 600 Companions, recruited from Macedonian nobles, and also organized an army of hoplite infantry recruited from the Macedonian peasantry. Thus his army comprised both heavy infantry and heavy cavalry, capable of working in combination: the infantry pinned the enemy down while the cavalry circled to charge into the enemy's flank or rear.

The phalanx in action
When the pikes were lowered to charge, the phalanx resembled a giant porcupine. This illustration of a battle of Macedonians against Persians conveys a striking impression of its irresistible advance. With these formations, Alexander conquered the Persian empire in three battles—the Granicus (334 BCE), Issus (333 BCE, *see page 34–5*), and Gaugamela (331 BCE).

See also
Weapons of reach, *pages 284–5*
Siege engines, *pages 294–5*

● Macedonian catapults

Both Philip II and Alexander were interested in siege tactics. Here, two torsion catapults are shown, a dart-thrower on the left and a stone-thrower on the right. Alexander's most famous siege was the siege of Tyre (332 BCE), a Phoenician city thought impregnable because it stood on an island half a mile from the shore. Alexander had to build a mole out from the shore to reach the walls with his catapults. Tyre fell after a seven-month siege.

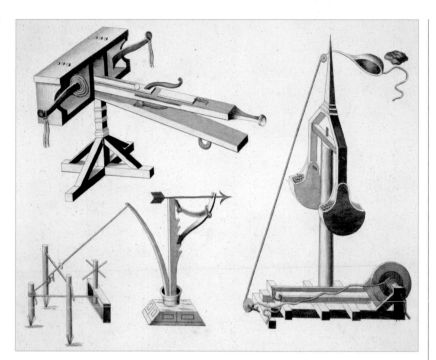

A fanciful battle ◀

In 335 BCE, Philip's son Alexander III, called "the Great," campaigned in the Balkans against Thracians and Illyrians. This mid-19th-century reconstruction of that campaign is colorful but almost totally fictional: the Macedonians are shown in combat with Dacians and Sarmatian cataphracts, who were not found in this region at the time; and using war elephants, which the Macedonians did not encounter until years later.

Anatomy of a Phalanx

The Macedonian phalanx was at
the heart of Alexander the Great's
war machine. While he might lead a
cavalry attack against his opponents,
his back would be protected by the
massive deadly presence of these
spear-armed men.

1 The basic unit of the phalanx was
the *speira*, which numbered about
256 men. They fought in tight order
some sixteen ranks deep. When the
phalanx advanced against the enemy,
the first five ranks would lower their
spears with their weapons carefully
passing between them. The remaining
ranks held their spears upward,
ready to step into any gaps caused
by casualties. The raised spears also
helped to deflect any arrows.

2 The long spear held by the
Macedonian *phalangite* was, in fact, a
pike, like that used by later warriors in
the Middle Ages and early gunpowder
period. It was about 14 cubits long,
just over 20 feet (6 meters), and was
called a *sarissa*. To help with handling
this extremely long weapon, it was
weighted at the butt end.

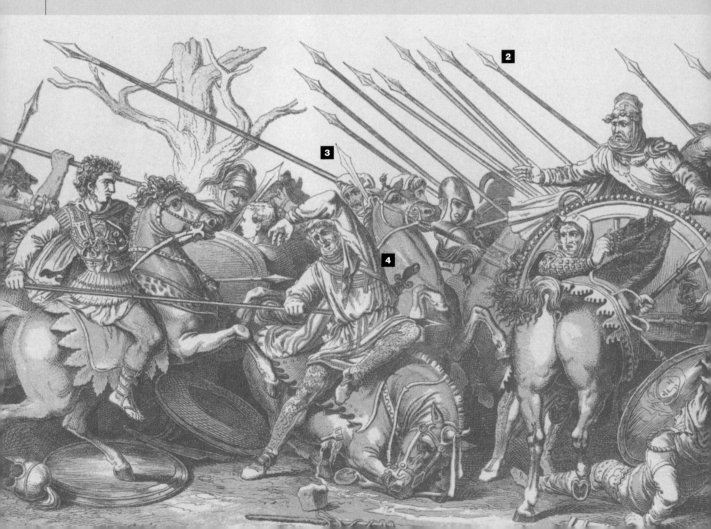

3 In addition to his pike, the *phalangite* carried a single-edged sword with a curved blade, called a *kopis*. He carried a small round shield called an *aspis*, made out of bronze, and wore body armor covering his torso and thighs made out of overlapping metal scales, interlinked mail, or reinforced linen. Typically, he wore a crested bronze helmet.

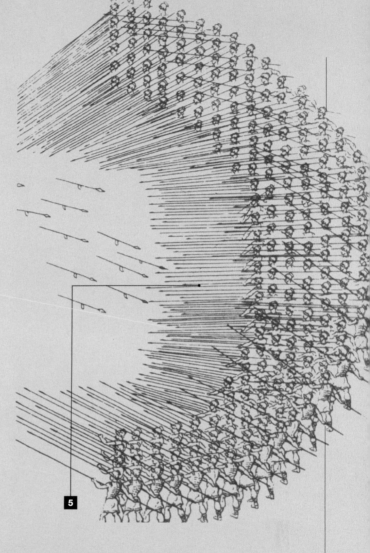

4 The impact of the spear-tipped phalanx could be devastating, especially to sword-armed warriors who had no way of cutting through the forest of points. Cavalry would not attack such a unit as horses could not be encouraged to charge against the hedgehog formation. No other spear-wielding enemy had weapons long enough to outreach the Macedonian *sarissa*.

5 This phalanx is formed in a crescent formation, perhaps to absorb and encircle attacking cavalry. In reality a phalanx would normally be formed *en echelon*, with blocks of spearmen covering each other at an angle to the enemy. The formation protected the Macedonians from a flanking attack with the phalanx acting as an anchor for the entire army to pivot around.

Rome and Her Enemies
509 BCE to 476 CE

The Greek contribution to warfare was more original, but the Romans exercised greater influence on Western civilization. The Greeks favored offensive tactics, but not necessarily offensive strategies. The Romans favored both. Roman warfare was an adaptation of Greek warfare, but with features that lent it an unprecedented capacity for aggression.

The original Roman "legion" was a Greek phalanx, but was eventually divided into three lines, each one broken into several units capable of independent maneuver. These innovations lost the depth and cohesion of the phalanx, but gave the legion far more flexibility.

Roman culture was more militaristic than Greek: Romans regarded almost constant war as a normal feature of society. "The Romans rely upon force in all their undertakings," wrote the Greek historian Polybius. The Roman republic's ability to wage war had no earlier parallel, and was not matched again until the rise of the modern European nation states.

Unlike most ancient oligarchies, membership of the Roman elite was not won by birth or wealth but through election to magistracies, the functions of which were military. Admission to the inner circle of the senate came through election to the consulship, the supreme magistracy, whose main function was leadership in war. There were only two consuls, elected annually, and election was usually a once-in-a-lifetime opportunity, so a noble who won the consulship had a single year to win glory for himself and his family. This system placed enormous pressure on the male members of the elite to compete with one another for military success. War was profitable for the elite above all, but also offered rewards to the entire citizen body—booty, land in new colonies, social advancement through a centurion's career.

The Roman alliance system also promoted war. Rome's allies rendered Rome only military service, not tribute, so Rome could only profit from them through war. By about 300 BCE, Rome had brought almost the entire Italian peninsula into a federation with the largest manpower reserves in the Mediterranean world, and was poised to begin unifying that world.

The Etruscans

Etruscans and Italics

In the last millennium BCE, central Italy was occupied by the Italic peoples, including the Latins, while northern Italy was inhabited by the mysterious Etruscans, whose language, written in an alphabet that has still not been deciphered, seems to have been a relic of the pre-Indo-European languages of Europe. Southern Italy and Sicily were dotted with Greek colonies, and by the 7th century BCE Etruscans were borrowing Greek institutions, including city-states and phalanx warfare. Through the Etruscans, Greek culture spread to the Latins and other Italic peoples. Some of the early kings of the Latin city of Rome had Etruscan names, and Rome may have been founded by Etruscans or passed through a stage of Etruscan rule.

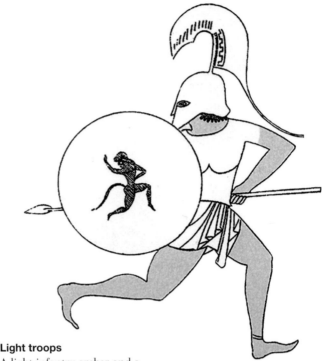

Light troops

A light infantry archer and a light cavalryman are shown here; the Etruscan phalanx may have been looser than the Greek, allowing more scope for these troops. The winged being beside the archer may be the goddess who led the ghosts of the dead to the underworld.

Etruscan hoplites

The Etruscan hoplites of the 6th century BCE used the same equipment as the Greeks of the period, designed for fighting in a phalanx formation: "Corinthian" helmet, round shield, cuirass, and long spear.

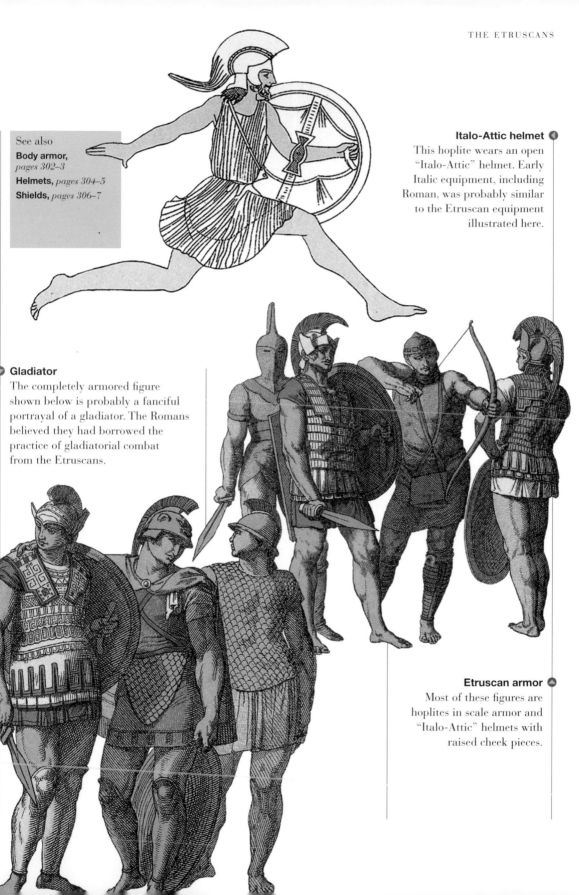

See also
Body armor,
pages 302–3
Helmets, *pages 304–5*
Shields, *pages 306–7*

Italo-Attic helmet
This hoplite wears an open "Italo-Attic" helmet. Early Italic equipment, including Roman, was probably similar to the Etruscan equipment illustrated here.

Gladiator
The completely armored figure shown below is probably a fanciful portrayal of a gladiator. The Romans believed they had borrowed the practice of gladiatorial combat from the Etruscans.

Etruscan armor
Most of these figures are hoplites in scale armor and "Italo-Attic" helmets with raised cheek pieces.

Hand weapons
• spear

Missile weapons

Defenses
• shield

Clothing
• "Corinthian" helmet
• "Italo-Attic" helmet
• scale armor

Warriors
• hoplites

Concepts & Tactics
• gladiatorial combat
• phalanx

Buildings & Transport

A Roman Legion

The manipular legion

The manipular formation was developed in the 4th century BCE during the constant wars by which Rome conquered Italy. It consisted of three lines of infantry, each line consisting of blocks of troops (maniples, or "handfuls") with wide spaces separating the maniples, enabling them to advance or withdraw independently of the movements of the battle line as a whole. Each line could be differently equipped. The origins of this formation are controversial, but it is widely thought that it was influenced by the Samnites, an Italic people of central Italy who were Rome's greatest enemy in the late 4th century BCE: Samnites seemed to have already adopted a loose formation that was ideally suited to their rugged terrain.

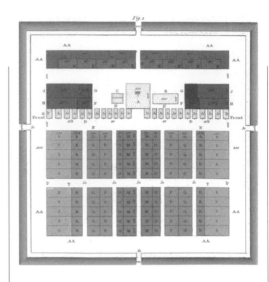

The Roman camp

The Greek historian Polybius left us a detailed description of a Roman camp, or *castra*, on which this drawing is based. The Roman army was unique in the ancient world in making a fortified camp every night. A camp for two legions was rectangular, surrounded by a ditch and rampart with a palisade. Every unit had a fixed place to pitch its tents. There were four gates (the main gate was the *porta praetoria*, the back gate the *porta decumana*, so called because it was near the tents of the tenth maniples), and two main roads 100 feet (30 meters) wide. The two legions, flanked by the auxiliaries, are camped near the *porta decumana*, with the tents of the tribunes before them. In the center of the camp is the *praetorium*, the headquarters of the commanders, where the standards were kept, and next to it the *quaestorium*, tent of the paymaster.

The testudo formation

The "tortoise" or *testudo* was a real formation used in sieges (*see pages 56–63*). It is unlikely that anyone tried to ride horses over it in this way, but the illustration is expressive of the formation's perceived impregnability.

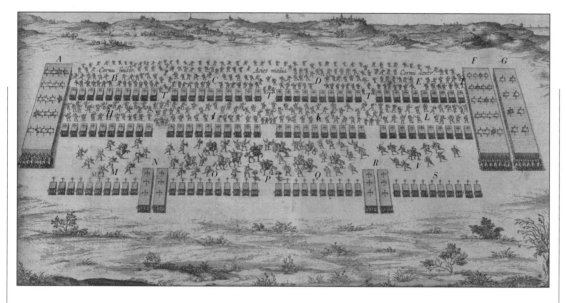

Hand weapons

Missile weapons

Defenses
• fortified camp

Clothing

Warriors
• *hastati*
• *principes*
• *triarii*
• *velites*

Concepts & Tactics
• boar's head formation
• manipular formation
• *testudo* formation

Buildings & Transport

The boar's head

Unlike the "tortoise" formation, the "boar's head" formation shown below is a Renaissance fantasy.

The manipular formation

This picture shows the Renaissance conception of the *acies veteris* (old formation), the manipular legion (3rd to 2nd century BCE), based on the detailed description by Greek historian Polybius. A consular army is depicted, consisting of two legions and an equivalent number of allies, about sixteen thousand infantry and two thousand cavalry. The legions are in the center, the allies on the wings, and the cavalry on the far wings (Roman cavalry *F*, auxiliary cavalry *A* and *G*). The legion is divided into three lines, and each line into ten maniples: first the *hastati* (Roman *C*, *D*, auxiliary *B*, *E*); second the *principes* (Roman *I*, *K*, auxiliary *H*, *L*); third the *triarii* (Roman *O*, *Q*, auxiliary *M*, *S*). The *velites* (*T*) were skirmishers who went before the legion. The two consuls, 12 military tribunes, and the eagles of the legions (*P*) stand between the *triarii* and the *principes*.

Rome at War, *509 BCE to 476 CE*

Evolution of the legion

In 509 BCE, the last Etruscan King was overthrown and replaced by an aristocratic council ("senate") and two consuls, whose main duty was to lead the Roman army ("legion"). In the 4th century BCE Rome fought a series of wars with other Italian city-states which resulted in the unification of Italy into a federation led by Rome. During these wars the legion developed the distinctive three-line formation described on pages 44–5. Each line was divided into ten maniples. The reforms of Gaius Marius, *c.* 100 BCE, replaced the three lines with a simpler division into ten cohorts, organized in one to four lines.

See also
A Roman legion,
pages 44–5
Swords, *pages 280–1*
Weapons of reach,
pages 284–5
Body armor,
pages 302–3

Hastati

The first line of the legion were called *hastati* and were armed with two *pila* (heavy javelins), short swords, and large oval shields. (The shield shown here did not come into use until the early 1st century CE.) They opened the battle by charging, throwing their javelins, and then closing with the sword.

Principes

The second line were called the *principes* and were armed exactly like the first line. (The republican shield is correctly shown.) If the charge of the *hastati* had not routed the enemy, the *principes* would come forward and repeat the maneuver. The third line, the *triarii*, composed of older men, were armed with long spears and formed a stable reserve.

Commander

Under the republic, legions were normally commanded by a consul or praetor. Under the principate, the monarchical system established by Augustus Caesar in 27 BCE, the commander was sometimes the Caesar (shown here) or a member of his family, or a legate appointed by the Caesar.

Signifer

Each of the 30 maniples and, after the Marian reforms, each cohort, had its own *signum* (standard), carried by a *signifer* wearing a bearskin.

Legionary of the cohort

After the Marian reforms all legionaries were armed alike, with *pilum* and sword. Each cohort had 480 men, giving a total of 4,800 for the legion. The mail or scale armor of the earlier legionaries was replaced *c.* 40 CE by a uniform segmented plate armor called the *lorica segmentata*, shown here.

Officers

On the far right stands a military tribune. Six of these, usually young aristocrats, were attached to each legion, and two of them shared command of the legion at any given time. Behind him stands a centurion, or noncommissioned officer; 60 of these were attached to every legion. On the left is the *vexillum*, the flag of the legion, carried by a *vexillarius*.

Hand weapons
• *pilum*
• short sword

Missile weapons

Defenses
• shield

Clothing
• bearskin
• segmented plate armor

Warriors
• *hastati*
• *principes*
• *triarii*

Concepts & Tactics
• manipular formation

Buildings & Transport

Rome at War

Evolution of the legion

The original Roman army was a citizen army, but in the last century BCE it became a volunteer professional army. The Roman republic was torn by civil war as the great families of the senate struggled for mastery. One of these families, the house of Caesar, won out, and its head, who assumed the honorary title Augustus, set up a system of disguised monarchy. Republican institutions continued, but the state was managed behind the scenes by Caesar. Caesar avoided royal titles and called himself the *princeps*, "first citizen"; historians call this system the principate. Eventually the ruler acquired the informal title Imperator Caesar: *imperator*, originally a title given to successful generals, was now restricted to the ruling family, and the family name Caesar became a title.

See also
The enemies of Rome,
pages 70–1

Defending the frontiers
Under the principate the legions were reduced in number to about thirty and were settled in permanent camps around the frontiers, especially on the Rhine and Danube, in Britain, and along the edge of the desert in Asia and Africa. The empire ceased to expand. These tombstone images show Roman cavalrymen trampling on German barbarians.

● Roman soldiers, 1st century BCE to 5th century CE

First in line (top left) is a legionary of the republic (*hastati* or *principes*), followed by a military tribune, a *vexillarius*, an *aquilifer* (eagle bearer), a centurion of the principate in *lorica segmentata*, an auxiliary, a legionary of the cohort, auxiliary cavalrymen, a legate, a late Roman emperor standing with three gladiators, and finally the general Aetius (5th century CE), called "the last of the Romans," in whose time the old Roman military system and equipment were nearly obsolete.

Rome at War

Roman standards

Originally there were five different legionary standards: the eagle, horse, bull, boar, and wolf. In the Marian reforms, *c.* 100 BCE, an image of an eagle (*aquila*), the bird sacred to the sky god Jupiter, became the uniform symbol and every legion had its own. Every cohort also had its own standard. Originally all standard bearers were called *signiferi*. After the reforms the officer who carried the eagle of the legion was called the *aquilifer* (eagle bearer) and was considered the senior *signifer*. The position of the eagle bearer was of vast importance. He was ranked just below the centurions and received twice the pay of the ordinary legionary. He was normally portrayed bareheaded, but probably put on a helmet if he participated in the fighting.

Vexillarius
Every legion had its own banner (*vexillum*), carried by a *vexillarius*, shown here.

Vexilla
The *vexillum* was decorated with the name and insignia of the legion. The legionary banner never left the legion, but when it was necessary to detach a special unit from the legion it was given its own *vexillum* and was called a *vexillio*. Under the principate, when the legions were settled in fixed camps and were no longer very mobile, use of these *vexilliones* became very common.

Hand weapons

Missile weapons

Defenses

Clothing
• bearskin

Warriors
• aquilifer
• draconarius
• imagnifer
• signifer

Concepts & Tactics
• Marian reforms

Buildings & Transport

Signa

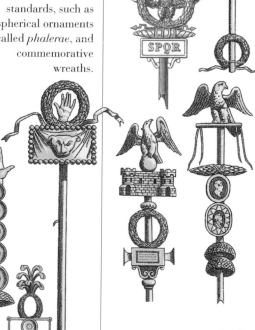

Every maniple and, after the Marian reorganization, every cohort, had its own standard, or *signum*, borne by a *signifer*, who wore a bearskin. The *signum* was a pole topped by an open hand or a spearhead, and bore various decorations to distinguish it from other cohort standards, such as spherical ornaments called *phalerae*, and commemorative wreaths.

Imagines

Legions commonly carried portraits of the emperor or members of the imperial family. The imago was carried by an *imagnifer* wearing a bearskin.

Dracones and other animals

The "dragon" was a standard borrowed from the Sarmatians and became a common cavalry standard in the 4th century CE. The *draco* was a windsock that flew horizontally when filled with wind and may also have produced loud noises. It was carried by a *draconarius*. A legion might also carry standards with astrological symbols, such as the signs of the zodiac, to mark the day of the legion's formation.

Aquilae

At first the eagles were made of silver; later they were gilded. Usually the eagle had raised wings surrounded by a wreath of laurel, symbol of victory. It was venerated and in camp was kept in a special shrine. The loss of it was a terrible disgrace to the legion.

The Roman Soldier

The cohort formation

In about 100 BCE, the consul Gaius Marius initiated a series of reforms that in the course of the next several decades transformed the legion from a citizen army into a professional army. The three-line formation was replaced by a simpler division into ten cohorts, all armed alike with *pilum* and sword, and organized in one to four lines. Each cohort had 480 men, giving the legion a total strength of 4,800. Thereafter there was no fundamental change in army organization until the 3rd century CE.

See also
Swords, *pages 280–1*
Body armor, *pages 302–3*
Shields, *pages 306–7*

Shields

The *scutum* was the shield of the republican legions. It was oval, typically 24 × 44 inches (60 × 112 centimeters) in size, made of planks glued together like modern plywood, with metal rim and boss (the shields were usually more elongated than they appear in these representations). Under the principate this type of shield was used only by the Praetorian Guard, the Caesar's bodyguard, and legionaries used a shorter shield with top and bottom cut off. Cavalry used a hexagonal shield of German origin.

Armor

The mail armor of the republican army was replaced by the *lorica segmentata*, or segmented plate armor (top row, left). The muscled cuirass (top right and above) was an expensive armor usually worn by high-ranking officers and members of the imperial family.

In the middle of the top row is scale armor, an inexpensive armor made of metal scales sewn onto a leather tunic.

Helmets from Trajan's Column, 2nd century CE

On the right is the standard legionary helmet of the principate. At this time crests were no longer worn except on parade. In the center is a light helmet of the type worn by auxiliary light infantry. On the left is a helmet of the "Italo-Corinthian" type, an archaic model probably worn only by auxiliaries at this time. The original "Corinthian" helmet (*see page 27*) had covered the entire head, but the Italic version was worn on top of the head, and the eyeholes had become purely decorative.

Swords

The standard legionary sword was often called *gladius hispanicus* because it was adopted in Spain in the 3rd century BCE. Top right is a Victorian depiction of a *falcata*, a short sickle-shaped sword with one cutting edge (the lower edge).

Daggers

The legionary also carried a short dagger, the *pugio*, although it went out of use in the 2nd century CE. The dagger was carried on the left hip, the sword on the right.

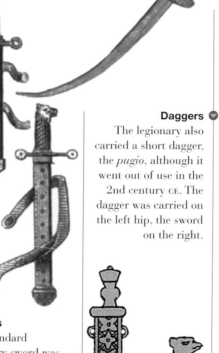

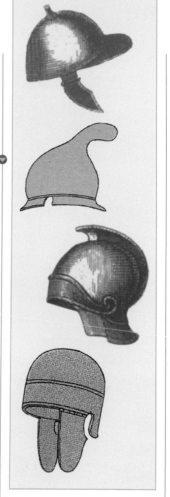

Assorted helmets

The two helmets at the bottom are alternative versions of the standard legionary helmet. The two at the top were probably worn by auxiliaries: second from the top is a version of the archaic "Phrygian" helmet, and above it is perhaps a light infantry helmet.

The Roman Soldier

Cavalry, archers, and auxiliaries

In republican times, auxiliaries were usually recruited from barbarian tribes living in the areas where the legions were campaigning, and were normally used as skirmishers. In the early principate regular auxiliaries were formed, equipped, and paid by the state. They were organized into cohorts of varying size, wore mail or scale armor, and were armed with spear and sword. Their methods of fighting did not much differ from those of the legions, but some auxiliaries provided cavalry and light infantry because after the Marian reforms those services no longer formed part of a legion. Latin was always the language of command. Auxiliaries enlisted for twenty-five years like the legionaries, and received Roman citizenship upon discharge.

See also
Sarmatian warriors, *page 31*
The enemies of Rome, *page 66–7*

Light infantry
Archers and slingers were recruited from various barbarian peoples, such as the Arab archers shown here.

Hand weapons

Missile weapons
• bow
• sling

Defenses

Clothing
• mail armor
• scale armor

Warriors
• Carthaginian
• Celtic
• Greek
• Numidian
• Persian
• Sarmatian

Concepts & Tactics
• auxiliaries
• heavy cavalry

Buildings & Transport
• elephant
• horse

Cavalry

Under the principate the Roman army made increasing use of auxiliary cavalry. In the early principate these were largely Celtic. In the scene below, horsemen charge past an *aquilifer*. In the 2nd century CE a type of very heavy cavalry called cataphracts, with both rider and horse in full armor, was introduced from the Sarmatians of the steppe (*see pages 30–1*).

Auxiliaries attack war elephant

Elephants were used by several of Rome's enemies under the republic—such as Greeks, Carthaginians, Numidians—and sometimes by Persians under the principate, but not by Romans themselves. In this illustration an elephant is attacked by infantry and cavalry. The use of the elephant is correctly shown. Elephants were often armored, and carried archers in a howdah, but the main weapon was the animal itself. They were not very effective as they could easily be maddened by missiles and might turn on their own troops. The chariot is an anachronism.

Roman Technology

Siege warfare

In the Hellenistic world siege tactics had been developed by professional engineers, who were often mercenaries. The Romans of the republic were backward at siege warfare, but the legions of the principate always included trained engineers who adopted all the Greek inventions. During a siege, battering rams breached city fortifications, artillery fired darts and stones at the defenders, and siege towers enabled the besiegers to reach the walls. To break the morale of the defenders, captives were crucified within sight and severed heads were flung into the city by artillery. If a city failed to surrender before the first ram touched the wall, the city was given over to a dreadful sack.

Siege engines

In this 19th-century reconstruction cities are attacked with rams, towers, and catapults. In the center is a *ballista* (*see pages 58–9*). There were many experiments with engines about which we know little. The dart-throwing catapult (lower right) looks implausible.

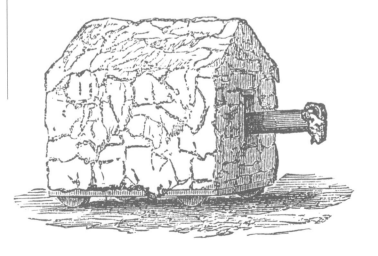

The battering ram

The battering ram had changed little since Assyrian times. It was a wooden beam up to 100 feet (30 meters) long, tipped with a metal ram's head. It hung in a frame, and soldiers swung it back and forth. To protect them, the ram was housed in a wooden shed, covered with fireproof clay or hide, and mounted on rollers.

See also
Anatomy of a ballista, *pages 58–9*
Anatomy of an onager, *pages 62–3*
Anatomy of a Roman siege, *pages 68–9*
Siege engines, *pages 294–5*
Shields, *pages 306–7*

Testudo formation

This formation, made by legionaries holding up overlapping shields to form a cover like a tortoise's shell, was used in sieges to allow soldiers to approach enemy walls.

Catapult

In this scene, the catapult is the late Roman type called an *onager* (*see pages 62–3*). The combination siege tower and ram behind it seems highly improbable.

Hand weapons

Missile weapons
• *ballista*
• battering ram
• catapult
• *onager*

Defenses

Clothing

Warriors

Concepts & Tactics
• siegecraft
• *testudo* formation

Buildings & Transport
• siege tower

Anatomy of a *Ballista*

The torsion catapult, with two levers powered by torsion springs (several loops of twisted skeins of hair or sinew) was invented in the early 4th century BCE by Greeks and adopted by Romans during the Punic Wars of the 3rd century BCE. Romans used the term *ballista* (from the Greek *baino*, throw) for the stone-throwing engine and called the dart-thrower a *catapulta* (from the Greek *katapeltes*, shield-piercer). But after 100 CE all catapults were called *ballistae*. They came in many different sizes. Some were small enough to be used by hand and resembled heavy crossbows. Two medium-sized *ballistae* are shown here.

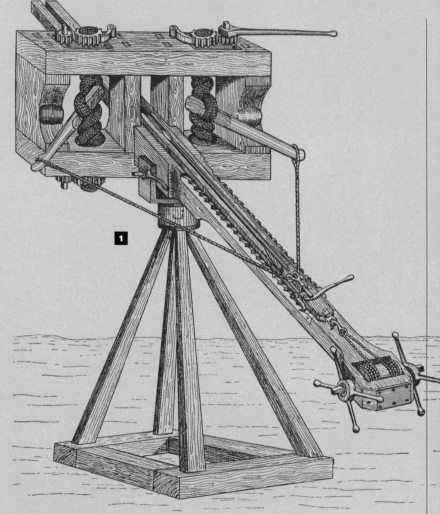

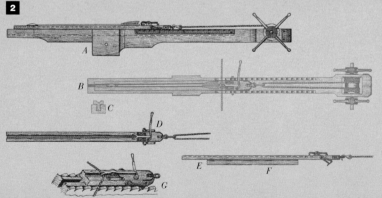

1 A dart-throwing *ballista* 6 feet (2 meters) high was used for discharging heavy arrows or javelins. In this image, the bowstring is drawn to its full extent. The dart rests in a shallow trough that runs along the stock.

2 Mechanism of the stock. *A*: side view of the trough. *B* and *D*: surface views. *C*: front view. *E*: side view showing keel (*F*). *G*: end of trough showing the catch for the bowstring.

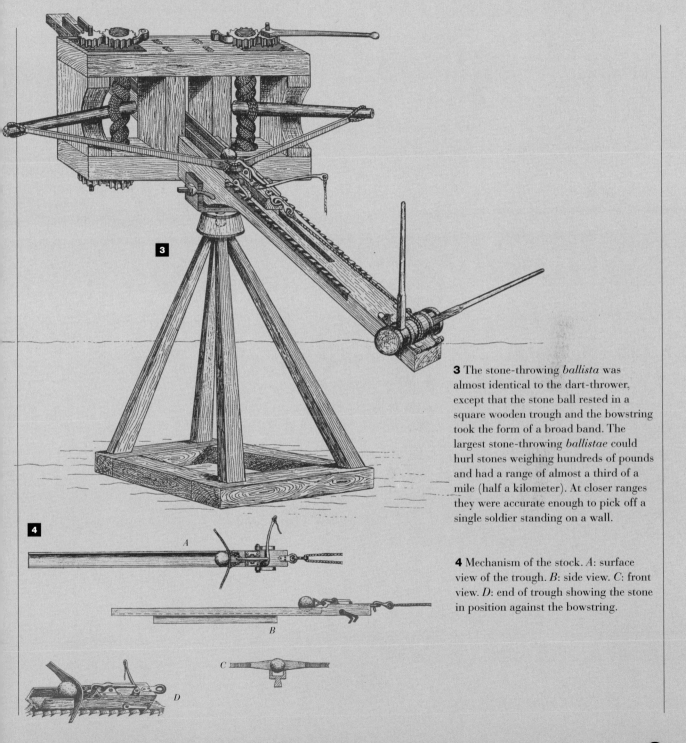

3 The stone-throwing *ballista* was almost identical to the dart-thrower, except that the stone ball rested in a square wooden trough and the bowstring took the form of a broad band. The largest stone-throwing *ballistae* could hurl stones weighing hundreds of pounds and had a range of almost a third of a mile (half a kilometer). At closer ranges they were accurate enough to pick off a single soldier standing on a wall.

4 Mechanism of the stock. *A*: surface view of the trough. *B*: side view. *C*: front view. *D*: end of trough showing the stone in position against the bowstring.

Roman Technology

The world in a ring

When conducting a siege the Roman armies built permanent camps, which were copies of the normal Roman *castra* (*see page 44*). By the early 2nd century CE, the empire ceased to expand and the legions, now numbering about thirty, were settled in permanent camps of this sort along the frontiers, especially the Rhine and Danube in Europe, and the edge of the desert in Asia and Africa. In an oration in 143 CE honoring the foundation of Rome, the Greek rhetorician Aelius Aristides compared the Roman empire to a walled city: "An encamped army like a rampart encloses the civilized world in a ring."

See also
The Roman camp, *page 44*
Anatomy of a Roman siege, *pages 68–9*
Siege engines, *pages 294–5*

Siege of Massilia

The last great Roman siege came in 49 BCE when Caesar's deputy Gaius Trebonius laid siege to Massilia (Marseilles). The Romans were protected from the defenders' *ballistae* by a six-story tower with brick walls some 5 feet (1.5 meters) thick and a wooden gallery 60 feet (18 meters) long stretching from the tower to the city wall. They used this to reach the city wall and undermine it. In this image by the Chevalier de Folard, the tower is on the left, and the gallery is incorrectly shown as not stretching all the way to the wall.

Roman fort

This image shows a typical Roman permanent camp. These forts were close copies of the original *castra*, but in the 1st century CE they were rebuilt with stone walls instead of earthen ramparts and huts instead of tents. In England, town names that include the word "chester" indicate the former sites of Roman legionary camps (e.g., Colchester, Leicester, Chester).

Siege of Numantia

One of the most famous Roman sieges was that of the Celtiberian stronghold of Numantia in central Spain by Scipio Aemilianus in 133 BCE. A ring of seven fortified camps was built around the town. Around this was built a ditch and rampart; then another ditch; and finally a stone wall 10 feet (3 meters) high and 8 feet (2.4 meters) thick. This 18th-century engraving by de Folard is not strictly accurate but shows how the 18th century envisaged a typical Roman siege.

Hand weapons

Missile weapons
• *ballista*

Defenses

Clothing

Warriors

Concepts & Tactics
• *siegecraft*

Buildings & Transport
• *fortified camp*

Anatomy of an *Onager*

In the 4th century CE, the two-armed *ballistae* were largely replaced by a one-armed stone-throwing catapult called an *onager* or "wild ass" because of its violent kick. It was simpler and easier to operate than the *ballista*. A single torsion spring was mounted in a wooden frame and a single wooden arm slotted into the spring so that it stood upright and traveled in a vertical arc. Four soldiers, two on each side, wound the arm down almost to the ground. A sling with a round stone was attached to the free end of the arm. When released, the arm sprung upright and hurled the stone. Because there was no bowstring, a huge padded buffer stuffed with chaff had to be placed in front of the machine to stop the arm (not shown in the picture below).

2 In this aerial view, the arm (*E*) is fully wound down. The ends of the cross-piece beams (*III, IV, V*) are stepped into the side-piece beams (*II*). The skein of twisted cord (*A*) is stretched between the large winding wheels (*B*). The ends of the spindles (*D*) are turned to rotate the pinion wheels (*C*), which rotate the large wheels (*B*), which twist the skein (*A*).

3 Surface view (*I*), side view (*II*), and perspective views (*V*) of the winding wheel and winch of the *onager*. One end of the skein is wound around the wheel (*III*). The winches generate the projectile power of the machine.

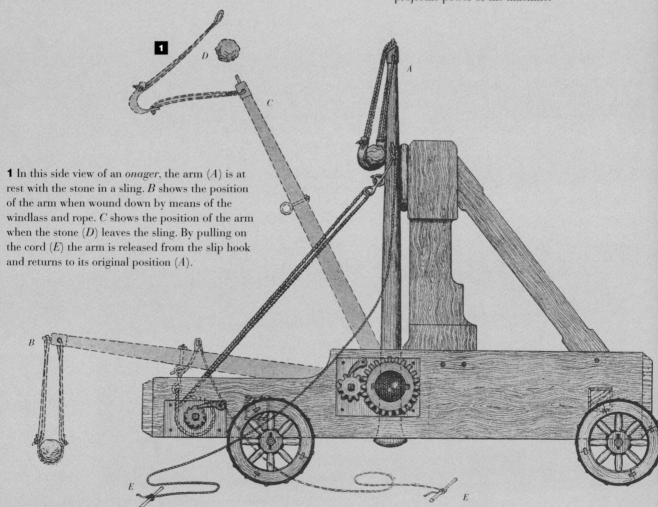

1 In this side view of an *onager*, the arm (*A*) is at rest with the stone in a sling. *B* shows the position of the arm when wound down by means of the windlass and rope. *C* shows the position of the arm when the stone (*D*) leaves the sling. By pulling on the cord (*E*) the arm is released from the slip hook and returns to its original position (*A*).

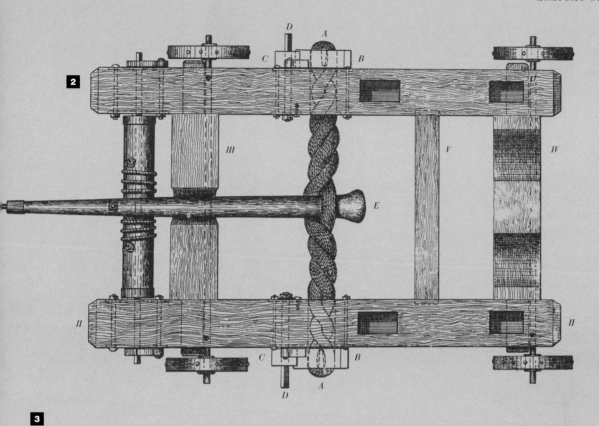

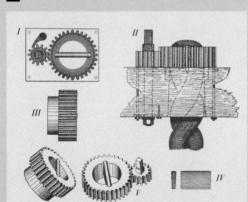

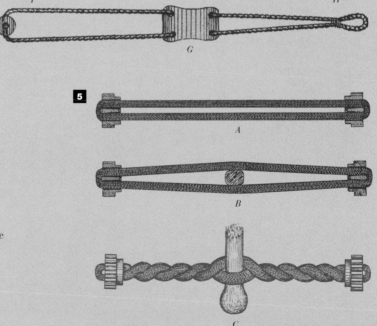

4 The sling, one end of which passes through a hole near the top of the arm (*F*). *G* is the leather pocket that holds the stone. The other end is looped over the iron pin at the top of the arm (*H*).

5 The skein of twisted cord is wound around the winding wheel (*A*). The end of the arm is placed between the two halves of the skein (*B*). The skein is tightly twisted by the winches (*C*).

The Enemies of Rome

Celts

In the last millennium BCE, peoples speaking Celtic languages inhabited most of central and western Europe. They were known to the Greeks and Romans as *Celtae* or *Galli*. It is not clear whether the Celts themselves used these names, or whether this huge collection of tribes had any sense of possessing a common cultural identity. Archaeology has identified them with the Halstatt culture of the Iron Age, which flourished in central Europe *c.* 600 BCE. Celtic peoples may have entered Britain *c.* 500 BCE. The La Tène culture appeared *c.* 400 BCE, and the Celts began their most vigorous age of expansion, occupying northern Italy and sacking Rome.

Celts in the 19th-century imagination

Most of the figures shown here are based on Meyrick and Smith's *Costumes of the Original Inhabitants of the British Isles* (1815), produced when there was little accurate information about the early Celtic inhabitants. The two figures on the far right represent Meyrick's notion of a Romanized Briton contrasted with a wild Celt from northern Britain. The latter is rather more accurate, for Roman authors testified that on the Continent Celtic warriors, as late as the 3rd century BCE, often went into battle stark naked, and the habit of British Celts of covering their bodies with paint and tattoos is also well attested. The Romanized Briton wears a Roman-looking tunic but has anachronistically been draped in plaid to make him look Celtic. Both the nude Celt and the horseman have been given very strange-looking weapons. The two figures on the left are supposed to represent early Irish people and are based on drawings of the early 17th century; the artist assumed that the ancient Irish looked like their contemporary descendants. Giving the man a spear to hold was his only attempt to avoid anachronism. But it is true that the ancient Celts wore trousers.

Helmets

Horned helmets were purely ceremonial. This example (bottom) was found in the River Thames at London.

Irish axman

This image represents a more believable attempt to envision ancient Irishmen. It is known that the ancient Irish warriors were very lightly armed by continental standards.

Tribal warriors

This is a somewhat fanciful attempt to reconstruct tribal warriors of barbarian Europe, probably supposed to be Celts. Early Celtic warriors did wear trousers, and the conical iron helmet of the man on the right is fairly authentic. But the armor is anachronistic. Celtic chieftains wore mail armor, which was probably invented by Celts in the 3rd century BCE. Common warriors went into battle stark naked at that time and continued to do so until at least *c*. 200 BCE.

Hand weapons
• ax
• spear

Missile weapons

Defenses

Clothing
• body paint
• conical helmet
• mail armor
• trousers

Warriors
• Celtic warriors

Concepts & Tactics

Buildings & Transport

The Enemies of Rome

Celtic warfare

Rome conquered the Celts of northern Italy in the 3rd century BCE and the Celts of Spain in the 2nd century; Julius Caesar began the conquest of Gaul, their major stronghold, in 58 BCE. Most of Britain was made a Roman province in the early principate. By this time most of the Celtic peoples were becoming Romanized, but Celtic languages have survived to this day in the northern and western fringes of the British Isles. The Greek geographer Strabo described the Celts as follows: "The whole race . . . is madly fond of war, high-spirited and quick to battle, but otherwise straightforward and not of evil character. And so when they are stirred up, they assemble in their bands for battle, quite openly and without forethought, so that they are easily handled by those who desire to outwit them; for at any time or place . . . you will have them ready to face danger, even if they have nothing on their side but their own strength and courage."

Celtic infantry

Celtic society was divided into three main castes: druids (priests), warriors, and peasants. Warriors were of four types: cavalry, charioteers, heavy infantry with swords (shown here), and light infantry with javelins.

Marks of wealth

Cuirasses of plate armor, finely embossed and incised, were worn only by wealthy chieftains. Most armor was mail and many warriors wore neither armor nor helmet.

Celtic cavalry

Celtic cavalry were highly esteemed. After the Roman conquest of Gaul, the Gauls provided the Romans with most of their mounted auxiliaries. Horsemen were armed with long spears. One figure carries a boar standard.

See also
Swords,
pages 280–1
Shields,
pages 306–7

Cavalry and chariots ◁

Cavalry and charioteers were recruited from the nobles. Cavalry would throw their javelins and then charge home with spear and sword. The Celtic cavalryman, like the Celtic infantryman, was primarily a swordsman. Two-horsed chariots were used only against cavalry; the warrior threw his javelins from the chariot and then dismounted and fought on foot with his sword. Celtic chariots were used for the last time in Britain in the 1st century CE.

Ceremonial shields ◁

Shields came in many shapes. Combat shields were of wood covered with hide; the ornate round shields shown here were probably ceremonial.

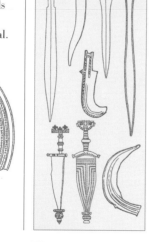

Ironwork ◁

The Celts were famous for their skills as ironworkers and probably invented mail armor (3rd century BCE), which was quickly adopted by the Roman army. These long iron swords come from the Halstaat and La Tène periods of the Celtic Iron Age, the classical age of Celtic culture, which lasted from the 7th century BCE till the Roman conquest.

Phrygian helmets ▲

These helmets are of the type called "Phrygian," widely used in the Hellenistic world and in barbarian Europe, but not particularly Celtic. The more typical Celtic helmet was pot-shaped and made of iron. The standard helmet used by the Roman army under the principate was based on it.

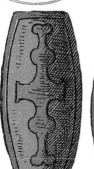

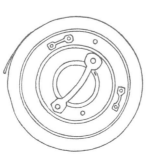

Hand weapons
• spear
• sword

Missile weapons
• javelin

Defenses
• shield

Clothing
• cuirass
• mail armor
• "Phrygian" helmet
• pot-shaped helmet

Warriors
• cavalry
• charioteer
• heavy infantry
• light infantry

Concepts & Tactics
• chariot

Buildings & Transport

Anatomy of a Roman Siege

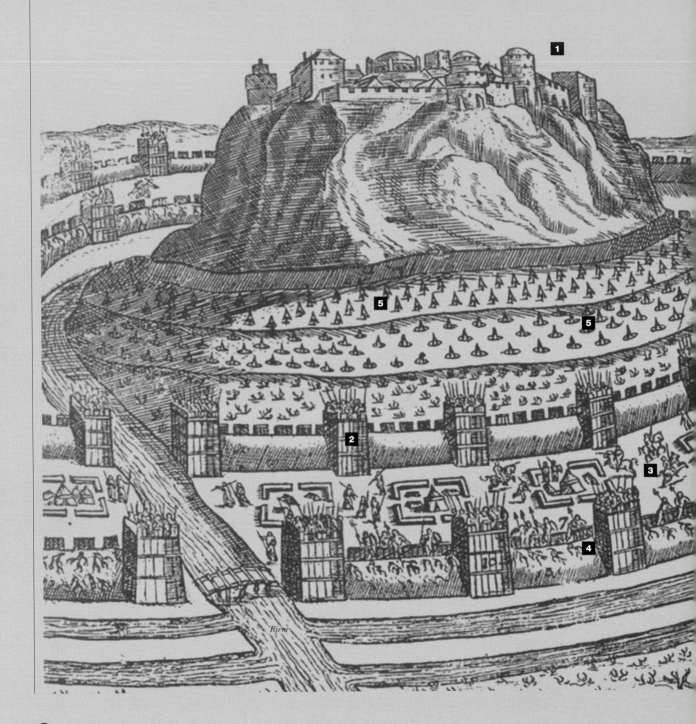

River

The siege of Alesia was the culmination of Julius Caesar's campaign of conquest in Gaul in 52 BCE. It demonstrated his mastery of Roman siege warfare. His earthworks and walls extended for 9 miles (14 kilometers) in two rings around the base of the hill fort. It was worth the enormous investment in labor as it brought Vercingetorix to his knees and virtually ended Celtic resistance in Gaul.

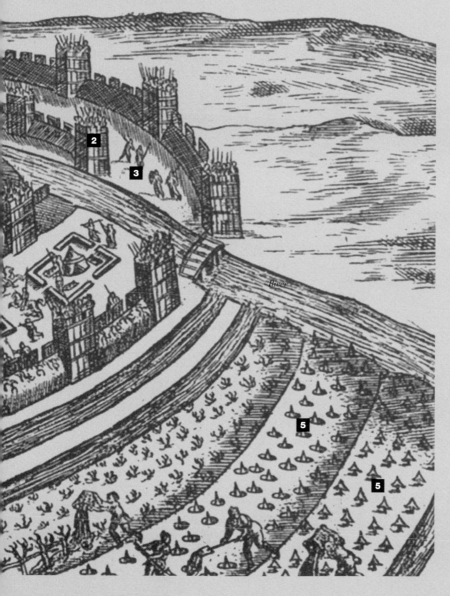

1 The Celtic hilltop fortress of Alesia was set upon a rocky plateau, now known as Mont-Auxois, 30 miles (48 kilometers) west of Dijon in south-east France. It was the impregnable base of Vercingetorix, leader of the Gauls. Surrounded by steep river valleys on three sides, it was protected by a wooden palisade and steep earth slopes.

2 The inner Roman wooden walls were designed to keep the Celts contained within their hill fort. In front of the wall was a ditch 8 feet (2.5 meters) deep and 15 feet (4.5 meters) wide. The earth dug from this was used to form a long mound on which was a wooden stockade with wooden towers built at regular intervals.

3 Roman camps within the two walls were laid out in ordered rows with tents and latrines. Up to fifty thousand soldiers in ten legions, with barbarian auxiliaries, formed the core of Caesar's force surrounding the hill fort. They could counter forays from both inside and outside Alesia. Merchants and camp followers kept the soldiers supplied with food and formed a mini-town within the walls.

4 The outer Roman ring of defenses was intended to protect Caesar's soldiers from attack by relieving Celtic forces coming from allied tribes. Trenches fronted this and some of them were filled with water diverted from nearby rivers. Roman field artillery could be fired from the towers situated along the walls.

5 Trenches and potholes were filled with stakes intended to trap Celtic warriors setting out on raids from the hill fort. The great strength of the Celtic tribes was their cavalry and Caesar wanted to neutralize their charges against his men and their fortifications.

The Enemies of Rome

Germanic peoples

Tribes speaking Germanic languages, a branch of the great Indo-European family, originally inhabited the area around the Baltic Sea to the north of the Celtic zone. In the later 2nd century CE, when the Romans had virtually eliminated the Celts, the Germans began to drift southward and came into contact, and often conflict, with Roman legions quartered along the Rhine and Danube. Over the next three centuries the German tribes borrowed much from the Romans, served in the Roman army in increasing numbers, and coalesced into larger, more formidable, and more Romanized chiefdoms.

When the Roman administration in the western empire collapsed in the 5th century CE, these barbarian tribes entered Roman territory en masse and established many semi-Germanic, semi-Roman states. These eventually became the kingdoms of medieval Europe.

See also
The Dark Ages, *pages 74–5*
A Carolingian knight, *page 80*
Swords, *pages 280–1*
Weapons of reach, *pages 284–5*
Clubs, maces, and axes, *pages 286–7*
Shields, *pages 306–7*

German weapons
Shown below is a collection of typical weapons used by the Germanic tribes: left to right, a *seax*, daggers, and a battle ax.

German chieftain
This German chieftain belongs to a later period when Germanic war leaders often wore mail armor acquired from the Romans. He has a long straight sword, derived perhaps from the Roman cavalry sword (*spatha*) and perhaps from the Celtic sword. He carries a wooden, hide-covered shield: this shield is round but Germans used many different shield types. By the 4th century CE there was little difference between Germans and Romans in technology and tactics, but Germans retained some peculiar weapons.

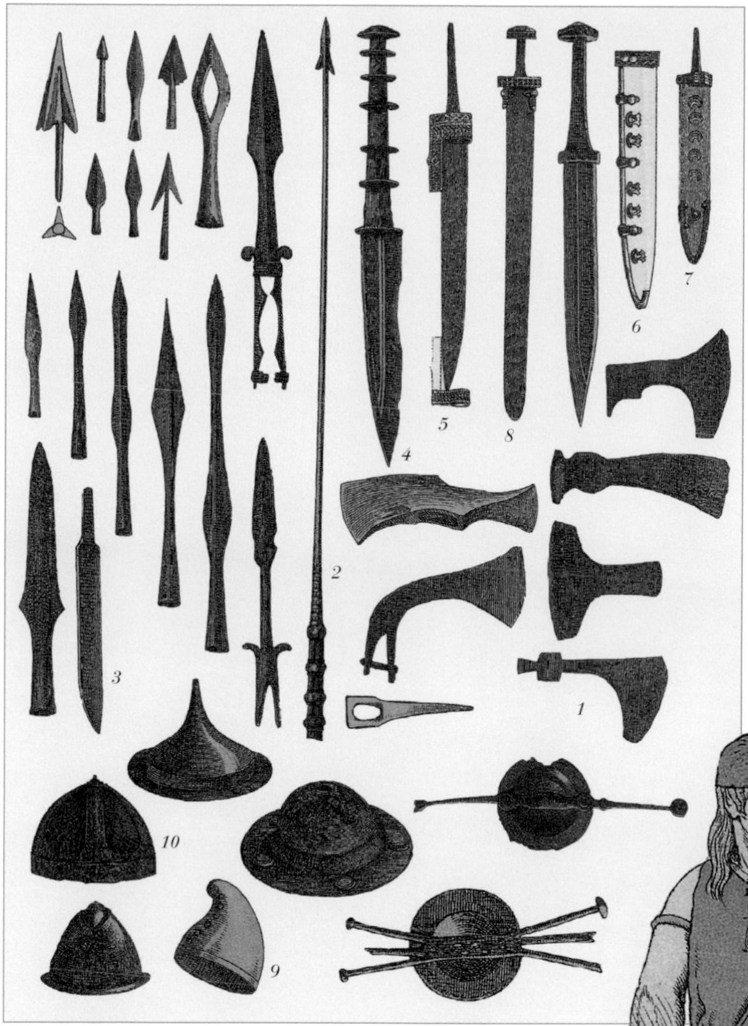

Hand weapons
• *framea*
• *seax*
• *spatha*

Missile weapons
• *angon*
• *francisca*

Defenses
• shield

Clothing

Warriors

Concepts & Tactics
• *furor teutonicus*

Buildings & Transport

▼ Teutonic fashion

When the Romans first encountered them, German warriors had no armor and often fought bare to the waist. Their basic weapon was a short-bladed spear called a *framea*, used both for throwing and fighting hand to hand. Their only tactic was a wild rush, called by Romans the *furor teutonicus*. Many tribes wore their hair in a topknot.

▲ Frankish weapons

The *francisca*, or Frankish throwing ax (*1*), resembled a Native American tomahawk but had an arch-shaped blade. Named after the great Frankish tribal federation on the lower Rhine, it was also used by many other German tribes, including the Anglo-Saxons. The Franks would open a battle by showering the enemy with these deadly hatchets. The heavy javelin or *angon* (*2*) appears to be modeled on the Roman *pilum*: it had a barbed iron head and a long iron shank set in a wooden haft. The long knife called a *seax* or *scramasax* (*3, 4, 5, 6, 7*) was used all over northern Europe. The word "Saxon" may have been derived from it. Other common German weapons were the long sword (*8*), the "Phrygian" helmet (*9*), and the Spangenhelm helmet (*10*).

Medieval Warfare
500–1500

Medieval societies devoted a great deal of time and energy to improving the technology of arms and armor, fortifications, and logistics, especially during the Crusades, when expertise at sea was required. Indeed, it is often forgotten what an important role naval warfare played in the medieval world.

Although a large amount has been lost to us from the period between 1000 and 1500 CE, enough remains to help us understand it, particularly evidence from the stone walls of the many castles that dot the landscapes both of Europe, where they originated, and the Holy Land, where they were established to protect the Crusaders' conquests.

Another glory of the period was the evolution of the knightly lifestyle, expressed through a love of horses, heraldry, and tournaments. From simple mail shirts, increasingly sophisticated body armor was developed, culminating in the full plate armor of the late 15th century. Not that the knights had it all to themselves, as modern myth suggests. Infantry armed with a variety of pole arms, as well as the longbow and crossbow, which were powerful enough bring down a mounted knight, also made their presence felt. In addition, at sieges, which were the predominant form of warfare, miners, engineers, and other experts were crucial to the successful prosecution of strategy and campaigns.

The development of effective siege weapons and other machines of war are other examples of medieval ingenuity. Catapults and siege towers had been used since antiquity, but the powerful trebuchet, developed in the mid-12th century, played a crucial role in battering down defensive walls. The increase in the use of gunpowder weapons in Europe from the mid-14th century finally spelled doom for the medieval castle with its tall but thin walls, as siege artillery that could destroy them were developed.

Finally, there is the heroism of the age, epitomized by war leaders such as Richard the Lionheart, King of England, a giant of the Crusades and a man whose name has rung down the centuries as a military hero.

Early Middle Ages, *500–1066*

The Dark Ages

The term "Dark Ages" is often applied to the Early Middle Ages (5th to 10th centuries) but only the early part of this period was lacking in civilization: roughly the two centuries following the end of the western Roman Empire in 476. By the 8th century the barbarian kingdoms of western Europe had stabilized and the Frankish kingdom had emerged as the dominant power. The Franks were Catholic Christians, not Arian heretics like most of the German tribes, and so benefited from the support of the Church. In the late 8th century their king, Charles the Great (Charlemagne), succeeded in uniting most of continental western Europe, and on Christmas Day 800 he was crowned "Roman Emperor" by the Pope. In the 5th century most of Britain was occupied by Germanic tribes from the North Sea coast (Angles, Saxons, and Jutes). In the 7th century they adopted Christianity and established several kingdoms, and by the 8th century they were an integral part of the unified Christian culture taking shape in western Europe and made major contributions to Charlemagne's revival of Latin learning (the "Carolingian Renaissance"). English warfare closely resembled that of continental Europe.

Medieval society

Like the ancient Celts, medieval scholars divided society into three functional classes: those who pray, those who fight, and those who work. The first class is represented here by a bishop and priest (below left); the second class by an armored thane and a king (below right); the last by peasants (left). The thane wears the conical iron cap and mail shirt (which would not, however, have covered his limbs) which by the 9th century were becoming the standard equipment of the Western military elite.

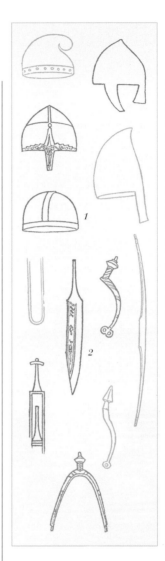

Carolingian horsemen

By Carolingian times the armored horseman (later called a "knight") was becoming the elite warrior, and the beginnings of feudal organization, in which vassals provided military service to their lords, can be discerned. But heavy cavalry were not so effective as they later became. Stirrups had not yet been adopted by the Franks. They held their spears in an overhand grip and stabbed with them in the ancient fashion. Often, Frankish cavalry rode to the battlefield but then dismounted to fight on foot.

Carolingian foot soldiers

The Roman legions were long forgotten, but the armies of Charlemagne were still mainly infantry armies. Most had only shield and spear. The more affluent soldiers pictured here wear scale armor; rich noblemen may have had mail, which was in use in contemporary Byzantine and Arab armies. Many soldiers used simple bows (top left) and possibly crossbows (bottom right), though this weapon, for some reason, did not become widespread until about the 11th century.

Helmets and weapons

Most helmets of the period were of the Spangenhelm ("strip helmet") type, a conical iron cap (*1*). The more ornate helmets shown here may be influenced more by late-Roman illuminated manuscripts than by actual usage. The *seax* was still in use (*2*) but was being replaced by the long sword.

See also
Swords,
pages 280–1
Body armor,
pages 302–3
Shields,
pages 306–7

Early Middle Ages

Viking invaders

At the end of the 8th century, when western Europeans were emerging from the Dark Ages, they were struck by a fresh wave of barbarian invaders more destructive than any before them. They came from Scandinavia, a land so remote that Christians had no name for them and could only call them "the Men from the North" (Norsemen, Normans). They proudly called themselves "Vikings" (pirates). Their advent was signaled by the sack of the great monastery of Lindisfarne in Northumbria in 793. In the years that followed they repeatedly raided the coasts of the British Isles and the Carolingian Empire. In the late 9th century they began to occupy permanent territories and founded the Viking kingdoms of York, Dublin, and Normandy.

Viking art

Ornamental plates originally attached to a king's belt, probably featuring berserkers—warriors who fought wearing the skins of bears or wolves and were believed to sometimes turn into bears or wolves in the frenzy of battle. One warrior wears a boar's-head helmet and another a horned helmet. Despite popular belief, there is no evidence that Vikings wore horned helmets.

See also
The Vikings: snekkes and drakkar, *pages 256–7*
Swords, *pages 280–1*
Body armor, *pages 302–3*

Norse attire

The man on the right wears a short mail shirt and iron cap and carries a round shield, long sword, spear, and javelin: this was all standard equipment for a wealthy Viking. The man in the center wears a ceremonial helmet with a boar crest; such helmets appear in Norse art.

The later Norsemen
These images show an 11th-century Scandinavian knight and a common soldier. By this time the kingdoms of Denmark, Norway, and Sweden had been Christianized and the Viking age was over. The mailed knight has a kite-shaped Norman shield, not the round one of his ancestors.

Viking weapons
A sword about 3 feet (1 meter) long was the favored weapon for hand-to-hand combat. Spears and javelins were also used both for throwing and hand-to-hand fighting. Scandinavia was rich in timber and iron and Norse metalwork was as famous as their shipbuilding.

The Viking longship
The Viking age was made possible by the invention of the longship, the first efficient oceangoing vessel. Longships could be more than 100 feet (30 meters) long and were powered both by oars and sails. Forty oars was considered standard. The long oar at the stern was used for steering, and the shallow draft enabled the ship to sail up rivers. Ships like these took the Vikings to Iceland, Greenland, and the North American mainland.

Viking atrocities
This embroidery from a Swedish church depicts the massacre of the innocents at Bethlehem. King Herod is saying *Occidite omnes* ("Kill all [the infants].") Scandinavia was a Christian land when these paintings were created, but the scenes depict what had happened, not too long before, when Vikings sacked a town.

Hand weapons
• long sword
• spear

Missile weapons
• javelin

Defenses
• kite-shaped shield
• round shield

Clothing
• animal skins
• iron cap
• mail shirt

Warriors
• berserkers

Concepts & Tactics
• coastal raids

Buildings & Transport
• longship

Early Middle Ages

The Normans

The Normans, whose origins were Viking, were the most renowned warriors of the Middle Ages. They were Danes who had invaded northern France under their leader Hrolf, who was granted territory by the French King in 911. Gradually they adopted the French language, religion, customs, and way of fighting, while not giving up their naval traditions. By the mid-11th century they were the leading exponents of cavalry and castle warfare. When, in 1066, William II, Duke of Normandy, laid claim to the English throne, he set about collecting a mighty fleet of longships and transports for his knights' horses in order to invade England. Landing in Sussex, he challenged King Harold to battle just north of Hastings on 14 October. After a long day's hard fighting William was victorious.

Norman knight

This Norman knight is fully armed for war. The pennon on his lance displays his status, but it is too early to be heraldic. His mail coat, a split tunic, is shown as rings sewn on to a leather backing but should really be mail. He would be accompanied by a squire, an essential support for a mounted warrior with more than one horse to manage.

> **See also**
> **The Viking longship,** *page 77*
> **The Norman invasion of England,** *page 257*
> **Swords,** *pages 280–1*
> **Clubs, maces, and axes,** *pages 286–7*
> **Body armor,** *pages 302–3*

Battle scene from the Bayeux Tapestry

Here we see Norman knights charging, lances lowered for the charge, against the English fighting on foot in a shield wall, carrying spears and long axes and supported by a lone archer.

Knight of the mid-12th century

The pointed helmet sweeping forward is in what was known as the "Phrygian" style, which was popular at the time. His sword in its lavishly decorated scabbard hangs from the belt, which is the symbol of his knighthood. The lions on his shield, one of the earliest heraldic arms adopted by a royal house, suggest that this figure is taken from the funerary plaque of Geoffrey le Bel of Anjou (d. 1152), the father of Henry II of England.

Hand weapons
• lance
• long ax

Missile weapons
• bow

Defenses
• kite-shaped shield

Clothing
• mail coat and leggings
• pointed helmet
• scale hauberk

Warriors
• Norman knight

Concepts & Tactics
• castle warfare

Buildings & Transport
• longship

William and his standard bearer

William, Duke of Normandy, accompanied by his standard bearer, at the crucial moment in the Battle of Hastings when he raised his helmet to dispel the rumor that he had been killed. He carries his baton of command that resembles a fighting club.

Count of Eu

This representation of the Count of Eu from the Bayeux Tapestry shows him carrying a long-handled Danish ax as a mark of his rank. His long cloak and scale hauberk also demonstrate his wealth. As a vassal of Duke William he wears his hair short and shaved at the back in the Norman manner.

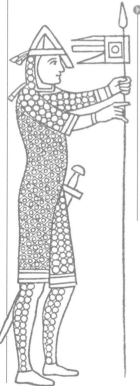

Norman shields

Norman shields were distinctively teardrop- or kite-shaped. The Bayeux Tapestry frequently shows them decorated with dragons. The large central boss is often surrounded by a pattern of rivet heads that also served to fix the long supporting strap (*guige*) to the back of the shield.

Duke William's ship

In this image from the Bayeux Tapestry, Duke William's ship *Mora*, a classic longship, leads the invasion fleet in 1066. He crossed at night carrying a lantern at the masthead (shown here), while the figurehead at the stern, a golden statue of a boy carrying a lance and blowing a horn, is described in contemporary sources.

Duke William of Normandy from the Bayeux Tapestry

The Duke is wearing a long mail hauberk with three-quarter-length sleeves. The mail leggings he wears were reserved only for the very rich in the mid-11th century. Carrying a sword shows him to be a knight, while his noble status is demonstrated by the banner on his lance and the ribbons falling from the back of his helmet and neck.

The Medieval Knight, *800–1500*

Origins and evolution

The medieval knight is an iconic figure, usually depicted in the full plate armor of the late 15th century. In fact, it took hundreds of years of development from much simpler forms of protection, different weapon types, and methods of riding to achieve this apogee. At the time of the Emperor Charlemagne, *c.* 800, armored horsemen rode without stirrups and carried round shields very much like the Roman cavalry centuries earlier. The introduction of stirrups in the 10th century changed the style of fighting, and knights began charging with lances, which they practiced by jousting in tournaments.

A Carolingian knight of the 9th century

The scale armor is rather clumsily represented in this reconstruction, and the round shield should be twice the size shown here. The two-part helmet, based on a Late Roman model, appears in contemporary manuscripts but may itself be a misunderstanding by Frankish artists.

A pair of jousting knights *c.* 1180

In order to engage in a head-to-head charge, the high saddle with its pommel and cantle wrapping around the rider's waist was firmly secured by double girthing and a breast strap. To withstand the shock of impact their legs are thrust out and upper bodies pushed forward to create a chevron shape braced against the saddle.

Late 12th-century knights

By the late 12th century mail armor for arms and legs had become usual, while the deeply curved teardrop shield seen here fits snugly to the body, providing better cover both on horseback and on foot. The figure on the left wears a barrel helm, which gave extra protection but restricted vision in comparison with the nasal helmet. He carries a long-handled, double-headed ax with which to fight when dismounted.

Hand weapons
• double-headed ax
• lance

Missile weapons

Defenses
• teardrop shield

Clothing
• full plate armor
• heraldic clothing
• scale armor

Warriors

Concepts & Tactics

Buildings & Transport
• horse-riding with stirrups

Knighthood ceremony

This depiction of the dubbing ceremony in the mid-13th century shows the symbols of knighthood. A king ties on the sword belt while servants affix golden spurs to the recipient's heels.

Late 14th-century knight

His coat of arms shows him to be Bertran de Guesclin, Constable of France, a hero in the war against the English. He wears a full "white armor" of plate with a dog-faced bascinet helmet.

See also
Heraldry and tournaments, *pages 82–3*
Anatomy of a knight, *pages 88–9*
Swords, *pages 280–1*
Weapons of reach, *pages 284–5*

Heraldry on clothing

Two young men prepare for a tournament in the mid-to-late 13th century. The standing figure wears an ermine-lined cloak, while the other man's surcoat is decorated with the heraldic symbol for water carriers. He wears shoulder protectors known as *ailettes*.

Late 15th-century knight

The knight in this illustration—possibly the King of Poland—is wearing the apogee of medieval plate armor, with protection for every part of the body. It is also a luxury item, and the belt supporting his sword and dagger is encrusted with jewels.

The Medieval Knight

Heraldry and tournaments

Tournaments were sporting occasions during which knights practiced the specialized skills of managing horse and lance. They had their origins in Carolingian and even Roman times, but in *c.* 1050 they took on the form of the joust that was maintained for 500 years. At the time of the Norman Conquest, although the Bayeux Tapestry shows decorated shields, warriors did not possess personal coats of arms. Heraldry first appeared in the 1130s as a result of the need to recognize individuals on the battlefield and as an indicator of status. Initially it was restricted to kings and great lords and became closely associated with the pageantry of tournaments. Heraldry developed its own language and strict rules of use, and disputes over use of the symbols were settled in special Courts of Chivalry.

The victor

This picture from the mid-13th-century Manasses Manuscript, which recorded the details of famous jousters, shows the victor of a tournament. It encapsulates the color and vivacity of what was in effect a sporting event. The spectators are beautiful women, whom the warrior fought to impress, and one is handing over a garland for the champion to wear. Also in the scene are musicians and acrobats. The knight has a whole team of supporters: a squire carries his master's lance, another valet his helmet, and a third, in a cap, holds a hammer for fixing armor damaged in the mock fighting.

Knights tourneying, *c.* 1500

In comparison with war armor, tournament armor often had a fixed leg protection and the barred helmet, which allowed better vision and did not have to protect against missile weapons as in warfare. The knights here also carry blunted swords for the encounter.

Personal identification

A group of late-12th-century knights wearing distinctive crests and one armorial shield. The kind of face masks worn here clearly made it impossible to identify a knight in any other way. Helmet crests were not functional in battle, as an opponent's weapon might catch on them, so they were worn more often at tournaments.

See also
Weapons of reach,
pages 284–5

Hand weapons
• blunted swords
• lance

Missile weapons

Defenses
• armorial shield

Clothing
• barred helmet

Warriors

Concepts & Tactics
• chivalry
• sport

Buildings & Transport

Noble opponents

The Duke of Brittany (left, wearing ermine) and the brother of the King of France (right, in fleur-de-lis) square up wearing armorial coats-of-arms and horse bardings. The illustration is based upon the lavishly illustrated *Tournament Book of René d'Anjou.*

Unhorsing

This picture of two mid-13th-century knights jousting shows the violence of even a nonlethal encounter. The victor (right), has broken his lance on the shield of the vanquished, hurling both man and horse backward. Jousters were rated according to the number of lances they shattered, and the best result was to dislodge an opponent and throw him a "full lance-length" from his horse.

The Medieval Knight

The knight's weapons

The medieval knight had to be expert in using a wide range of weapons. In order to achieve this a young squire practiced from the age of seven, reaching the age of knighting between fifteen and eighteen years old. The primary weapon was the sword, the symbol of knighthood, which was girded on at the time of dubbing. The lance measured 10–12 feet (3–3.5 meters) and took great strength and skill to manage. When knights fought on foot, as they often did, despite the myth that they were always charging cavalry, they cut the lance in half for easier handling. In the 15th century a specialized weapon, the poll-ax, was introduced. It required martial-arts training to use effectively.

See also
Knighthood ceremony,
page 81
Anatomy of a knight,
pages 88–9
Swords, *pages 280–1*
Clubs, maces, and axes,
pages 286–7

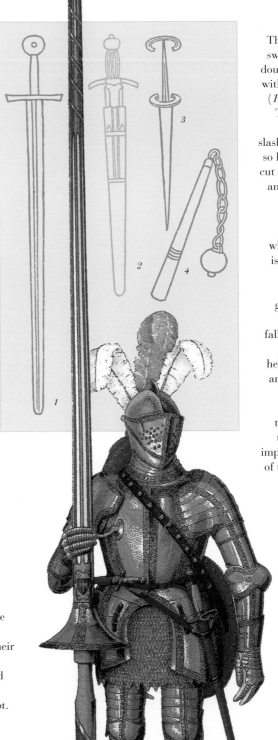

Lance and sword

This 16th-century lancer is probably a member of the Gens d'Armes, the elite heavy cavalry of Francis I of France. Although such troops were near the end of their usefulness—as was shown by their defeat at Pavia in 1525 by Spanish arquebusier infantry—they still had a role to play as impetus cavalry. He carries a round buckler, showing that he also expected to fight on foot.

Hand weapons

The classic medieval sword was a straight double-edged weapon with a rounded point. (*1*) The great sword. This was primarily used to deliver a slashing blow and was so heavy that it could cut off limbs or cleave an unprotected head in two. (*2*) The shorter sword was used for stabbing, while the dagger (*3*) is of the rondel type (named after the shape of the hand guards), often used for dispatching a fallen enemy through the eye-slits in his helmet. (*4*) The ball-and-chain mace was designed to crush armor, especially the helmet, denting the metal so that it impacted on the brain of the recipient of the blow, stunning or killing them.

Methods of hanging the sword

(*1*) Sword hanging from a double belt, 14th century. (*2*) The simple knightly belt of the 12th century. (*3*) Mid-13th-century method of hanging a knight's sword. (*4*) Sword hanging from a single belt, 15th century. (*5*) Sword hanging horizontally; used for shorter weapons.

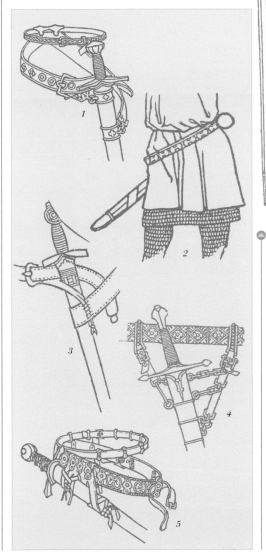

Chained swords

In the 14th century it became usual to attach both sword and dagger to a knight's armor by chains known as guard chains. Their principal function was to allow the sword to be retrieved if it was dropped or knocked from the hand in combat. The chains attached to the tassets of the 15th-century armor (below right) are the suspension chains of the scabbard. The guard chain of the sword is attached to the breastplate worn under the gamboised jupon, which is the visible outer covering.

Deadly weapon

A knight in a German-style armor, *c.* 1480, carrying the deadly poll-ax. Knights were fully armored at this time, so the weapon, with its point, blade, and pointed hammer head acted as a kind of can opener. To use it effectively required extensive training.

The Medieval Knight

The knight's armor

When fully armored a knight was protected from most weapons of his day. Mail provided a secure defense against swords and slashing weapons, although it could be penetrated by a lance point. From the mid-13th century onward an up-armoring began, first using padded additions, then hardened leather, and, by the mid-14th century, additional plates of metal. Each piece of armor had its own technical term relating to the part of the body that it was designed to cover. In response to the introduction of powerful longbows and crossbows, later plate armor was shaped into glancing surfaces to deflect the deadly missiles.

Development of the great helm

Square-topped helms with face masks (top) began to be used in the 1180s, appearing on the Third Crusade of 1189–92. The domed helmet with a cross-shaped viewing slit (center and bottom) is typical of the 1290s.

Collection of 12th-century knights

The pointed helmets are earlier than the square or domed ones. The illustrator has attempted to show different types of armor but has misunderstood contemporary illustrations, as most, if not all, would have worn conventional mail.

15th-century helmets

A bascinet with movable visor c. 1400 (top). A mid-14th-century bascinet with movable visor and fixed bevor (throat protector) worn by Gottfried von Eppstein (center). Strap and buckle securing a bascinet at the rear c. 1400 (bottom).

Hand weapons

Missile weapons

Defenses
• bevor
• cervelliere
• couter
• fauld
• poleyn

Clothing
• coif
• mail armor
• plate armor

Warriors

Concepts & Tactics

Buildings & Transport

Knight c. 1320

A composite armor of mail and plate. Metal poleyns protect the knees, while the shoulder (pauldron) and forearm (lower cannon) guards were often leather at this date. The mail ventail surrounding his face has a piece that attaches to the helmet for nasal protection.

15th-century armor

These figures show the full suit of armor at its point of highest development in the 15th century. Of particular note is the introduction of plates to cover the groin and thighs, known as faulds, with horizontal plates and, later, tassets hanging from them.

Coifs

Protection under the helmet was of great importance to the wearer. Initially just a padded cap (top), the coif soon became another mail defense (center) and by 1300 had assumed the same shape as the great helm that it supported (bottom). By 1400 it had developed into a cervelliere, or brain guard, which fitted under the bascinet.

Mid-14th-century knight

This knight wears a coat of plates comprising four large plates, front and back, covered by fabric with his coat of arms. The pieces protecting the knees, elbows, and shoulders are metal. The arms and legs are protected by splinted armor of metal strips riveted on to a leather base. His feet are protected by scale armor. (Gunther von Schwarzburg, from his tomb in Frankfurt cathedral, 1349).

See also
Anatomy of a knight, *pages 88–9*
Armor, *page 301*
Helmets, *pages 304–5*

Anatomy of a Knight

This magnificent representation of mail armor from the mid-12th century epitomizes the chivalric warrior of that era. Chivalry was a relatively new concept at that time, with its code of etiquette, courtly love, and a battlefield culture that allowed noblemen to be ransomed rather than killed if they were defeated. The figure actually represents Count Roland, one of Charlemagne's commanders, whose legendary exploits were celebrated in the *Chanson de Roland* after he had been killed fighting the Saracens in Spain in 798. Placed in charge of the rearguard and attacked at the Pass of Roncesvalles, he carries the horn that he refused to blow to recall his king as he considered it dishonorable not to carry on the fight alone.

1 The figure wears a long mail coat, split at front and back to make riding easier. It has long sleeves and would often have gauntlets that were rolled back to free the hands when not needed. Hidden from view by the long, ankle-length tunic, he would also be wearing mail hose to protect his legs.

2 The gird on his left side is a fine example of an early medieval sword, broad, and double-bladed. The belt is also in two parts, tightly cinched in at his waist to reduce the drag of the mail coat on his shoulders, and with another strap to support the sword.

3 The long shield is a development of the 11th-century kite style but with a straight top to allow the knight to peer over it when jousting. The prominent boss was often gilded as a form of display, and the lions represent an early form of heraldic device. The strap across his shoulder, or *guige*, is necessary to bear the weight of the heavy shield, especially when the warrior needed both his hands to manage his lance and his horse.

This plate armor belonged to Charles the Bold, Duke of Burgundy (1467–77). The duke would no doubt have approved of this rather romanticized representation of himself. His self-image was that of the perfect chivalric knight, and, in truth, he was almost the last of that breed. When he succeeded his father Philip the Good in 1467 he was one of the richest princes in Europe, not a king but with estates stretching from Flanders to southern France, along the rivers Rhine and Rhone, that contained some of the most populous and richest lands in the region. Unfortunately, his dreams of becoming the Holy Roman Emperor encouraged him to attack the Swiss Cantons in 1476. Defeated in three battles, he was killed at the last, and his lands went to the Habsburg Charles V by marriage.

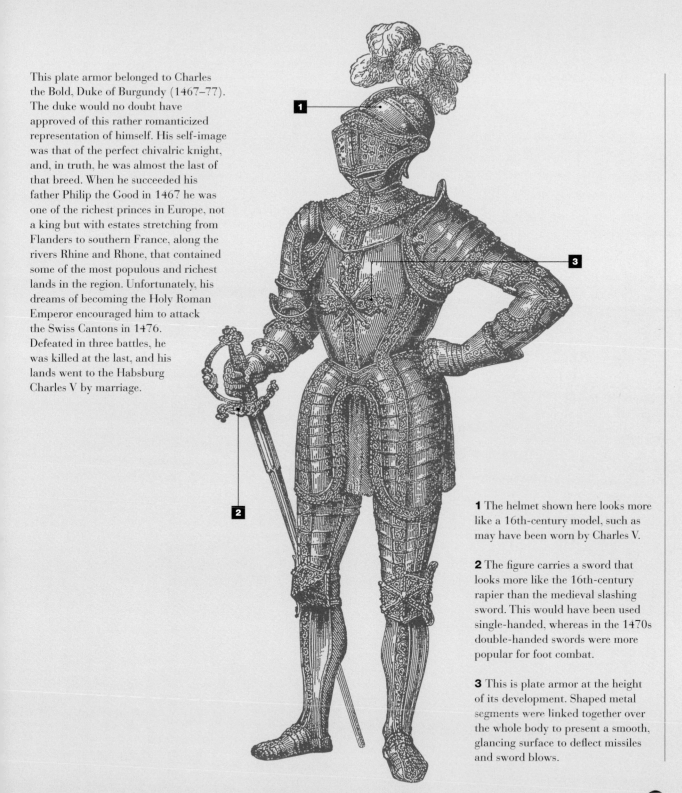

1 The helmet shown here looks more like a 16th-century model, such as may have been worn by Charles V.

2 The figure carries a sword that looks more like the 16th-century rapier than the medieval slashing sword. This would have been used single-handed, whereas in the 1470s double-handed swords were more popular for foot combat.

3 This is plate armor at the height of its development. Shaped metal segments were linked together over the whole body to present a smooth, glancing surface to deflect missiles and sword blows.

The Medieval Knight

The horse and horse armor

The knight's most prized possessions were his warhorses, and he usually took more than one on campaign with him. The warhorse, or *destrier*, was a highly trained animal, and the techniques it learned to maneuver in battle are now represented in modern dressage. The early Crusaders soon discovered that unprotected horses were very vulnerable to Turkish archers, who aimed at the mount rather than the rider. As a result, horses were provided with armor, known as barding, from the mid-12th century onward. In the later Middle Ages, and in response to the longbow and crossbow, plate armor for the entire body was created. In this way the development of horse armor matched that of the rider.

Full metal jacket
A warhorse in full mail barding from the 1170s. The pommel is incorrectly shown, as its horns should be facing backward to grip the rider's waist.

Knight charging
This magnificent representation of a charging knight comes from the mid-13th century. The horse's barding displays its rider's heraldry to great effect.

Colorful cavalry
A trio of late 13th-century Spanish knights displaying their heraldry on every aspect of the equipment of both men and horses.

Foot armor
Combined armor for the foot with spur, mid-14th century.

Hand weapons

Missile weapons

Defenses

Clothing
• horse barding

Warriors
• full body armor

Concepts & Tactics
• early Crusaders
• Turkish archers

Buildings & Transport
• armored horses

Gothic architecture

Full Gothic or German armor for man and horse, c. 1480. Metal plates cover the horse's head, neck, chest, and rump, and even its throat is protected by mail armor.

Flank guard

Late 15th-century tournament armor, including a circular leg guard.

Spurred into action

With his legs thrust forward during the lance charge, a knight needed a long spur to allow him to reach the aid points (just behind the girth) on his horse's flank.

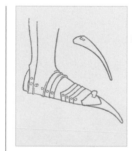

Knight's armored shoe (sabaton)

In the 15th century it was fashionable to wear very long-toed shoes, a style that was also used for armor. When dismounted, the knight could remove the additional projection. When fighting on foot, it was normal to dispense with sabatons altogether.

Crinet and plastron

Full armor for the horse's head and chest, c. 1500.

The well-dressed horse

(1) Decorated tail protector with tassels.
(2, 3) Tournament saddle, front and side view. The rider's thighs received extra protection from the leg guards. This special form of saddle has no cantle, as the rider sits on the bars at the back of the saddle, providing a particularly secure seat. (4) Horse shoe.
(5) Armor for a horse's hoof.

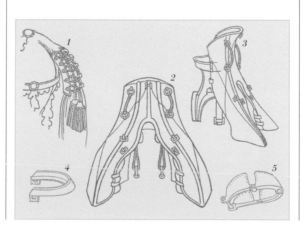

See also
Heraldry and tournaments,
pages 82–3

The Medieval Knight

The knight in battle

Battle is a notoriously difficult subject to portray in art, as it is about tactical movement and kinetic energy, both of which are impossible to show in the snapshot of a static picture. After the invention of printing in the late 15th century it became possible to show various stages of a battle in a series of prints but, from medieval art and the people who copied it, we are mostly left with a simple stage set upon which the main actors are displayed. Medieval manuscript illustrations also tend to concentrate on the activities of the knights, for reasons of their noble and heraldic status, so they can create a false impression of actual tactical deployments and progress on the encounter depicted.

Battle of Ampfing, 1322

The horses are shown unarmored, although many would have had at least a felt barding by this date. The artist has represented the different protagonists with different helmets: open-faced bascinets to the right, closed helms for the king and his companions in the center, and, behind, the chapeaux-de-fer, iron hats, of the sergeants, the non-noble mounted auxiliaries to the knights. Note the mounted crossbowman at the extreme left. Such troops were available from *c.* 1200, but were too lightly armored for combat as they would have been easy prey for knights, so their role was mostly confined to skirmishing.

Hand weapons
• halberd
• mace
• spear

Missile weapons
• longbow

Defenses

Clothing

Warriors

Concepts & Tactics
• ambush

Buildings & Transport

Theatrical Agincourt

This early 19th-century print of an imagined medieval battle is the kind of picture that would have been used to advertise a performance of Shakespeare's *Henry V* at that time. It shows knights fighting on foot with a variety of pole arms: spears, halberds, and maces. On the left, another knight dismounts to join the fray, dispelling the myth that chivalrous knights could only fight on horseback. This was common practice both during the Hundred Years War (1338–1453) and the Wars of the Roses (1455–85).

Siege of Thérouanne

A print showing the Battle of the Spurs between Henry VIII of England and Francis I of France fought outside English-besieged Thérouanne in 1513. It is shown as a glorious chivalric melee, and the only archer figure is shown shooting mounted, an unlikely occurrence. In fact, the English won the battle because they positioned a body of dismounted longbowmen in ambush on the flank of the advancing French. Surprised by their shooting, the French knights spurred their horses into flight, hence the name of the battle. This region of northern France is very flat, so the mountains in the background are a romantic addition.

The Medieval Soldier, *1000–1500*

Infantry and men-at-arms

Although the Middle Ages are usually represented as the time when knights and cavalry dominated the battlefield, this was only ever partly true. From around 1300 onward, infantry forces grew in importance. In 1302, at Courtrai, Flemish townsmen on foot defeated the flower of French chivalry. Following their ambush of the Austrians at Mortgarten (1351) and another victory at Sempach (1386) the Swiss became popular as mercenaries. Welsh longbowmen proved to be a vital component in English armies, contributing to victories over the French at Crécy (1346), Poitiers (1356), and Agincourt (1415). From 1419, in Bohemia, Jan Ziska taught the Czechs a way of fighting from wagons using cannon and handguns that completely overwhelmed the knights who opposed them.

Two Swiss hornblowers
These musicians played a crucial role in keeping the pikemen in step, giving directions in battle and raising their own morale while lowering that of the enemy.

Swiss foot soldiers *c.* 1500
These are mostly pikemen; those who fought in the front rank wear armor, the rest are without. The crossbowman, who would have operated outside the pike block as a skirmisher, is also unarmored. His companion the handgunner, in contrast, is shown wearing a full suit of armor. While men using a weapon so slow to reload would undoubtedly wear some armor, they more often sheltered behind a large shield known as a *pavise*.

Hand weapons
• pike
• pole arms

Missile weapons

Defenses
• buckler

Clothing

Warriors
• *bidaut*
• Flemish townsman
• sword-and-buckler man
• Welsh longbowman

Concepts & Tactics
• music for morale

Buildings & Transport

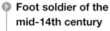

Sword-and-buckler men

These soldiers carry a small round shield known as a targe and represent a troop type whose mobility made them useful in battle, although they could not stand up to the more heavily armored spearmen. As infantry began to adopt pikes in the mid-15th century and maneuvered in clumsy formations, the sword-and-buckler men formed crucial links between the pike blocks.

Two-handed blades

Infantry pole arms came in many shapes and sizes: (*1*) a pike with subordinate blades; (*2*) early form of halberd; (*3*) morning-star; (*4*) glaive; (*5*) war-flail.

Foot soldier of the mid-14th century

This soldier represents the type of skirmishing infantryman that was increasingly common on the battlefields of Europe at this time. Unarmored, he relies upon his mobility to survive and harry the enemy. Such soldiers were known as *ribauds* and *bidauts*, and they often hailed from mountainous zones such as the Pyrenees. In battle they would slip under the bellies of the knights' warhorses and wound or kill them.

See also
Swords,
pages 280–1
Clubs, maces, and axes, *pages 286–7*

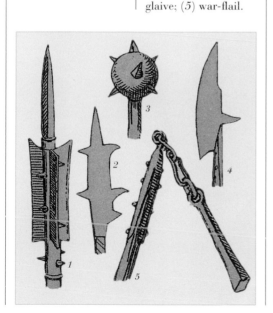

The Medieval Soldier

Infantry: tactics and technology

In a society where military skills were associated with noble birth it was difficult for non-noble soldiers to assert themselves on the battlefield. They were not even considered to be proper warriors but rather as upstarts. Consequently, they were despised and hated by their chivalrous opponents, who often killed them out of hand, in contrast to the mercy the knights showed their noble enemies. This meant that they had to display a particular kind of bravery when entering battle. Between the knights and peasants or townsmen lay a class of non-noble cavalrymen variously called *hobilars* (Britain), *valets* (France), or *genitors* (Spain and Italy). Any fully equipped warrior could be called a man-at-arms whether he fought on horse or foot.

Swiss horsemen
Although they look like cavalry, since they are carrying halberds and their leader an ax, it is more likely that they are infantry fortunate enough to have acquired mounts for the march.

Foot soldier, late 14th century
This member of the Paris militia is well-equipped compared with most infantry of the period, and he may be a prosperous burgher. His spear would have been longer than this illustration suggests. In battle he would have acted mainly on the defensive behind his large shield. He wears the chapel-de-fer helmet, which combined protection with good visibility.

The Ghent Militia, *c.* 1350

Seeking independence from their French feudal overlords, the Flemish marched under the banners of their towns and their guilds, which gave them a strong sense of identity and, with music provided by hornblowers, played a crucial role in raising morale and helping to maintain order on the battlefield. Their arms were often limited to simple pole arms or maces. Here, the main body behind the banner are carrying a mixture of spears, which could be planted in the ground to hold mounted knights at bay, and *goedendags*. The *goedendag*, which means "good day" in Flemish, is an ironic name for a heavy wooden club, about 4 feet (1.2 meters) long, with its top tipped by an iron band and a spike, thus providing both a sharp and a crushing weapon against knightly armor. Watching from the town walls are the crossbowmen, whose role in battle was to shoot down the knights' horses with their heavy bolts.

See also
Weapons of reach,
pages 284–5

Genitors

Genitors were a lightly armored cavalry common in Spain, who used many tactics learned from the Moors. Their descendants, the conquistadores, later used these to great effect in America. Here they are shown wielding fearsome falchions, but they would also have used lances and javelins.

The Medieval Soldier

The longbow and the crossbow

Missilemen became increasingly important on the battlefield during the Middle Ages. Originally a hunter's weapon, the longbow became widely used throughout the Kingdom of England, and compulsory practice at the archery butts was brought in by the mid-14th century. A powerful weapon with a 220-yard (200-meter) range and great penetrating power at 50 yards (45 meters), it made English armies feared all over Europe. Crossbowmen were also a dangerous enemy to the knights, although their weapon was slower loading. With a belt-and-claw mechanism they could shoot eight shots a minute in comparison to the longbow's twelve to twenty. Heavier models could shoot only two, so their users sheltered behind the cover of a large shield, or *pavise*.

Missilemen

Two missilemen from the Ordinance Companies (regular forces) of the King of France, dating from the mid-15th century. The French recruited mostly foreign missilemen—crossbowmen from Italy, notably Genoa, and archers from Scotland, with which France was allied.

Loading a crossbow

A mid-15th century crossbowman loads his quarrel into his spanned bow. He keeps a supply of these bolts in a pouch on his right hip.

Polish crossbowman, mid-15th century

Crossbows were important weapons for fighting the Ottomans, as their heavy bolts kept the Turkish horse-archers at bay.

See also
Anatomy of a crossbow, *pages 100–1*
Thrown weapons, *page 288–9*
Bows, *pages 290–1*
Crossbows, *pages 292–3*
Body armor, *pages 302–3*

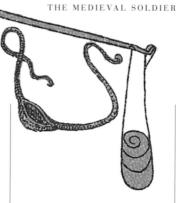

10th-century archer
An early medieval archer is shown using a recurved bow. In fact, most Western European bows were simple staves throughout the Middle Ages.

Slings
The sling was a weapon as ancient as the conflict between David and Goliath, but, despite its simplicity, it never went out of use in war. The staff sling (right), known as a fustibal, was employed extensively in naval warfare. It was particularly useful for hurling pots of Greek fire from land or sea.

Spanning a crossbow
These late 15th-century crossbowmen in the service of the King of France both wear armor for the upper body and, in the case of the figure on the right, plate-armor arm protection. Crossbowmen needed to be armored because it took a long time to span their bows. Both have a winding device, called a windlass, to do this.

Longbowman
The equipment of this heavily armored archer of the late 15th century marks him out as a member of the French King's Garde Ecossais, formed of noblemen. In battle they actually served as heavy cavalry.

A war arrow
About 30 inches (75 centimeters) long, with three feathers; most effective at 100 yards (90 meters).

Pavise from the Vienna armories
The front is highly decorated. The rope grip on the back is for adjusting its position when propped up by a wooden strut.

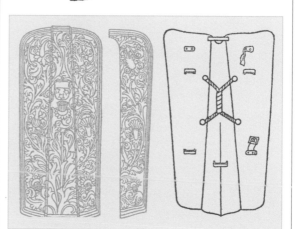

Anatomy of a Crossbow

The crossbow is a weapon of great antiquity. Archaeological evidence has revealed its use from as early as the 6th century BCE in China. The first example of its use in Western Europe is during the Late Roman Empire in the 4th century CE, when some of the skirmishing troops of the legions appear to have had them. But, in fact, these *ballistiarii* may have been managing larger artillery pieces rather than the handheld kind. A stone carving from around 400 CE does show a crossbow, but this is probably in a hunting rather than a fighting context. Crossbows do not appear in art again until the late 10th century, when they are shown in use by the besiegers of a walled city. Written evidence from the mid-11th century onward attests to their more widespread use, usually associated with the Italian maritime states and the Crusades.

1 This illustration shows a simple stave crossbow from *c.* 1100. It has a wooden stock about 3 feet (1 meter) long, and its bow is made of wood, bone, and sinew to give it a similar flexibility to the nomadic horse-archer's composite bow. This meant that it was susceptible to damp, which could lead to its parts separating. Despite this it was a popular weapon aboard ship and was commonly used by Italian sailors.

2 The cord, made of twisted twine, is much thicker than a bowstring and could only be drawn back by the user putting his foot in the stirrup at the front of the bow and pulling using both hands.

3 When in position it would be locked in place by the nut, usually made of bone, until the time came to shoot. This meant that, unlike an ordinary bow, it could be kept loaded.

4 Squeezing the long-handled trigger tripped the nut and released the bolt to an effective range of about 200 yards (180 meters). Crossbow bolts could pierce any mail armor and even go through a shield.

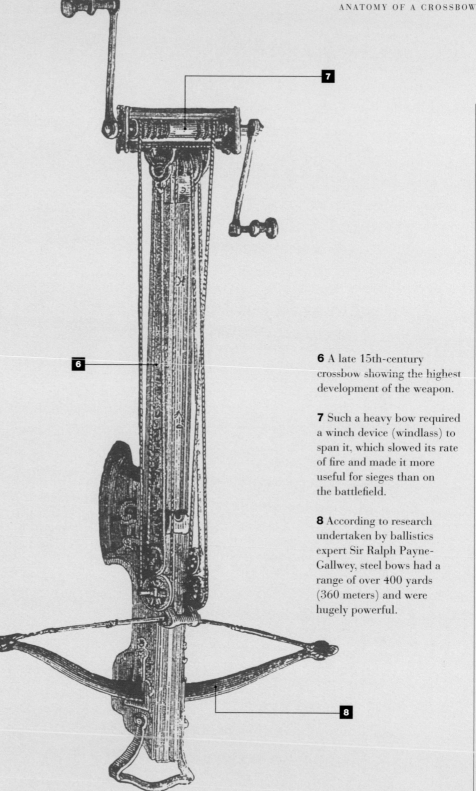

5 A quarrel, or crossbow bolt, was much shorter than an arrow at less than 12 inches (30 centimeters) long. The bulge behind the head of the bolt here suggests that it was intended to be used as an incendiary device.

6 A late 15th-century crossbow showing the highest development of the weapon.

7 Such a heavy bow required a winch device (windlass) to span it, which slowed its rate of fire and made it more useful for sieges than on the battlefield.

8 According to research undertaken by ballistics expert Sir Ralph Payne-Gallwey, steel bows had a range of over 400 yards (360 meters) and were hugely powerful.

The Crusades, *1095–1272*

Battle for the Holy Land

The Crusades were born out of the idea that the Holy Land, which had been under Muslim control for over 400 years, should be returned to Christian rule. When Pope Urban II called for volunteers in 1095, thousands of knights and others responded. Despite their lack of knowledge of the terrain and tactics of their enemies, the First Crusaders captured Jerusalem in July 1099. Many then returned home, and it proved difficult to defend the new conquests. One answer was the novel idea of warrior-monks devoted to the service of God. The first military order was that of the Templars; their patron, St Bernard of Clairvaux, achieved papal endorsement for them in 1129. Other orders were the Hospitaller Brothers, the Teutonic Knights, and many orders in Spain, where Christians were reconquering land that had been under Moorish rule.

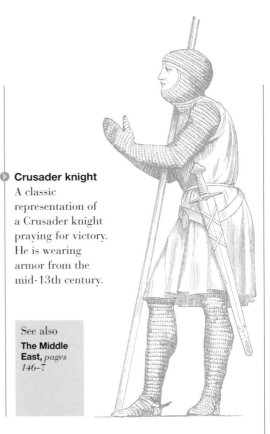

Crusader knight
A classic representation of a Crusader knight praying for victory. He is wearing armor from the mid-13th century.

See also
The Middle East, *pages 146–7*

Crusaders in Egypt
This 16th-century print illustrates the arrival of the Crusaders of the Seventh Crusade under King Louis IX of France, later St Louis. They arrived in Egypt in 1248 at Damietta, a fortified port at the mouth of the Nile. This had to be taken from the Ayyubid Sultan before marching south to capture Cairo as a base from which to recover Jerusalem, which had been lost to the Khwarzmians in 1244. The costumes and equipment are those of *c.* 1520, and the mounted enemy on the far bank are labeled Turks, a generic name for the Muslim enemy but accurate for the time of printing, when the Ottomans threatened Europe.

Hand weapons

Missile weapons

Defenses

Clothing
• cassocks
• mail armor

Warriors
• Hospitaller Brothers
• Knights Templar
• Teutonic Knights

Concepts & Tactics
• religious war
• warrior-monks

Buildings & Transport

Knights Templar

Knights Templar wore white cassocks similar to those of Cistercian monks—the order to which their patron, St Bernard of Clairvaux, belonged— emblazoned with a red cross. The mounted figure's armor is not easy to date but looks later than the order's dissolution by the French king in 1307. The figure on the left is a Teutonic Knight from around 1410.

Teutonic Knights

Military monks were supposed to dress very simply, although as their orders grew rich through donations their masters took on the status of great princes. The grand master here (left), accompanied by a brother knight, bears the distinctive Teutonic Cross on his chest and wears both a sword belt and, apparently, a crown. This may be because in the 1220s German knights became more involved in the Northern Crusades along the Baltic coast. Here they established their Ordenstaat, or state of the Teutonic Order, which played a major role in the region until its defeat by an allied force of Poles and Lithuanians at the battle of Tannenberg in 1410.

The Crusades

Richard the Lionheart and the Third Crusade

The Third Crusade was called after the recapture of Jerusalem and most other Christian territory in Syria by Saladin in 1187. When Guy de Lusignan, King of Jerusalem—who had been captured at the battle of Hattin—was released in 1189 he began a siege of Acre, but with only a small force he could not manage more than a blockade. King Philip II of France reached the Holy Land in April 1191 and Richard I of England in early June. In fact, the two kings were sworn enemies, but they collaborated for the sake of the Crusade. After constant attacks by siege engines the city eventually surrendered on July 12, leaving six thousand of Saladin's men prisoner, a great blow to his prestige.

Richard the Lionheart at the siege of Jaffa, 1192

After failing to take Jerusalem in June, Richard led his forces to secure fortifications along the Syrian coastline. Saladin thought he saw an opportunity to recapture the strategically crucial port of Jaffa and launched a heavy assault on July 27. When Richard, who was at Acre, heard the news he scraped together a small force of fifty knights and two thousand infantry. Sailing down the coast, he arrived four days later and went straight into the attack, wading from his ships wielding a battle ax. On August 4 Saladin tried again. Outnumbered ten to one, Richard set up his infantry outside the town in teams of one crossbowman and one archer behind a line of shielded spearsmen and resisted every attack of the Muslim cavalry. Saladin was forced to withdraw. This picture shows a romanticized view with Richard on horseback, although he mainly fought on foot in the battle line to encourage the foot soldiers.

City of Acre

This map of Acre was drawn in the 14th century. The city was effectively the capital of the Crusader States, being the richest port in the Levant and fortified by a double line of tall walls. In the center stands the castle, or citadel, while in the bottom right lies the tower of the Templars. The sea tower was connected to the walls by a chain to prevent enemy vessels sailing into the harbor.

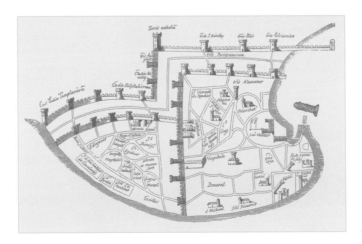

Richard the Lionheart

Taken from his royal seal, this shows Richard I, "the Lionheart," King of England from 1189 to 1199, mounted and fully armored for war, his drawn sword symbolizing military virtue. His barrel helm sports a magnificent crest, and his shield bears three lions. This is the earliest representation of the English royal coat of arms: gules three lions passant guardant.

Siege of Antioch, 1098

This image of the siege, during the First Crusade, is from a 15th-century manuscript. By this time, expeditions to the Holy Land were no longer realistic as Europe struggled to fend off the Ottoman Turks.

See also
The Crusades,
page 102–3
The Middle East,
pages 146–7

The Castle, *1000–1500*

Castle design and defenses

The castle is central to our understanding of medieval warfare. The original motte-and-bailey structures were built of wood and earth banks. Soil was excavated and piled into a mound (motte) up to 100 feet (30 meters) high and strengthened by timber beams. The surrounding area, protected by a wooden palisade, was known as the bailey, a term that survived into the era of stone building. The first stone towers appeared *c.* 1000 and soon developed into impressive buildings— the Tower of London, built after 1066, is a good example. In the 13th century the defensive emphasis switched to the walls and saw the building of concentric castles. But gunpowder weapons spelled doom for the castle with its tall, thin walls, so it began to be replaced *c.* 1500 by low, earthen-bank redoubts, known as star forts.

Fortified entrance

A double-towered fortified gateway with a portcullis for extra security. A lookout window can be seen to the right of the heraldic shield over the entrance.

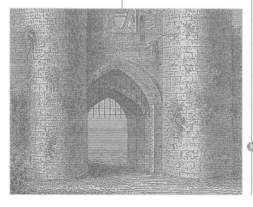

Towered gateway

A double-towered gateway shown in plan. Above the entrance is a machicolation (*A*), from which defenders could hurl down missiles on attackers. The gateway is divided into two chambers (*B, C*) by the heavy wooden portcullis. Arrow slits on the interior walls of the towers (*D*) would allow defenders to shoot into the gateway at anyone trying to gain entry.

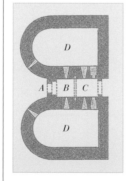

Drawbridge

A heavily fortified drawbridge gateway. Above each one is a turret, with arrow slits capped by a triangular roof, and between them another roofed structure. The drawbridge itself can be lifted by means of chains in order to close. A small gateway or sally port to the right of the main gateway also seems to have its own drawbridge.

Drawbridge interior

A view showing the operation of the drawbridge.

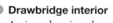

Hand weapons

Missile weapons

Defenses
• crenellation
• drawbridge
• machicolation
• portcullis

Clothing

Warriors

Concepts & Tactics

Buildings & Transport
• castle
• concentric castles
• motte-and-bailey
• stone towers

Lookout tower
This square tower has a round turret at each corner. This is more for decoration than military effectiveness.

Crenellated tower
This square tower is topped by square crenellations above the wall and machicolations in front of the wall, allowing defenders to throw projectiles on attackers below.

See also
Anatomy of a castle, *pages 108–11*
Siege engine technology, *pages 112–13*

Window embrasure seen from inside the wall
Windows were potentially weak places in castle walls, so embrasures were cleverly designed as reinforcement, making them as strong, sometimes stronger, than the walls themselves.

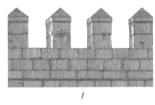

1

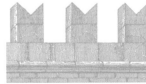

2

3

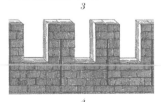

4

Different types of crenellations
These allowed the defenders to take cover while reloading weapons and then to shoot at attackers from between them: (*1*) diamond topped; (*2*) V shaped; (*3*) rounded; (*4*) square—note that each square crenellation is provided with an arrow-slit which afforded further protection of the archer or crossbowman using it.

Anatomy of a Castle

1 Kidwelly stands high above the western bank of the River Gwaendraeth at its upper tidal limit in west Wales. The riverside needed no further strengthening by defenses, and in the 12th century a motte-and-bailey castle of wood and earth was constructed behind a deep ditch on the landward side. Much of the castle remains today, largely of 13th-century build or later.

2 The frontal (southern) elevation of Kidwelly's impressively fortified gatehouse has two round towers flanking the entrance, while on the left side the chamber tower rises a full story higher. The doorway is deeply inset allowing for the construction of a three-arched machicolation to defend it from attack. Although there are windows higher up in the walls, the lower floors have only observation or arrow slits in them, allowing the attacker no possibility of breaking in through these openings.

3 The view from the inside the gateway shows its present ruined state, but the three windows of the first-floor hall hint at its original splendor.

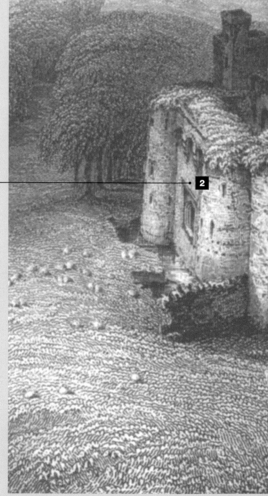

4 This section view across the castle is taken from just inside the western wall. The two storys of the gatehouse can be clearly seen, as can the gateway chamber that would have contained the portcullis.

The two towers shown are the southwest and northwest round towers of the keep, with the lesser fortifications of the northern curtain wall to the right.

Anatomy of a Castle

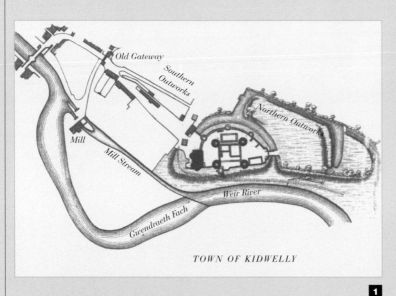

2 Viewed from the southwestern, or river, side the castle provides a most imposing aspect. On the left-hand side of the engraving is the gatehouse tower, linked by a wall to the southernmost (southeast) tower of the keep.

3 Directly in front of that projects the chapel tower, supported, because of the steepness of the slope, by two huge spur buttresses.

4 To the right of this is the great hall of the keep, which was used by its lord for everything from handing down justice and formal audiences to feasting and merriment.

5 Further right is the northeast round tower.

6 At the extreme right is the northern gatehouse. This is not as impressive a structure as the main gatehouse, but it is also flanked by two round towers and leads to a bridge across the moat.

7 Beyond the gatehouse lies the northern bailey, with additional earthen-bank fortifications.

8 A point to note is that the openings at ground level on the gatehouse and the chapel tower are not windows, as this would make the castle vulnerable to attack, but latrine chutes. Contrary to popular wisdom about the hygiene standards of the Middle Ages, the inhabitants of fortresses had to be most particular in disposing of their waste in case an outbreak of disease should occur among the garrison at the a of siege.

1 This map shows Kidwelly's semicircular 110-yard (100-meter) enclosure on its rear wall above the river. Two outer enclosures, or baileys, lie on either side. The one to the south later developed into a town with its own wall, showing that it was normal for a castle to be part of a wider defensive fortification. Owing to its height above river level the surrounding moat was dry.

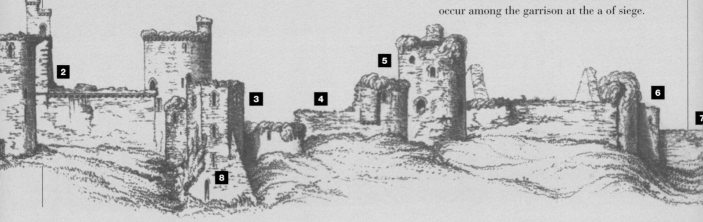

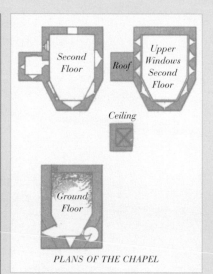

Second Floor

Roof

Upper Windows Second Floor

Ceiling

Ground Floor

PLANS OF THE CHAPEL

9

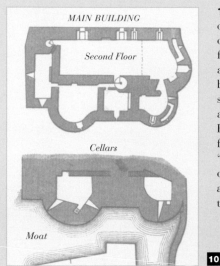

MAIN BUILDING

Second Floor

Cellars

Moat

10

10 Plans of the gatehouse show the cellars, their thick walls pierced with only three slits for light. The second floor, above the gateway, comprises a single larger room and chamber behind the towers. The first floor, not shown here, has a chamber and a hall and kitchen to the right (western) side. Being directly above the gateway its floor is pierced in two places by "murder holes" for throwing projectiles down on the heads of anyone attacking the portcullis guarding the entrance.

9 These plans of the chapel area remind us that a castle was also a Christian community of many souls, whose spiritual needs were met by the ministrations of the lord's chaplain. The chapel tower juts out from the walls on the scarp slope running down to the river. It comprises a basement and an upper floor that is the chapel itself, with an upper range of clerestory windows to bring in light. The small room on its south side was the sacristy that contained the sacred vessels and vestments for services, and the priest's bedroom was situated below it.

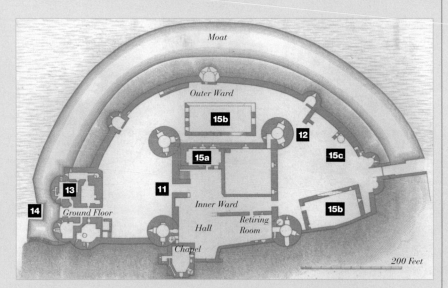

Moat

Outer Ward

15b

12

15a

15c

13

11

14

Ground Floor

Inner Ward

Retiring Room

15b

Hall

Chapel

200 Feet

11 The central tower, or keep, measures 30 square yards (25 square meters) and dates from *c.* 1275.

12 The keep's four round towers protect the corners of the structure as well as providing mutually supporting lines of fire from their arrow slits.

13 The great southern gatehouse and curtain wall were added in the early 14th century, both to strengthen the castle and to provide a more impressive status symbol.

14 The barbican, the outwork that protected the gatehouse tower from across the moat, is no longer visible.

15 In the more peaceful Tudor period of the early 16th century, when the requirements of defense became secondary to greater comfort, more domestic buildings were added: (*a*) kitchen in the central tower; (*b*) two rectangular halls in the outer ward; and (*c*) an oven inside the east wall.

The Castle

Siege engine technology

The Middle Ages are not usually associated with rapid technological developments, but many inventions had their origins at this time, including windmills, printing, and, in the case of warfare, gunpowder weapons. Prior to the development of cannon powerful enough to smash down stone walls, medieval soldiers had recourse to many other types of siege engine. These could be in the form of artillery hurling huge stone balls. One, inherited from antiquity, was the *ballista*, a form of giant crossbow, although this was largely replaced by the trebuchet from the mid-12th century. Another way of bringing down walls was to use battering rams, usually under cover of wheeled sheds. Wooden siege towers were also constructed to allow the attackers to scale enemy fortifications.

Bridge on wheels

This late-medieval manuscript dating from *c.* 1400 shows a siege tower being used against a fortress that is surrounded by water. As a result, it has been necessary to construct a huge bridge projecting from the tower across the intervening space. The bridge has then been provided with crenellated wooden hoarding along its length to protect the attacking troops. Needless to say, this was a very dangerous operation, not least because any man falling into the water while wearing heavy armor had no chance of survival.

See also
Anatomy of a trebuchet, *pages 114–15*
Siege tactics, *pages 116–17*
Siege engines, *pages 294–5*

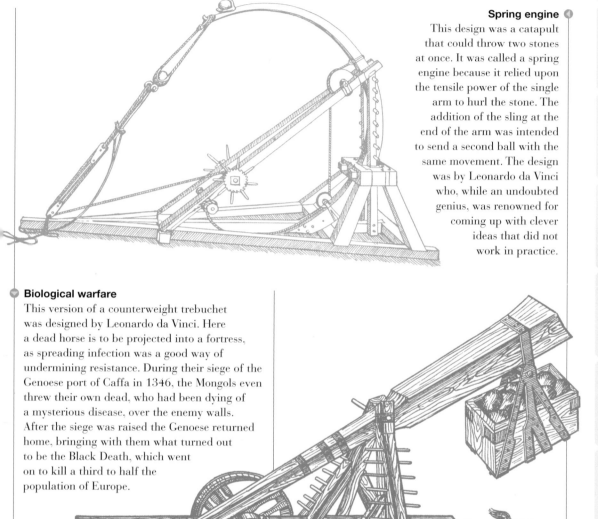

Spring engine

This design was a catapult that could throw two stones at once. It was called a spring engine because it relied upon the tensile power of the single arm to hurl the stone. The addition of the sling at the end of the arm was intended to send a second ball with the same movement. The design was by Leonardo da Vinci who, while an undoubted genius, was renowned for coming up with clever ideas that did not work in practice.

Biological warfare

This version of a counterweight trebuchet was designed by Leonardo da Vinci. Here a dead horse is to be projected into a fortress, as spreading infection was a good way of undermining resistance. During their siege of the Genoese port of Caffa in 1346, the Mongols even threw their own dead, who had been dying of a mysterious disease, over the enemy walls. After the siege was raised the Genoese returned home, bringing with them what turned out to be the Black Death, which went on to kill a third to half the population of Europe.

Anatomy of a Trebuchet

1 The trebuchet is the most iconic and powerful siege engine of the pre-gunpowder era. Its name comes from the Old French verb *trebucher*, to throw over, which exactly describes its unique action. Unlike the most popular type of siege engine in the medieval era, the *ballista*, which operated like a huge bow on the horizontal plane, the trebuchet's single arm swung through the vertical axis, releasing its missile at the highest point for the farthest range.

2 The first reference to the use of trebuchets in Western Europe is associated with the attacks of the nomadic Avars on Constantinople in the 6th century CE. The earliest examples were traction operated, teams of men pulling on ropes to bring down the front end of the beam. Depending upon the size of the weapon these teams could vary in size from just a few operators to a hundred men.

3 The finest development of the trebuchet was the counterweight weapon shown in this illustration. These came into use around the middle of the 12th century. The technology seems to have reached the West via Arab scientific manuscripts, although European narrative histories attribute the development to Christian engineers. Certainly, they are mentioned during the Third Crusade when Richard the Lionheart deployed two— nicknamed "God's Own Catapult" and "Bad Neighbor"—in the attack on Acre in 1191.

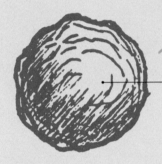

4 Standing up to 22 yards (20 meters) high, a large trebuchet could hurl stones over 275 yards (250 meters). Recent reconstructions have demonstrated their fearful power. At Castelnaud Castle in France, an experimental machine with a 6.6-ton (6 metric ton) counterweight was able to cast a 300-pound (136 kilogram) ball some 200 meters (220 yards) with extraordinary accuracy. A similar model built in Scotland proved capable of getting its shots repeatedly through an aperture as small as a normal-sized window.

5 The importance of this ability to hit the same spot consistently was that a defensive wall or tower would be seriously weakened by repetitive impact, causing it to crack and fall. In 1304, when besieging Stirling Castle, Edward I had a machine called "Warwolf" constructed, which took five master carpenters and fifty others some three months to complete. The mere threat of its awesome power was enough to make the garrison offer to surrender before it had fired a shot.

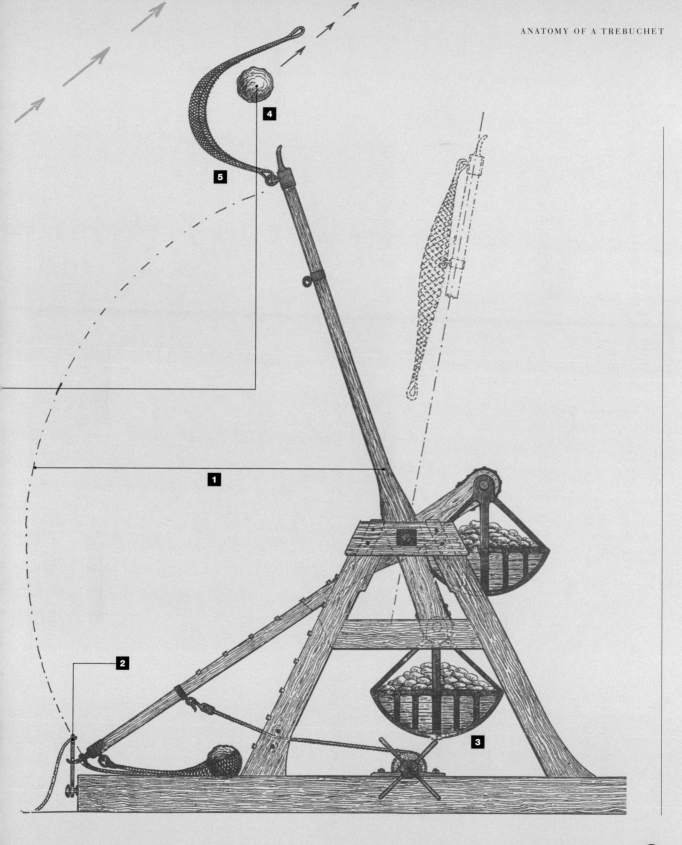

The Castle

Siege tactics

When faced with high and fiercely defended stone walls, medieval armies often struggled to overcome them. The most usual form of siege was that of blockade, by which the attackers attempted to cut off any means of relief or supply in order to starve out the defenders. If the ground was suitable, mining was attempted. A tunnel would be dug under the walls and shored up by timber supports. Combustible material would then be brought in and set on fire. As the timber supports burned they collapsed, bringing the walls down above them and causing a breach for the attackers to storm.

Attackers and defenders
A mid-13th-century representation of two counterweight trebuchets bombarding a stone tower. The only apparent recourse of the defenders is to throw stones by hand.

Crusaders besiege Jerusalem
This powerful image by the 19th-century artist Gustave Doré shows the First Crusaders attacking Jerusalem in 1099. In the foreground is a torsion engine (*petrary*). Behind it, a counterweight trebuchet is about to be released. Unfortunately, both engines are anachronistic, the *petrary* being of the Roman *onager* type and the trebuchet not arriving for fifty years after the siege in question.

Hand weapons

Missile weapons
• cannon
• *petrary*
• trebuchet

Defenses
• scalding water
• sharpened stakes
• stones

Clothing

Warriors
• archers
• crossbowmen

Concepts & Tactics
• blockade
• mining
• siegecraft

Buildings & Transport
• belfry
• castle
• siege tower

Methods of siege warfare

Here the many methods of attacking a castle are shown in one mid-19th-century print. A belfry, a movable wooden tower, is wheeled into position and its bridge lowered to allow the troops access to the castle walls. Archers and crossbowmen shoot at the defenders from below. The cannon show this to be the 15th century, although such weapons would not actually have been placed so close to the action.

Combined operations

This illustration from a mid-14th-century manuscript shows a fortress being assailed by land and sea. On the land approach, the besiegers have erected a wooden tower from which to shoot while other archers shoot from below. On the seaward side are two ships also filled with archers, one of whom is in the crow's-nest. In reply, the defenders are delivering a barrage of stones and arrows.

Undermining the walls

This mid-13th-century manuscript detail shows an attempt to mine the walls of a castle. The attackers have wheeled a wooden framework with an armored roof up to the base of the walls that they are attacking with their picks. The defenders are attempting to interrupt the attackers' progress by hurling down stones, scalding water, and sharpened stakes, although without much apparent success.

See also
The Crusades, *page 102–3*
Siege engine technology, *pages 112–13*
Anatomy of a trebuchet, *pages 114–15*
Early cannon, *page 118*
Anatomy of an early cannon, *pages 120–1*
Siege engines, *pages 294–5*

Gunpowder, *1240–1500*

Early cannon

The Mongol invasion of Europe in 1240–41 first brought Chinese gunpowder technology to the West. Soon afterward, the English monk and scientist Roger Bacon described the component parts of charcoal, sulphur, and saltpeter. A century later the first guns were deployed. These were simple, vase-like objects with a touchhole leading to a chamber in which the explosion was contained. A 1326 manuscript by Walter de Milemete shows one of these discharging a heavy arrow toward a fortress. Developments gradually made a better airtight seal and a longer, stronger barrel possible, and effectiveness was also increased by better methods of combining the three constituents of gunpowder. By 1400 cannon were regularly used in sieges, and by 1500 a wide array of handguns and field pieces was used in open battle.

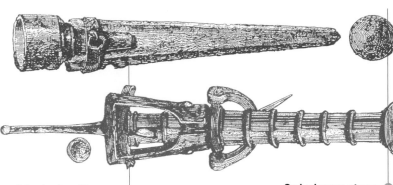

Swivel guns at sea
These two early cannon were for use on warships. One has a simple stock and small barrel, suggesting it was probably a one-shot weapon from about 1400. The other is a more sophisticated 16th-century development. The spike was pushed into the ship's gunwale and the handle allowed the gun to be trained up or down as required. A further development was the swivel gun, which could also be swung from side to side.

Siege gun and mantlets
Owing to the very slow reloading process, siege guns needed to be protected against defending fire from inside the fortress, and it was usual have wooden shielding. Here, two soldiers provide extra cover with their large portable shields, or *pavises*.

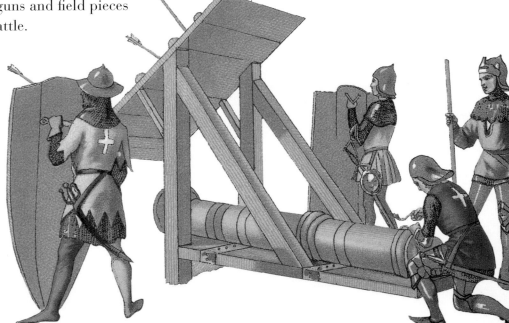

See also
Methods of siege warfare,
page 117
Anatomy of an early cannon,
pages 120–1
The wider world,
page 125
Artillery and fortifications,
page 160
The evolution of artillery,
pages 210–11
Artillery,
pages 296–7

Mobile field cannon

This mid-16th-century cannon has developed to the stage where it is fully mobile. It sits on a carriage and has a trail that connects to a limber drawn by several horses in traces. Now capable of being easily moved on campaign and deployed in battle, it also has a device for raising and lowering the barrel for shooting at different ranges.

Siege battery in action

Here two cannon are protected by a hinged mantlet, which is being raised to allow them to fire. The one on the left is the old form of bombard, stubby and wide-mouthed. Carried on a cart to the siege, it was bedded into the ground with a wooden framework behind it to prevent recoil. On the right is a longer-barreled gun, probably cast in bronze; this was to be the future for gunpowder artillery.

Missile weapons
• cannon

Defenses
• mantlet
• *pavise*
• shield

Clothing

Warriors
• Mongols

Concepts & Tactics
• development of gunpowder
• siegecraft

Buildings & Transport
• carriage to transport cannon
• warship

Anatomy of an Early Cannon

1 Siege gun *c.* 1400. Before the introduction of cast-bronze cannon in the 16th century, the barrel was constructed of long strips of iron tightly bound by constricting bands along its length. This construction technique was borrowed from wooden barrel making and did not make for a particularly airtight tube. Such weapons were breech-loaders, with a pre-prepared charge screwed into the rear end, which was a slow and cumbersome job.

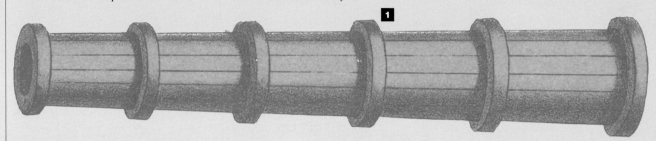

2 When early cannon were deployed at sieges, and because they were only simple tubes, it was normal to provide them with a timber framework. Unfortunately, the frame shown here would not have supported such a heavy gun, which would normally be buried in the ground.

3 Single-piece-cast cannon *c.* 1500. A great technological advance was in casting cannon in bronze in one piece. This did away with the problems of the force of the ignition escaping through any gaps in the stave-construction barrel.

4 A bronze breech-loading cannon *c.* 1500. This piece was probably used aboard ship. It combined the advantages of bronze casting with the flexibility of the breech-loader. Using a removable charge chamber enabled the gunners to prepare charges beforehand, which greatly speeded up the firing procedure.

5 There was a fashion in the late 15th century for multibarrelled guns, known as the ribauldquin. They were one-shot weapons and not to be confused with modern machine-guns. Producing a spray of lead balls, they were most useful in an anti-personnel role—when defending a breach in a fortress wall against storming troops, for example.

6 Following the execution of Jan Hus for heresy at the Council of Constance (1415), his Bohemian followers, known as the Hussites, fought for independence against the Holy Roman Emperor Sigismund. Jan Zizka, their brilliant leader, devised a way of using the wagon-fort formation to defeat all comers by equipping it with cannon. This late 15th-century print shows ordinary wagons behind, which could be filled with soldiers, and, in front, battle-wagons filled with handgunners.

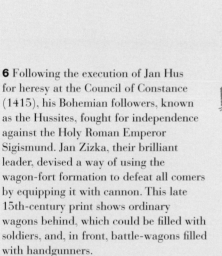

7 A late 15th-century battle-wagon. Although it looks like a tank the vehicle could not be used in the same way because the horses would have been too vulnerable to missile fire. They would normally have been unhitched and the wagon drawn up in a defensive circle. The scythed wheels are a romantic and unlikely touch added by the artist.

Gunpowder

Early firearms

Early gunpowder weapons came in a variety of sizes, and handguns appeared at much the same time as the larger cannon. They proved notoriously difficult to use, however, as they took a long time to load, tended to misfire, and were very susceptible to wet weather, which could render them useless. Despite these obvious disadvantages they remained in use, and technological developments gradually made them more effective. By 1500 the arquebus, a muzzle-loading weapon fired from the shoulder by applying a lighted match (cord soaked in saltpeter) had taken on the form it was to keep for hundreds of years.

Incendiary weapons
This picture from the mid-15th-century treatise called *The Firework Book* shows how guns and crossbows were used for shooting incendiaries during a siege. The intention was to set fire to the wooden hoardings around castle ramparts and the thatched roofs of the outbuildings within the castle walls.

See also
Firearms, origin and evolution, *pages 154–5*
Anatomy of a matchlock, *pages 158–9*
Handheld firearms, *pages 298–9*

Wallgun, *c.* 1380
This weapon is nearly 5 feet (1.5 meters) long and weighs nearly 42 pounds (19 kilograms), suggesting it was intended to be used from castle walls. The short barrel on a long wooden stock is muzzle-loaded and is typical of the earliest forms of handgun.

Handgun *c.* 1400
With a small barrel on a long wooden stock, this gun is of particular interest because the spike on the muzzle cap could be swung into position to turn the weapon into a spear, anticipating the later bayonet.

Hand weapons

Missile weapons
• arquebus
• handgun
• musket

Defenses

Clothing
• armor
• mailcoat

Warriors

Concepts & Tactics

Buildings & Transport

Handgun and musket
These two late 15th-century handgunners are shown as helmeted soldiers in mailcoats and full leg harness. However, such troops would usually be more lightly armored. One fires his gun from under his arm, while the other has an early form of musket supported on a rest.

Sharpshooter
This well-armored late 15th-century soldier carries an early form of arquebus and has a lighted match in his left hand that he will put to the touchhole to fire the weapon. The firing position, which looks strange today but was quite normal at time, used a butt that nestles on top of the shoulder.

Mounted handgunner
Despite the obvious problems it was not uncommon for firearms to be used from horseback. This late 15th-century figure, in full knightly armor, shows how this could work. The tail of the gun is fixed to the breastplate and steadied by a support attached to the pommel of the saddle. The reins run through another hook on the breastplate, but this is probably artistic license.

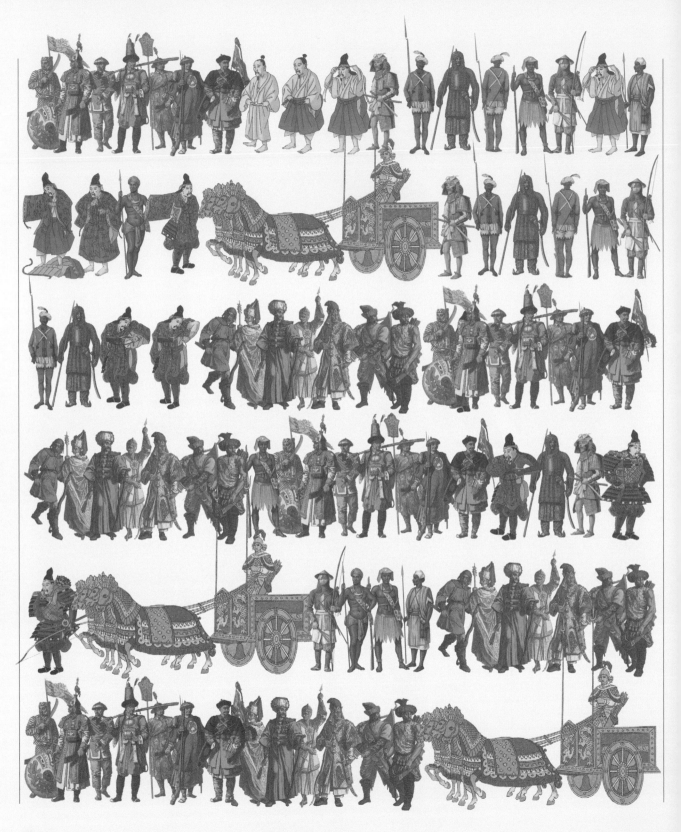

The Wider World

c. 2000 BCE to 1865 CE

Beyond the Western world the technology of warfare progressed at different speeds. As late as the 16th century in Central America the Aztecs were fighting with Stone-Age weaponry. In contrast, the Chinese were the first to pioneer gunpowder weapons in the 11th century. The Islamic world proved a vital conduit for the passage of military innovation east and west. The Chinese fire-lance of the 12th century became a firearm in the hands of the Turks and Europeans in the 14th century. Likewise, the technology of siege weapons passed back and forth between Arabs, Crusaders, and the Far East. It is interesting to note that while the Mughals of India had a full array of cannon and firearms in their armies in the 16th century, they—and even China—failed to keep up with subsequent European innovations.

Empires rose and fell on the strength of their military expertise. In the 13th century the Mongols rode out from the impoverished steppes of their homeland to topple dynasties in China and the Middle East. In the early 19th century brilliant military reforms among the Zulus allowed them to conquer much of southern Africa. But that was not the only talent needed by a conqueror. The triumph of the Mongols was due in part to their mastery of horsemanship and war techniques but also to Genghis Khan's ability to unite his tribes into a world-beating force thanks to his political skills. Similarly, the Mughals ruled for so long in India because they recruited Hindu officials alongside their own Muslim governors, and when the time came for the British to succeed them, it was not because they were outfought but because they were outmaneuverd politically.

Different levels of military technology made some civilizations vulnerable. The Aztec realm fell quickly to gun-armed Spaniards, while the Chinese Empire suffered as it fell behind the West technologically. The Japan of the samurai tried to keep out foreign ways of warfare but rapidly adopted them when it could see no alternative, both in the 16th century with guns from Portuguese traders, and then in the 19th with the complete remodeling of its armed forces after the British and German armies.

China

Chinese warlords: tactics and technology

The story of Chinese warfare is one of constant tension between the warriors of the steppes to the north of China and her sedentary civilization. Fortified walls were built to protect her people from the barbarians, but sometimes it was these horse-mounted tribes that settled on Chinese soil to create their own dynasties—such as the Mongolian Yuan in the 14th century or the northern Manchu in the 17th and 18th centuries. Chinese warfare blended the horse-borne skills of steppe warriors, such as excellent mounted archery, with the talents of Chinese military technicians, who created early gunpowder weapons and siege weaponry. Armor ranged from lightweight but tough leather—sometimes rhinoceros or sharkskin—to iron scale corselets.

Fortifications along the Great Wall of China
Although ancient walls had been raised to protect the northern border of the Chinese Empire, the Great Wall of China was constructed during the Ming dynasty, from the 15th to 17th centuries. The defense of the Great Wall centered on fortified towers and garrisons positioned at strategic points, with the wall itself being used as a method of transferring troops rapidly along its length.

Chinese weapons
Unlike the curved blades of Japan, Chinese swords were often straight with two cutting edges. Sometimes beautifully decorated with gilt, iron swords were used by senior warriors, while the majority of soldiers in a Chinese army were usually armed with spears or bladed pole-weapons, as seen here, derived from agricultural tools.

Chinese cannon and giant mortar
The Chinese pioneered the use of gunpowder in warfare, with the first recipe dating back to the 11th century, but it was used mainly in the form of bombs packed in bamboo canes. A gunpowder flamethrower was deployed in the 13th century and rockets in the 14th century—the same time that cannon first appeared in China.

Hand weapons
• pole arms
• spear
• sword

Missile weapons
• cannon
• mangonel
• mortar

Defenses
• fortified towers

Clothing
• iron corselet
• leather armor

Warriors
• Manchu
• Mongolian Yuan

Concepts & Tactics
• border protection

Buildings & Transport
• Great Wall of China
• war chariot

Imperial conquest
The Chinese Emperor Ch'ien Lung leads his army against the Gurkha tribes of Nepal in 1791. The Manchu Ch'ing dynasty was a period of great prosperity, with the Chinese population rapidly growing from 143 million to 360 million people between 1741 and 1812. The expansion of this empire brought it into conflict with distant countries and cultures.

See also
China: imperial ambitions, *pages 128–9*
Siege engines, *pages 294–5*

Chinese siege weapons
On the left is a mobile ladder for storming fortresses and on the right a mobile bridge. Mangonels were used to throw stones that battered enemy walls or fling clay pots containing flaming materials. The counterweighted trebuchet with its greater range was introduced into China from the Muslim world. Walls were protected against these devices by raising barriers of rice-stalk netting.

Chinese war chariot
A fanciful illustration of a Chinese war chariot with armored horses. Chariots were deployed early on in Chinese warfare, with evidence of their use dating back as far as the Bronze Age. The Chou dynasty devised a method for harnessing four horses abreast, but by the 4th century BCE the impact of steppe warriors was proving effective, and chariots were replaced by cavalry in Chinese armies.

China

Imperial ambitions

The widening technological gap between China and Europe made the country vulnerable to Western imperial adventures. Central authority in China was weakened greatly by the Taiping Rebellion in the mid-19th century (1851–66)—a tremendously destructive civil war that left 25 million people dead. The Chinese Empire's inability to protect itself from outsiders was exposed in defeats by both Britain and France, and this led the way for the eventual Western occupation of Peking—a humiliation that profoundly shook faith in the old imperial system. The Manchu Ch'ing dynasty ruled during this period of turmoil. An ethnic minority within the Chinese population, the Manchus maintained control over their vast empire by reserving half of all civil service posts for themselves. But this ensured their own decline as more able Chinese administrators were kept out of power.

Chinese Imperialist troops attack Taiping rebels in 1853

From Muslims in the west of the country to Triads in the south, numerous armed groups revolted against their Manchu overlords and nearly brought an end to the Ch'ing dynasty in three decades of fighting. Several Western adventurers trained troops for the Imperialists, among them Charles Gordon, later known as Gordon of Khartoum.

Chinese warriors of the mid-19th century

The Ch'ing dynasty originated in the northern steppes of Manchuria and so recruited many Mongol and Manchu tribesmen into their army. This indicates that expert archery was still important even in an age of firearms. Among the figures, second from right, a musketeer stands next to a Tatar horse-archer.

The British invasion of the Canton River during the Opium War of 1839–42

The British victory of musket-armed modern soldiers over the antiquated Imperial forces still using swords, shields, and spears—as shown here in this primitive illustration—undermined the authority of the Ch'ing dynasty and was one of the causes of the subsequent Taiping Rebellion.

Manchu horse-archer

This late 19th-century engraving is based upon a photograph of a Manchu horseman. He is equipped with a composite bow—one of the most powerful forms of bow, gaining its strength from a combination of wood, animal sinew, and horn glued together. It could penetrate armor from 30 yards (27 meters).

Arms and armor worn by an Imperialist Tigerman warrior

Although few in number, the Tigermen wore outlandish costumes with a tiger-head hood and tiger-head shield. Their main purpose was to frighten the enemy with their wild actions and shouting, enhanced by scattering firecrackers beneath their feet.

Japan

The samurai: technology

Japanese fighting skills were honed in a series of civil wars that saw the samurai class of professional warriors challenge the authority of their emperor. The rise of the shogunate signified the arrival of the samurai as the ruling class of their country. At first samurai were noted for their skill at riding and archery, but by the 13th century it was their swordsmanship that had become famous. During the 16th century bitter civil wars continued, as samurai clans fought each other for supremacy, but with the emergence of Tokugawa Ieyasu the Japanese found a skilled politician as well as a competent warlord. He established peace and unity in the form of the Tokugawa dynasty that would survive for two and a half centuries from 1603.

Japanese knives
The *aikuchi*, or dagger, was distinguished from short swords by having no hand guard, or *tsuba*. It was usually carried by older samurai in semiretirement. Scabbards could be highly decorated with natural motifs of insects or snakes. A smaller knife is inserted in the scabbard shown second from right.

Japanese arms and armor
The classic armor worn by samurai—the *haramaki*—remained largely unchanged for centuries and consisted of body armor made of numerous overlapping plates of leather and metal laced together. To this was added large shoulder guards and a boxlike skirt-guard. The ornate armor depicted here, belonging to a nobleman, includes further leg and arm guards and a face mask.

Hand weapons
• aikuchi
• katana
• wakizashi

Missile weapons

Defenses

Clothing
• haramaki
• mempo
• war helmet

Warriors
• samurai

Concepts & Tactics
• swordsmanship

Buildings & Transport

Japanese swordsmith

Numerous craftsmen working in wood, leather, and metal lavished their skills on all aspects of Japanese arms and armor, but the most celebrated were the swordsmiths. Famous makers established their own schools and were known for different styles of blades. The most famous swordsmith was Masamune, who has a premier blend of sake named after him today.

Two swords

Below is a samurai carrying a long sword, or *katana*, and a short sword, or *wakizashi* (above). The *wakizashi* was a backup weapon to the longer *katana*; it was worn indoors when the *katana* was set aside. Blades were strengthened by folding and hammering the heated steel to make them tough but not brittle.

Japanese armor with face masks

The mask, or *mempo*, often had a moustache attached to it, sometimes even teeth, all contributing to a fierce expression. The inside of the mask could be lacquered red, and the reflected light of this enhanced the warrior's angry appearance. On the chin of the *mempo* was a hole for draining away the sweat of a very hot warrior encased in armor.

War helmets

Japanese helmets were made from several steel or leather plates with a distinctive flared neck guard. Those worn by leading warriors could be very ornate indeed, with crests made out of lacquered and gilded leather, signifying references to their name or clan. On hearing that his rivals called him The Cow, Tokugawa Ieyasu had great horns fixed to his helmet and the plates covered in cowhide.

See also
Anatomy of a Japanese warrior, *page 134–5*
Swords, *pages 282–3*
Bows, *page 291*
Body armor, *pages 302–3*
Helmets, *page 305*

Japan

The Samurai: tactics

Civil war between rival clans preoccupied Japanese warlords and their samurai throughout the medieval period, but sometimes the Japanese were challenged from abroad. In the 13th century the Mongols tried twice to invade Japan, but on both occasions a typhoon destroyed the invading fleet, and this was dubbed the "divine wind," or *kamikaze*—the inspiration for Japan's suicide pilots in the Second World War. Toyotomi Hideyoshi was one of Japan's greatest warlords in the 16th century, and after a string of successful campaigns he proclaimed himself ruler of the country. He embarked on overseas adventures, but his invasions of Korea ended in failure. His death allowed Tokugawa Ieyasu to take over and establish a peaceful domain in the country.

Japanese sword practice
Essential for the samurai was the learning of swordsmanship, as the sword became his primary weapon. The most strenuous blow was the *kesagiri* cut, which began at the left shoulder and cut diagonally down through the body. The sport of kendo today continues the tradition with fighters using bamboo swords.

Japanese archer
Archery was the primary martial skill of the early samurai and remained a revered talent and pursuit for the nobility. Long composite bows were made of wood glued together with strips of bamboo; arrows were made from bamboo. There were a variety of arrowheads for different purposes, including two-pronged forks designed to cut the lace of armor or cripple horses.

Japanese actor with a giant gun

The first firearms, matchlock guns, were introduced into Japan by Portuguese merchants. They were quickly adopted by the samurai and used by their foot soldiers to great effect in the battles of the late 16th century, which led to the strengthening of samurai armor.

Fighting with sword and pole-arm

Effective—and cheap—Japanese pole-arms derived from farm implements, *naginata*, and spears were used by foot soldiers to bring down mounted samurai. They were, famously, wielded by Buddhist warrior-monks, and they were also used for hunting.

See also
Swords, *pages 282–3*
Bows, *page 291*

Japanese infantryman

The *ashigaru* were the supporting foot soldiers in samurai armies. They were lightly armored with bows, spears, or firearms and sometimes fought behind fieldworks. Under the Tokugawa dynasty the status of warriors was rigidly enforced, with only samurai allowed to wear their characteristic two swords, and the *ashigaru* were very much of a lower caste.

The ronin

After the death or dishonor of a samurai master, his samurai became masterless *ronin*. A famous 18th-century Japanese story tells of the forty-seven *ronin* who avenged their master by slaying his killer but were then ordered to commit suicide, which they all did. This was a demonstration of *bushido*—the warrior spirit.

Anatomy of a Japanese Warrior

1

2

This sequence of illustrations shows an early samurai putting on his clothing and armor. He would normally be assisted by a retainer, as much of the process involved the complicated lacing of individual pieces.

1 The first two sequences show the warrior putting on his underclothing followed by a thick embroidered robe. This provided layers of padding that were essential when wearing armor, as any blow might fail to break the armor plate but could create a shockwave that would rupture internal organs unless insulated. He attaches his first pieces of armor, called *suneate*, to his legs. He wears shoes of bear fur.

2 In this sequence the warrior attaches further pieces of padding and little plates of shaped leather armor to his arms. He also begins to attach the large plates to his boxlike skirt armor, or *kusazuri*, that protects him beneath the waist.

3 The warrior continues to attach the pieces of his waist armor that usually hang from his breastplate, or *do*. The majority of the weight of the armor was borne on his shoulders. Massive shoulder guards, the *o-sode*, were attached to the breastplate to cover the smaller arm pieces. Such an outfit would normally be finished off with a helmet.

4 The fully clad warrior is armed with two swords—the indicator of his samurai status—one short, the *wakizashi*, and one long, the *katana*. He also carries a short box-quiver filled with arrows and a long wood-and-bamboo composite bow.

The Americas

Aztec warfare

In Central America, Aztec warfare was driven by one gruesome necessity—the demand for enormous numbers of prisoners for human sacrifice. Their tactics and stone weapons were not designed to annihilate the enemy but subdue him so he could be dragged off for sacrifice later. This meant the Aztecs were highly vulnerable to a culture that did not play by the same rules. When Hernando Cortés arrived in Mexico with a handful of Spanish conquistadores looking for silver and gold and armed with steel swords and firearms, he allied himself with the Aztecs' enemies. Although heavily outnumbered, the Spanish triumphed over the Aztecs in 1521 after only two years.

See also
Swords,
page 280

Aztec weapons

These were Stone Age weapons, with arrowheads made out of a volcanic glass called obsidian, knives and spearheads made of flint or chalcedony, and wooden clubs tipped with flakes of obsidian. Clubs were the preferred weapons as they were perfect for disabling enemies, mainly by lashing at their legs so the rest of them could be used later for sacrifice.

Aztec jaguar warrior

Like any medieval army the Aztecs could raise large numbers of peasants to form the bulk of their forces, but the professional warriors comprised a small elite, and these were called jaguar and eagle warriors after the most formidable animals in their world. Jaguar warriors wore the full skin of the big cat and wielded obsidian-edged clubs, fighting at the front to capture as many prisoners as possible.

Aztec warriors armed with clubs

The other elite Aztec warriors were named after the eagle and were used mainly for scouting. They were clad in feathers, as shown in this picture drawn by a Spanish missionary. While the eagle warriors derived their authority from the Aztec god of the sun, the Jaguar warriors represented the god of the night.

Montezuma

Montezuma, Emperor of the Aztecs, ruled his realm from Tenochtitlan, and his people regarded him as a living god. He invited Cortés to his capital but then ambushed the Spaniards. Cortés later made Montezuma prisoner in his own palace and had him executed. He eventually defeated the Aztecs and founded his own capital nearby—Mexico City.

Tlaxcalan warriors

When Cortés first arrived in Mexico he defeated the Amerindians of Tlaxcala and founded the city of Vera Cruz. The Tlaxcalans then joined with the conquistadores to attack their enemies, the Aztecs. The Tlaxcalans were armed with similar Stone Age weapons, notably the obsidian-edged club and flint-tipped arrows.

Cortés takes the surrender of Aztec warriors outside Tenochtitlan, 1520

Cortés's own Spanish soldiers, armed with muskets and wearing armor, can be seen to the left. Although their weapons were greatly superior to those of the Aztecs they were vastly outnumbered, and they had to recruit local tribes as well as using their own warships—loaded with cannon and transported overland—to capture the Aztec capital.

Hand weapons
- clubs
- flint knives

Missile weapons
- bow & obsidian arrows

Defenses

Clothing
- animal skins
- feathers

Warriors
- eagle warriors
- jaguar warriors
- Tlaxcalan

Concepts & Tactics
- human sacrifice

Buildings & Transport

137

The Americas

Native American warfare

The Native Americans ruled their lands for centuries before the coming of the European settlers. However, they fought fierce wars among themselves, so when the European colonists first settled along the east coast the tribes formed alliances with them to fight against their enemies. But as the colonists moved west and grabbed more land, many tribes came into direct conflict with them. The strongest resistance came from the Plains Indians—tribes that included the Sioux, Cheyennes, Comanches, and Kiowas. More devastating than warfare, however, was the impact of Western disease, which severely reduced the strength of native tribes. Added to this was the introduction of western liquor, which led to an epidemic of alcoholism among tribal warriors.

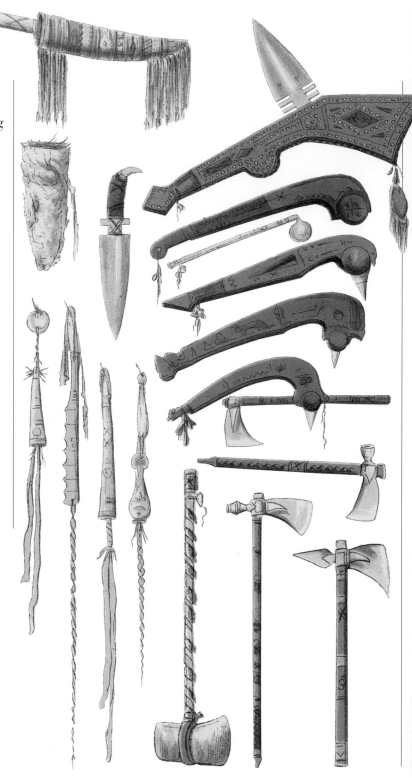

▶ Native American knives, axes, and clubs

Thousands of European-made iron knives were traded with Native American tribesmen for furs, after which they would be decorated in local styles with animal-hide sheaths covered with beads and tassels. The carved clubs and axes are of traditional form, but the pipe combined with tomahawk was a European innovation adopted keenly by senior tribesmen, who carried them as a mark of status.

Hand weapons
• ax
• club
• tomahawk

Missile weapons
• flintlock

Defenses

Clothing

Warriors
• Hidatsa
• Mandan
• Mohawk
• Omaha
• Plains Indians

Concepts & Tactics
• European colonization

Buildings & Transport

Omaha warrior

Black Elk of the Omaha tribe, which migrated from Ohio and settled in South Dakota, where they continued their traditional way of life until smallpox reduced them to only a few hundred. The black-painted face of the warrior signified he had recently killed an enemy. He was painted by George Catlin in the 1830s.

See also
Clubs, maces, and axes,
pages 286–7

Stone-headed club

Native Americans had lived in North America for thousands of years before the arrival of Europeans, and they fought tribal wars with one another. This primitive tomahawk is typical of this earlier period of warfare, although it might also have been used to finish off a wounded animal during a hunt.

Mohawk warrior from Canada

Native Americans living on the northeast coast of North America fought alongside the British and French as they battled to see who would win control of Canada in the mid-18th century. This Mohawk was armed by the British with a flintlock and acted as a skirmisher for the Redcoats.

Hidatsa warrior

This warrior is wearing the flamboyant costume of the Dog Society—a group of young warriors pledged to fight bravely in battle. Like their neighboring Mandan, the Hidatsas lived in earth-domed lodges and grew corn. In the 18th century they clashed with the Sioux and moved across the plains to settle near the Missouri river. This engraving is from a painting by Karl Bodmer in the 1830s.

Africa

African warriors

Many great African kingdoms rose and fell long before European colonization. Much of their wealth and power derived from trade with Arabs and Europeans—but this also fuelled a darker business, as the victims of wars between African kingdoms were sold on as slaves, and in exchange Africans received iron weapons and guns. When Europeans began to colonize Africa they expected easy victories, but many African warriors had been trained since childhood and were highly effective in battle. In Ethiopia the King of Shewa's army adopted European firearms and decisively defeated the Italians. The French had a tough time against the elite female warriors of the West African kingdom of Dahomey. The reputation of the Masai was so fierce that colonial powers avoided any direct combat with them.

Throwing-knives of the Balegga and Wahuma tribes

These weapons were characteristic of many North African and Central African warriors, and their shapes became increasingly elaborate, some taking abstract animal forms. Weapons of this kind served more of an ornamental purpose, signifying status, and it is unlikely that such valuable blades were actually thrown in battle.

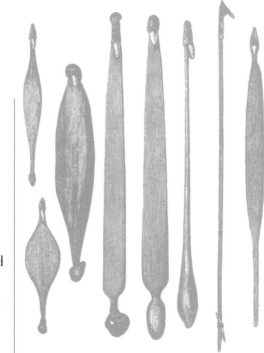

African spear-launching sticks

These were used to give extra impetus to a thrown weapon by extending the throwing arm. A spear would have a hollow at one end that would fit over the spur on the stick. In one motion the warrior would swing the launcher forward, letting go of the spear and gaining greater range for his weapon.

Elephant-hide shield with spears

African warriors were also accomplished hunters and made military equipment out of animal trophies. Masai warriors fought with shields made from the hides of water buffalo, which they believed were strong enough to be proof against European muskets. Sadly, this was not true, and the Masai learned to duck down to avoid a volley of gunfire.

Senegalese warriors of the 19th century

These warriors are equipped with spears and muskets. In the 13th and 14th centuries, the Senegalese grew rich on their trade connections with the Islamic world and founded the powerful Mandingo and Jolof kingdoms, but by the mid-19th century they were absorbed into the French Empire and provided soldiers for their army.

See also
Thrown weapons,
pages 288–9

Tree fort

When attacked by their slave-hunting neighbors, the Gaberi of Chad fought from trees, hurling spears and sticks at their enemies from above. Other natural features could also be useful in battle. When the Dahomey fought the French, they hid behind giant anthills.

Kanuri cavalry

Cavalrymen of the Kanuri—who live in northern Nigeria—wearing quilted-cotton armor to protect themselves and their horses. When colonial troops faced such warriors they seemed like something from the Middle Ages, especially when the horsemen of northern Cameroon clad themselves in mail armor.

Hand weapons
• spear

Missile weapons
• musket
• throwing knives
• throwing sticks

Defenses
• elephant-hide shield

Clothing
• mail armor
• quilted-cotton armor

Warriors
• Dahomian
• Ethiopian
• Gaberi
• Kanuri
• Masai
• Senegalese

Concepts & Tactics
• European colonization
• slave trade

Buildings & Transport
• tree fort

Africa

Zulu warfare

Under the rule of their chief Shaka, the Zulus became the most powerful tribal force in southern Africa in the 19th century. Shaka improved the already strong military skills of these warriors by devising a deadly method of close-combat warfare. He discarded their light shields and throwing spears to replace them with broad-bladed stabbing spears and a large, heavier shield. The shield was used to hook away the opponent's protection, exposing him to the stabbing blade. Shaka combined this new fighting technique with the Zulus' traditional buffalo-horn formation that enveloped an enemy before annihilating him. Thus armed, the Zulus quickly expanded and took over the lands of their neighbors. In 1828 Shaka was assassinated but his brilliant reforms were continued under the rule of chief Cetchewayo, who became one of the few native commanders to inflict a major defeat on a colonial power.

Zulu warriors and their shields
Introduced by Shaka, these large oval shields were made out of cowhide. To strengthen them, extra strips of hide were threaded through parallel slits cut down the middle. A stick was then pushed through these strips at the back and decorated with a piece of fur on the top.

Zulu warrior of the 1840s
Drawn by European traveler and artist George French Angas, this warrior is decorated with streamers and beads. These, with the smaller size of his shield, suggest that he is dressed to impress a woman rather than fight on the battlefield.

Close combat
Zulu warriors attack a Boer defensive wagon formation, or *laager*. The success of the Zulus depended on them rapidly coming into close combat with their enemy, but a Boer *laager* or British square prevented this and kept them at sufficient distance to be shot down. Zulus can be seen here returning their own firepower.

Zulu boys in dancing dress
Training to become a Zulu warrior began young, with boys learning fighting techniques and stick combat. Small shields were carried in dancing displays that helped teach the young men to coordinate their movements within a battle formation.

Zulu blacksmiths at work
Here the Zulus are making the blades of the broad stabbing spears devised by Shaka. He called the weapon *iklwa*, from the sucking sound it made when drawn out from a body. One of the craftsmen is using a goatskin bellows to increase the heat of the furnace; another man beats the hot metal into shape.

Hand weapons
• stabbing spear

Missile weapons
• throwing spear

Defenses
• laager
• large shield
• light shield

Clothing
• beads
• streamers

Warriors
• Cetchewayo
• Shaka

Concepts & Tactics
• buffalo-horn formation
• close combat

Buildings & Transport

Central Asia

Mongol warfare

The Mongols rose to the status of a world power in the 13th century under the leadership of Genghis Khan. He united previously obscure Mongolian tribes into a powerful force that terrorized and conquered territories from China through the Middle East to eastern Europe. After Genghis Khan's death his successors continued to rule highly successful Mongol dynasties, including the Golden Horde in Russia. The Mongols' military success was built on their magnificent horsemanship and their tactics of false retreats and harassing attacks, but they also adopted the military techniques of the people that they conquered, including Chinese and Arab methods of siege warfare and their use of gunpowder weapons. Their mastery of naval warfare was poor, however, and they failed in their attempted invasions of Japan.

See also
Body armor,
pages 302–3

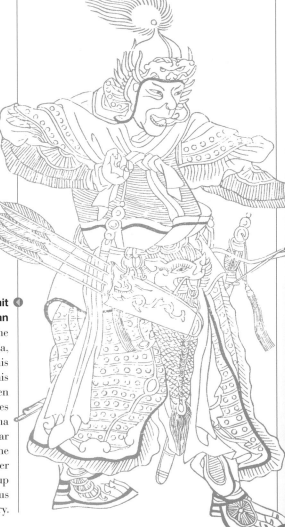

Subotai, one of Genghis Khan's greatest generals
Beginning as a lowly guard to Genghis Khan's tent, Subotai ended up commanding Mongol armies on far-reaching campaigns in China, Persia, Korea, and Russia. On his advance west he rode as far as Hungary, and it was only because of his master's sudden death that he retreated eastward and spared Europe from Mongol dominion.

Chinese portrait of Genghis Khan
Born *c.* 1162 on the steppes of Mongolia, the secret of Genghis Khan's success was his ability to defeat then incorporate warring tribes into one mighty army. China was the first target of his war machine, and although he initially came only as a raider Khan's successors ended up ruling the largest contiguous empire in human history.

Hand weapons

Missile weapons
• gunpowder weapons

Defenses

Clothing
• Arab-style helmet
• leather-and-mail armor
• Mongol helmet
• Shoulder armor

Warriors
• Genghis Khan
• Golden Horde
• Subotai
• Tatars

Concepts & Tactics
• false retreat
• harassing attack
• horsemanship
• siege warfare

Buildings & Transport

Mongol arms and armor

Wearing the traditional leather-and-mail armor of the Mongolian steppes, the Mongols also adopted many of the weapons and military costumes of the people they conquered, including the Chinese-style shoulder armor and Arab-style helmet seen in this collection.

Tatar warriors

The name Tatary was given to the lands ruled by Turkic tribesmen in southern Russia and Central Asia. At one time they formed part of the Mongol Golden Horde, but during other periods they were independent tribes who raided the cities around their steppe lands. The Russians recruited many of these fierce Tatar warriors into their own armies. They were bitter enemies of the Christian Cossacks.

Mongol helmet

The Russians paid heavily for their failure to halt the Mongols and lived under the yoke of the Golden Horde for over a century. This helmet, from a Russian collection, is strongly influenced by Persian or Turkish models and reflects the wide variety of military cultures present in medieval Russia.

145

The Middle East

The Arab world

With the slow decline of the Byzantine Empire in the eastern Mediterranean, Muslim Arabs and Turks filled the vacuum. In North Africa, Arabs conquered the entire coast and entered Spain. Here, they were known as Moors and created a dazzling civilization. In Asia Minor the Turks became firmly established, eventually capturing the capital of the Byzantine Empire, Constantinople, in 1453. From the 11th century onward Europeans led military expeditions to Palestine—the Crusades—to recapture holy cities revered by Christians. Islamic warlords fought back, and the most famous of these was Saladin. Western and Eastern methods of warfare clashed, with European knights learning to value the importance of horse-archery and Islamic warriors respecting the heavily armed military holy orders, including the Hospitaller Brothers and Knights Templar.

An 11th-century Arab army advances to the sound of its musicians
Known as Saracens by their Christian opponents, Islamic armies fighting in the Crusades were usually a combination of Arab and Turkish warriors, strong in cavalry with heavily armored lance-carrying horsemen and lightly clad horse-archers.

Portrait of Saladin
Saladin, a Kurdish warlord, commanded the Saracen forces during the Third Crusade and was the implacable enemy of Richard the Lionheart. Although defeated by Richard at the Battle of Arsouf, he took control of Jerusalem. However, he allowed Christian pilgrims to visit the city after a treaty with the Crusaders.

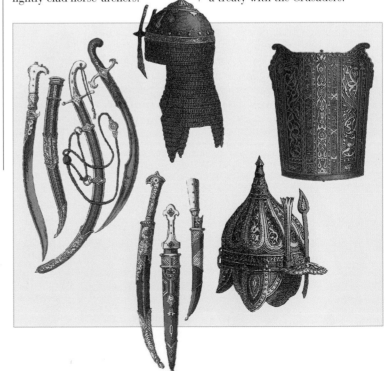

Arms and armor from Persia
The Persian armor shown here includes a damascened breastplate and helmets with mail. The Timurid and Safavid dynasties made Persia the other great Islamic military power in the Middle East and a relentless opponent of the expanding Ottoman Turks.

Hand weapons
• lance
• three-pointed dagger

Missile weapons
• bow

Defenses

Clothing
• Persian armor

Warriors
• Hospitaller Brothers
• Knights Templar
• Moors
• Saladin
• Saracens

Concepts & Tactics
• horse-archery
• strong cavalry

Buildings & Transport
• Krak des Chevaliers

Krak des Chevaliers, Syria

This was one of the greatest castles of the Crusader period and home to the Hospitaller Brothers, one of the elite martial holy orders, whose raids against the Saracens proved a constant thorn in their side. Their task was to protect the caravans of Christian pilgrims heading towards the Holy Land, but they also looted the surrounding settlements.

Moorish three-pointed dagger

This was worn over a gauntlet by a horseman and worked in the same way as the Mughal *katar*—a broad-bladed weapon intended to punch through enemy armor. Throughout the Islamic world, from Moorish Spain to Mughal India, weaponry showed many similarities.

Moorish military figures from the Alhambra, Granada, Spain

Recruiting warriors from North Africa, the Moors hung on to many of their Spanish lands until the late 15th century. Frequent raiding on both sides meant both Moors and Christians were highly militarized in Spain and adept at all kinds of warfare, including siege tactics. The Moors borrowed some of their military techniques from the Byzantines.

See also
The Crusades,
pages 102–5

147

India

The Mughal empire

Muslim Turkic invaders from Central Asia had always had an impact on northern India, ruling various sultanates throughout the Middle Ages, but the greatest of these conquerors arrived in the 16th century. Babur, descended from the Mongol ruler Tamerlane, rode into India from Afghanistan in 1526 and established the Mughal dynasty—a name derived from Mongol—that continued to dominate India until eclipsed by the British Empire in the 18th century. Akbar, Babur's grandson, was the greatest of the Mughals, and he extended his rule throughout the subcontinent. His administrative talents were as sophisticated as his art of war and, by recruiting Hindu princes to high office in his government, he ensured his Muslim dynasty continued in power for at least another 150 years.

Body armor

Mughal damascened body armor of the 17th century was made of steel engraved with intricate floral patterns of gilt inlay—a method of armor decoration that originated in Damascus in Syria. Such plate armor was usually worn over a shirt of mail that helped protect the wearer from enemy archers.

Tulwar

A Mughal *tulwar* was a steel sword with a curved blade, which could be beautifully decorated with gilded inscriptions. Mughal military culture combined that of the Turkic steppe tribes with Islamic Persia to produce a highly sophisticated, but tough, martial elite.

Mughal saddle-ax

This has a damascened head with a silver-gilt floral design. Mughal armored cavalry were heavily armed with bow, quiver, sword and lance, with an ax for close combat to hack through an opponent's mail armor.

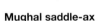

Khanjar

This 18th-century *khanjar* was a knife with a 9-inch (23-centimeter) curved blade strengthened by a central rib. Decorated hilts could be made of elephant ivory or damascened steel.

Katar

The *katar* was a distinctively Indian weapon with a broad armor-piercing blade and square double grips. Some unusual versions of the *katar* had a double blade or even pistol barrels attached.

See also

Mughal warfare, *pages 150–1*

Swords, *pages 282–3*

Body armor, *pages 302–3*

🔹 Babur, the conqueror of India

Babur, the Mughal Emperor (center), leads his army on a military expedition. Babur's early conquest of Central Asian cities gave him the funds to raise a powerful army for his invasion of India. Note the bactrian camels used by some of his soldiers, many of whom would have been recruited in Afghanistan. A typical Mughal army would have more cavalry than infantry.

India

Mughal warfare

Akbar's successors extended Mughal rule throughout India, but by the late 17th century there was a new power rising in southern India—the Hindu Marathas. They fought the Mughals and reduced the extent of their rule to the north of the subcontinent. Between these two warring powers came European merchants and their soldiers. By the middle of the 18th century, the British and French were fighting for control over the lucrative trade in the region. The Mughals responded early to modern methods of warfare and deployed their own artillery and troops armed with guns, but they were outmaneuverd by their enemies. The British were particularly adept at both winning battles and securing treaties with all remaining Indian rulers, so by 1805 the Mughal time was over and its last emperor departed the region.

Armored Mughal cavalryman
Coming from Central Asia the Mughals favored a strong cavalry dimension to their armies, with both heavy cavalry for close combat and light-cavalry archers. Archers would torment and weaken an enemy, encouraging it to charge forward and break its formation, thus allowing the heavy cavalry to crash through and scatter the remaining forces.

See also
Katar, *page 148*
Moorish three-pointed dagger, *page 147*

An Indian prince on an elephant

War elephants, some of them heavily armored with plate and scale armor, formed an important part of Mughal armies. With soldiers mounted on howdahs the animals would advance in front of their commander to intimidate the enemy horses, which fled from their size, noise, and smell. The elephants would be guarded by an escort of soldiers to stop enemy infantry from attacking the animals.

18th-century sepoy

A sepoy of an East India Company battalion from Bombay in the mid-18th century. The British recruited many Indian soldiers and equipped them with muskets and red jackets, although they kept other aspects of their local dress. British victories in India against the Marathas put pressure on the Mughals, who eventually gave up their rule of the subcontinent.

Mughal military encampment of the late 16th century

Note the soldiers at the bottom of the illustration carrying firearms. Already familiar with rockets and other gunpowder weapons, the Mughals were quick to adopt guns, and they manufactured their own muskets, the finest ones being inlaid with gilded damascened steel.

An array of Mughal weaponry

Seen here is the unusual armor-piercing *katar* knife (center right) and the tiger-claw weapon (center left). The ax-shaped weapon (right) is used for controlling war elephants. A typical Mughal cavalry helmet (left) has a straight, adjustable nose guard and neck-protecting mail.

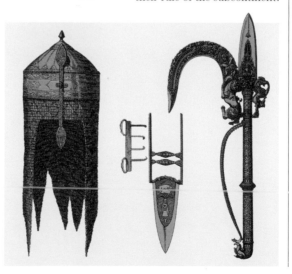

151

The Firearms Revolution
1500–1650

The increasing use of gunpowder weapons brought about, over time, a transformation in the practice of warfare and the composition of armies. Artillery's greatest influence was felt initially in the realm of siegecraft because the power of gunpowder and shot made the medieval form of castle obsolete. In contrast, handheld firearms could not replace crossbows and longbows until technological developments made them more efficient.

The wars and campaigns that disfigured European history during this period proved critical for military developments, and the influence of commanders who were also innovators was crucial. These included Gonzalo de Cordoba, Maurice of Nassau, and King Gustavus Adolphus of Sweden.

The evolution in methods of warfare was not solely dependent upon the increasing use of gunpowder. The battlefield could no longer be dominated by the knight; vulnerable to missile weapons, he could also be resisted by formations armed with the pike, which became even more potent when associated with other weapons. Effective use of pike formations demanded coordinated and disciplined movement by a more professional class of warrior than the feudal assemblies of men whose principal training was for individual skill-at-arms. From the massed formations of pikes there developed more subtle tactical units, in which missile weapons were integrated. The Spanish tercio formation combined blocks of pikemen with bodies of musketeers, who were vulnerable while reloading their weapons. The pikemen protected the musketeers while retaining their own offensive abilities, and became the most effective element in land warfare.

Cavalry tactics also changed to include troops who were more lightly armed and equipped and thus more suited to some tasks than the armored warrior. Portable firearms provided the cavalry with its own missile capability, although the ability to discharge a firearm from horseback could tend to stifle the offensive power of the cavalry, until the merits of the charge were reasserted.

Firearms

Origins and evolution

The first handheld guns were rudimentary and operated on the same principle as that of the cannon: a metal barrel or tube into which a propellant charge was inserted via the muzzle, with ignition being achieved by the introduction of a spark through a touch-hole in the barrel. Early illustrations suggest that this was first attained by the use of a straight rod, said to be of red-hot iron. However, the difficulty of keeping iron so hot in the field suggests that, in some cases, the rods may have been holders for some form of burning match. Among the earliest of these portable hand-cannon were some that had the metal of the barrel extended to form a long handle to facilitate use, and from this stocked weapons were developed. The first hand-cannon were small, a tube of about 8 inches (20 centimeters) mounted on a wooden tiller.

Handgun supports

Some early gun stocks had very curved butts; others were straight, designed to fit over the shoulder or under the arm. As one hand was needed to ignite the charge and the other to hold the barrel, supports were devised, either a rest or a pole-arm on which the barrel could be lodged, as in this illustration. Here the soldier holds the gun stock under his arm, operating a serpentine with one hand and holding the rest with the other.

See also

Matchlock and wheel-lock, *pages 156–7*

Anatomy of a matchlock, *pages 158–9*

Handheld firearms, *pages 298–9*

Early handgun

This illustration depicts an early version of the handgun. The weight of the barrel is supported while the gunner ignites the propellant charge of gunpowder with a rod or match-holder.

"Holy water sprinkle"

This weapon, dating from the first half of the 15th century, combines a multibarreled handgun with a "holy water sprinkle," a somewhat ironic name for a form of spiked club or mace. Originally devised in the later 14th century, by the early 16th multibarreled guns included weapons mounted on carriages to produce a form of light artillery—sometimes called organs, from the resemblance to organ pipes—as well as handguns.

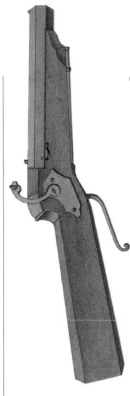

Early matchlock

The difficulty of holding a handgun with one hand and igniting its charge with the other led to the invention of the matchlock. An S- or Z-shaped lever, called a serpentine, was devised so that movement of the trigger part of the lever lowered the other end with its lighted match into the priming-pan that held the gunpowder. Further developments changed the one-piece serpentine into a separate but connected trigger and match-holder, as here.

Arquebus

The first simple bronze or iron tubes were fitted with "tillers" or wooden stocks, similar to those fitted to crossbows, to enable them to be used by hand. Some had a socket at the sealed end of the barrel, permitting the insertion of a wooden haft; others were bound to a wooden stock by iron bands. This example, apparently dating from the late 14th century, has the barrel fitted into a wooden stock.

Arquebus, *c.* 1420

Many early guns had a hooklike projection on the underside to allow the gun to be rested securely upon a wall or stand to reduce the effect of recoil. From this the name *Hackenbüchse*, or hook guns, developed, which became harquebus or arquebus in French and hackbut or hagbut in English. Subsequently the term arquebus came to be used to describe all portable firearms.

Firearms

Matchlock and wheel-lock

The smoldering match held in a serpentine gave its name to the matchlock musket, but another technological development, devised certainly by the early 16th century and perhaps earlier, was derived from the method of kindling a fire by flint and steel or a similar material. It involved a serrated wheel, revolving rapidly to strike sparks from a piece of iron pyrites. Affixed to the side of a firearm, the wheel was powered by a strong spring connected to the spindle of the wheel by a chain. A spanner, or key, was used to turn the wheel, winding the chain around the spindle and compressing the spring; pressure on a connected trigger released the wheel, which spun and struck sparks from a piece of pyrites held in the jaws of a cock. The cock was pivoted so that it could be held against the wheel, ready for firing.

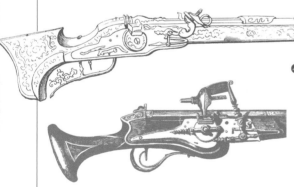

Breech-loading wheel-lock pistol

Most hand firearms were loaded by the muzzle. Both matchlock and wheel-lock breech-loaders existed but were never in common usage. This mid-16th-century example shows the cock in position for firing, with its jaws, the clamp that held the iron pyrites, placed against the serrated wheel.

Wheel-lock carbine

This highly decorated short-barreled wheel-lock carbine shows the wheel mechanism and the priming-pan containing the gunpowder; the pan had a cover that was closed manually and opened as the wheel revolved. Note how the cock could be positioned to lie alongside the barrel, allowing the gun to be carried safely even if the wheel were wound up ready for release.

Powder flasks and spanners

The cartridge—a measured charge of powder and ball made up into a paper tube—was not available until the 17th century, and instead loose powder and projectiles were used. Powder flasks, which deposited the propellant into the muzzle of the gun, often by means of a spring-loaded measure, were sometimes highly decorated, like the carved example shown here, while balls were carried in pouches. Also shown here are the spanners, or keys, used to wind a wheel-lock into firing mode.

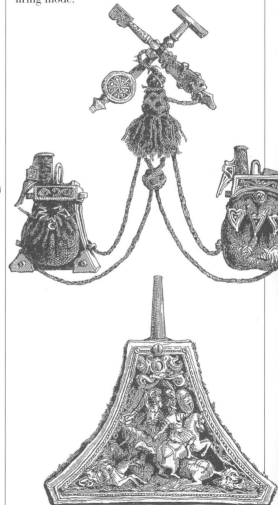

Hand weapons

Missile weapons
• breech-loading pistol
• matchlock musket
• wheel-lock musket

Defenses

Clothing

Warriors

Concepts & Tactics

Buildings & Transport

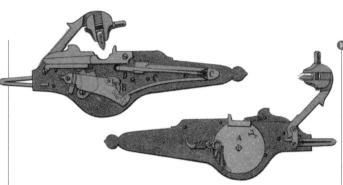

Wheel-lock

The inner mechanism (top) and outer appearance (bottom) of a wheel-lock lock. Even the simpler type of wheel-lock was mechanically quite complex, a factor reflected in the relative expense of the wheel-lock when compared with other mechanisms. In 1631, for example, a firelock was quoted as costing only two-thirds the price of a wheel-lock. The internal view of the mechanism shows the cock, with a piece of iron pyrites clamped in its jaws, poised over the priming-pan.

Elaborate wheel-locks

More complicated wheel-lock mechanisms included an automatic pan cover that opened as the wheel revolved. In the internal view here (top) the cock is in firing position over the wheel. In the external view (bottom) it is drawn back into a safe position. The technology of the wheel-lock made it more fragile than other mechanisms, and attempts were made to reduce the chance of damage by enclosing the external mechanism with a cover. Other expedients included combining the wheel-lock with a matchlock mechanism, or providing a second cock to keep the firearm operational even if the pyrites broke in one cock.

Matchlock and wheel-lock muskets

These illustrations—showing muskets dating from the early to mid-16th century—compare the appearance of the matchlock (top) with the wheel-lock (bottom). The shape of the stock, notably the butt, varied considerably, requiring the arquebusier to hold it against his breast or at the shoulder, depending on the design.

> See also
> **Anatomy of a matchlock,** *pages 158–9*
> **Handheld firearms,** *pages 298–9*

Wheel-lock musket

Muskets with wheel-lock mechanisms were not generally used for ordinary military purposes, the wheel-lock being less robust than other systems. They were used for hunting, however, and by those able to afford the considerable expense. Such firearms could be elaborately decorated, to a degree that matched the technological complexity of the mechanism, with the metal engraved and the stocks carved or inlaid.

Anatomy of a Matchlock

1 This early matchlock shows the match-holder poised alongside the touch-hole in the barrel through which the flame from the priming powder penetrated to the propellant charge.

2 The long-barreled matchlock firearm came to be known as a musket (the early English spelling was sometimes musquet). The term was derived from the Italian *mosquetto*, sparrow-hawk, following the practice of naming weapons after birds or animals. The early use of the term implies that it described a weapon somewhat lighter than the heaviest hook-gun arquebus, but it was still a heavy weapon. The size was never fully standardized, but in the earlier 17th century English muskets were described as about 48 inches (1.22 meters) long in the barrel—total length about 62 inches (1.57 meters)—with a bore taking ten or twelve balls to the pound. A lighter form of musket became known as a caliver, a term seemingly derived from "calibre." In 1630 measurements were established for English firearms: musket, barrel length 48 inches (1.22 meters); caliver, barrel length 39 inches (99 centimeters); arquebus, barrel length 30 inches (76 centimeters); carbine, or petronel, barrel length the same as an arquebus but with a smaller bore.

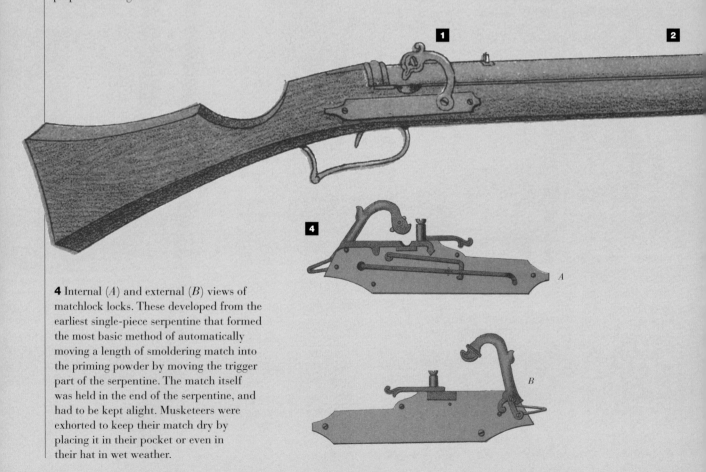

4 Internal (*A*) and external (*B*) views of matchlock locks. These developed from the earliest single-piece serpentine that formed the most basic method of automatically moving a length of smoldering match into the priming powder by moving the trigger part of the serpentine. The match itself was held in the end of the serpentine, and had to be kept alight. Musketeers were exhorted to keep their match dry by placing it in their pocket or even in their hat in wet weather.

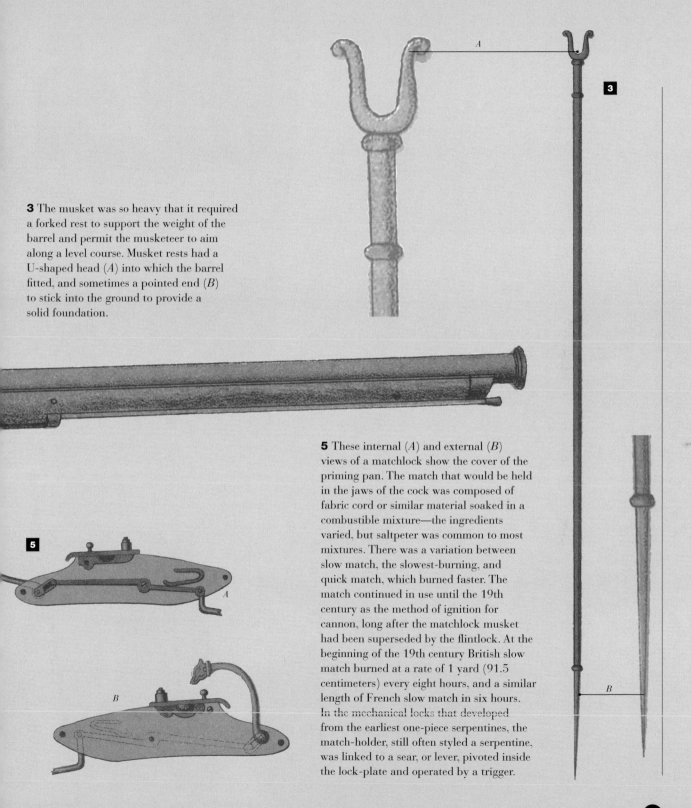

3 The musket was so heavy that it required a forked rest to support the weight of the barrel and permit the musketeer to aim along a level course. Musket rests had a U-shaped head (*A*) into which the barrel fitted, and sometimes a pointed end (*B*) to stick into the ground to provide a solid foundation.

5 These internal (*A*) and external (*B*) views of a matchlock show the cover of the priming pan. The match that would be held in the jaws of the cock was composed of fabric cord or similar material soaked in a combustible mixture—the ingredients varied, but saltpeter was common to most mixtures. There was a variation between slow match, the slowest-burning, and quick match, which burned faster. The match continued in use until the 19th century as the method of ignition for cannon, long after the matchlock musket had been superseded by the flintlock. At the beginning of the 19th century British slow match burned at a rate of 1 yard (91.5 centimeters) every eight hours, and a similar length of French slow match in six hours. In the mechanical locks that developed from the earliest one-piece serpentines, the match-holder, still often styled a serpentine, was linked to a sear, or lever, pivoted inside the lock-plate and operated by a trigger.

Artillery and Fortifications

The technology advances

Although not especially effective during this period, artillery formed a significant part of an army. The standard piece consisted of the barrel or tube, mounted upon a two-wheeled carriage, many of which were large, heavy, and difficult to move. Improvements in the casting of barrels enabled larger charges and projectiles to be used. The different sizes of artillery piece were generally given names rather than, as later, being named according to the weight of their projectile. These varied, but English terms in the 17th century included, from smallest to largest: robinet, falconet, falcon, minion, saker or drake, demi-culverin, culverin, demi-cannon, cannon, and cannon royal. Guns larger than the culverin were largely restricted to siege and fortress duty.

Early artillery piece

An early depiction of a small fieldpiece mounted on a two-wheeled carriage. Elevation of the barrel could be achieved by inserting a wedge, or quoin, under its sealed end. Here the gunner is about to discharge the gun by applying a smoldering match in a holder to the touch-hole. The rate of fire was slow, around twelve shots per hour for a lighter gun and eight for a very heavy piece.

French artillery piece

A French piece of the third quarter of the 16th century with a two-wheeled carriage. The standard projectile was a simple ball made of iron, or sometimes stone, loaded via the muzzle At close range, case shot, packages containing a number of small balls, or loose shot, a fearsome antipersonnel weapon, could be fired.

See also
The evolution of artillery, *pages 210–11*
Fortification and siege warfare, *pages 212–13*
Anatomy of a cannon, *pages 224–5*
Artillery, *pages 296–7*

Hand weapons

Missile weapons
• artillery
• case shot
• loose shot

Defenses
• bastioned fort
• ravelin

Clothing

Warriors

Concepts & Tactics
• siegecraft
• trenches

Buildings & Transport
• fort design

▲ Star fort

When artillery became sufficiently powerful and mobile to batter down the walls of the old style of fortification, there occurred a complete change in the theory of fortifications, beginning in Italy in the early 16th century. New styles were devised, both to resist and accommodate artillery, and the design of forts, as shown here, was now along precise geometrical lines.

▲ Fortifications

From the later 16th century there were further developments in fortification design, including emphasis on defense in depth. Forts consisted of a series of low-lying banks and walls surrounded by open ground, giving the attacker no cover. Additional fortifications extended beyond the main defenses: ravelins, triangular detached works between two bastions, and outlying hornworks as shown.

▲ Siegecraft

In response to the improvements in fortification design, siegecraft reached a peak of efficiency in the later 17th century. Successive lines of trenches, or parallels, were pushed toward the defenses by zigzag saps, with positions constructed for the artillery trained upon the fortress, as in this illustration. When the trenches were sufficiently close to the defenses, an assault could be launched.

▲ Bastioned fort

The new design of fortification was low-lying, providing an effective artillery platform while presenting as small a target as possible to the enemy. Corner towers were replaced by the bastion, a four-sided projection from the corners of the fort that opened the entire approach to the wall to crossfire, eliminating any dead ground in which the attacker was safe.

▲ Culverin barrel

One of the classic heavier guns was the culverin, named after the French *couleuvre*, or snake. Its shot weighed about 15 pounds (6.8 kilograms) and its barrel length could be about 11 feet (3.35 meters) or more; it was believed that a longer barrel increased the range. Barrels might include cast decorations.

The Last Knights, *1500–1530*

The rise of the infantry

In the high Middle Ages the armored cavalryman—often referred to as the knight—represented the most potent military asset and was associated with the higher echelons of society and its ruling elite. This began to change as other weapons became more prominent: the English longbow, wielded by those of lesser social standing, cut down the chivalry of France, and the diminution in the effectiveness of the knight was accelerated by the development of firearms and of the pike when used in formation. The Battle of Pavia (February 24,1525), where the army of the French King, Francis I, was defeated by a Spanish Imperial force that had a larger proportion of firearms than the French, demonstrated the need for the cavalry to change and make use of the new technology.

Helmet styles

Styles popular from the early 16th century included, from top: the burgonet, which unlike earlier visored helmets left the face exposed, which could be protected by a separate plate, or buffe; the cabasset, a conical form with shallow brim; the high-combed morion; and the lobster-tail, named after the articulated neck-guard.

16th-century knight

A fully armored knight in the magnificent equipment that is characteristic of the early 16th century. He is armed with a war hammer, which was for use against armor, in addition to his sword. This also illustrates horse armor, including for the head (chanfron), neck (crinet), breast (poitrel), sides (flanchards), and hindquarters (crupper).

Emperor Maximilian I

Following the so-called Gothic style of armor, which reached the height of its development in the late 15th century, a fluted design became popular from *c.* 1500, reaching its zenith in about 1530. It was sometimes named the Maximilian style after the Emperor Maximilian I (1459–1519), illustrated here.

Hand weapons
- pike
- war hammer

Missile weapons
- matchlock arquebus

Defenses

Clothing
- burgonet helmet
- cabasset helmet
- lobster-tailed helmet

Warriors

Concepts & Tactics

Buildings & Transport
- armored horse

Burgonet helmet
Helmets like the burgonet and lobster-tail might be worn with an armored neck protection, or gorget (bottom). They might also have a barred face guard attached to the peak or a sliding nasal bar that passed through the peak.

Swords
A sword that attained the highest level of decoration in the 16th century was the rapier, a straight-bladed weapon designed for thrusting. It usually had an elaborate guard to protect the hand, composed of quillons (bars at a right-angle to the blade) and either curved bars, as illustrated, or cup-shaped guards.

16th-century armor
In the 16th century some of the finest examples of the armorers' art and skill were produced, including armors with elaborate engraved and gilded decoration. By the later 16th century there was an increasing use of half-armors, such as those illustrated here, in which the defenses for the leg were abandoned.

Warriors
Armor from the second half of the 16th century, including half-armor worn by a man armed with a matchlock arquebus (far left), a decorated armor of the smooth plates that succeeded the fluted style (center), and an armor of very elaborate construction, including a sculptured grotesque style of helmet and a skirt (or "tonlet") replicating fabric clothing (far right).

See also
The medieval knight, *pages 90–1*
Body armor, *pages 302–3*
Helmets, *pages 304–5*

The Development of Cavalry

Light horse and firearms

From the beginning of the 16th century a greater degree of discipline was introduced into cavalry tactics, and there was a growing use of lighter horsemen. Cavalry began to use firearms, not just the light troops but the heavy, armored horsemen as well. In Germany there developed a form of cavalry, often mercenaries, known as reiters, literally horsemen, although this was usually a contraction of the term *Schwartzreiter*, or black horseman, derived from the blackened armor that became popular during this period. They carried pistols, wheel-locks being especially suitable for use on horseback, and used these in addition to their swords. One of the older cavalry weapons, the lance, declined in use, and by the early 17th century it was rarely seen, although it remained a traditional arm in certain regions, notably Poland.

Cavalrymen
Two contrasting styles of cavalry from the late 16th and early 17th centuries. The armored cavalryman, known as a cuirassier from his cuirass, or breastplate, might carry a lance in addition to his sword and firearms. The lighter-equipped trooper (left), protected by a helmet and a coat of thick buff leather, was sometimes termed a carabine from his light musket or carbine.

Mounted trooper
A mounted light horseman from the end of the 16th century, still wearing half-armor, including body and arm protection and a burgonet helmet. He carries a carbine and pistols as well as a sword, the former being his principal weapons.

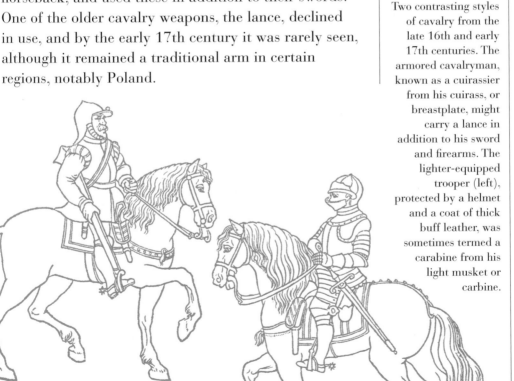

See also
Weapons of reach,
pages 284–5

Hand weapons
• lance
• sword

Missile weapons
• arquebus
• pistol

Defenses

Clothing
• burgonet helmet
• cuirass
• half-armor

Warriors
• arquebusier
• genitour
• stradiot
• *Schwartzreiter*

Concepts & Tactics
• increasing use of firearms on horseback

Buildings & Transport

Light horseman

From the later 15th century there was an increasing appreciation of the merits of lighter-armed cavalry, suitable for such tasks as skirmishing and reconnaissance. They emulated the effective light troops of Turkish, Hungarian, and Albanian origin. Venice had the stradiots, and the Spanish had the genitors. Such troops wore reduced armor and could be armed, as illustrated here, with firearms.

Battle of Dreux

Cavalry are depicted in action in this early illustration of the Battle of Dreux of December 19, 1562. This was an engagement at the beginning of the French Wars of Religion, conflicts that took place in the later 16th century between Protestants and Roman Catholics. Bodies of pikemen are visible in this illustration, one being assailed on all sides by cavalry, while armored horsemen, including lancers, are engaged in the foreground.

Infantry

The Landsknechts

Infantry tactics were revolutionized by the Swiss, who, lacking cavalry, evolved a devastatingly effective lightly armored infantry. Armed with pikes of up to 21 feet (6.4 meters) in length, they marched in disciplined, massed phalanxes, impenetrable to cavalry and capable of rapid offensive action. They were supplemented by missile-armed troops, acting mainly as skirmishers, and halberdiers, but it was the pike that defined their system. The weapon proved so successful that many became mercenaries, often in French pay. To counter them, Emperor Maximilian I created a similar force in Germany, the Landsknechts, organized in regiments with discipline and rank structure, making them in a sense the forerunners of modern armies. In addition to Imperial service, many Landsknechts also became mercenaries.

◗ Landsknecht costume

Landsknechts were often characterized by flamboyant costume, including garments of puffed-and-slashed construction—an outer layer with cuts, or slashes, revealing an inner layer of a contrasting color. Headdresses were often equally elaborate.

See also
Emperor Maximilian I,
page 162
Weapons of reach,
pages 284–5

◗ Landsknecht weapons

A group of Landsknechts in typical costume, including an arquebusier (left) with a bandolier of powder-tubes, a fifer (second left), a man armed with a pole-arm and the characteristic short sword with curved quillons, sometimes referred to as a *Katzbalger*, and, on the right, a man with a two-handed sword.

French soldiers

This image of troops in French service in the first half of the 16th century shows costumes in the popular contemporary style of contrasting colors, and includes Swiss pikemen and a Landsknecht armed with a characteristic, two-handed sword.

Two-handed swords

The huge two-handed sword was a popular infantry weapon, designed for a slashing blow. There was also a long-bladed weapon termed a hand-and-a-half sword, which could be used either one- or two-handed.

16th-century warriors

On the left is the Emperor Rudolf II, wearing engraved and gilded half-armor. In the center is a junior officer wearing a form of pikeman's armor—breastplate and thigh-guards (tassets)—and armed with the Landsknechts' favored two-handed sword. On the right is a halberdier; the halberd was an infantry weapon especially useful for engaging a cavalryman.

Infantry

Infantry drill

Tactical changes required a greater degree of discipline than had previously been necessary. Because of its length, movements of the pike had to be coordinated with others in the formation, or confusion would ensue—the Swiss were among the first to require this level of discipline, and they were trained to adopt a number of suitable formations. Similarly, musketry was most effective when delivered systematically, especially when successive ranks might be required to fire in sequence, leading to a more formalized style of firing drill. In addition to a massed volley, other methods of firing included that in which the rear ranks would advance successively between the forward ranks, firing when they reached the front of the formation.

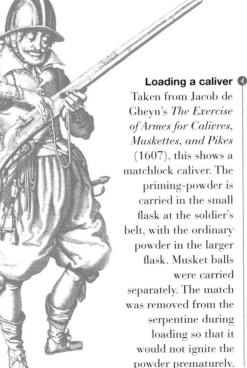

Loading a caliver ◗
Taken from Jacob de Gheyn's *The Exercise of Armes for Calivres, Muskettes, and Pikes* (1607), this shows a matchlock caliver. The priming-powder is carried in the small flask at the soldier's belt, with the ordinary powder in the larger flask. Musket balls were carried separately. The match was removed from the serpentine during loading so that it would not ignite the powder prematurely.

Pike drill ◗
A number of illustrated guides were produced in the 17th century to show the drill for pike and firearms. This pike drill shows how the weapon was transferred from the shoulder position for marching (*XXIX, XXX, XXXIV*) to "charge your pike" (*XXXV*), in which the weapon was leveled for action. Figure *XLI*, and left, shows the pike positioned against cavalry, sloping the weapon so that the points were at the horses' breast height.

See also
Anatomy of a matchlock, *pages 158–9*
Weapons of reach, *pages 284–5*
Handheld firearms, *pages 298–9*

⬤ Firearms drill

This complicated drill for loading and firing is taken from one of the manuals by Johann Jacobi von Wallhausen, who wrote a number of military studies. It shows the caliver, the lighter musket that did not require the use of a rest. Beginning with a loaded musket, the soldier readies his match, fires (*12*), and reloads, first placing powder into the priming-pan, and then loading the powder and ball via the muzzle, using the ramrod (*23–30*).

Hand weapons
• pike

Missile weapons
• caliver
• musket

Defenses

Clothing

Warriors
• Swiss infantry

Concepts & Tactics
• drilling and formation

Buildings & Transport

War in Europe, *1618–1651*

The Thirty Years War

The Thirty Years War (1618–48) was probably the greatest and most destructive conflict in Europe before modern times. It began as a religious struggle between Protestant and Roman Catholic princes in Germany, represented at the outset by the Protestant Evangelical Union, formed in May 1608, and on the other side by the Catholic League. The religious element featured throughout the war, but it took on an increasingly political dimension, that of a conflict between the Habsburg Holy Roman Empire (centered on Austria) with the associated Roman Catholic princes of Germany and Spain, and those who wished to check Imperial power—the Protestant princes of Germany, the Kingdoms of Sweden and Denmark, and Roman Catholic France.

See also
Matchlock and wheel-lock, *pages 156–7*
Anatomy of a matchlock, *pages 158–9*
Weapons of reach, *pages 284–5*
Handheld firearms, *pages 298–9*

Officer of pikemen, early 17th century
Pikemen's armor usually consisted of a combed helmet, or morion, or a conical cabasset helmet; breast-and-back plates and lamellar (armor made of overlapping lames, which were small plates similar to those on scale armor); thigh guards, or tassets; and sometimes a gorget to protect the throat. The body armor was sometimes referred to as a corselet or cuirass.

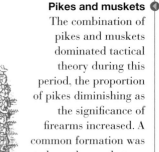

Pikes and muskets
The combination of pikes and muskets dominated tactical theory during this period, the proportion of pikes diminishing as the significance of firearms increased. A common formation was to have the musketeers deployed in two equal bodies on either side of a body of pikemen; other musketeers might be positioned as skirmishers ahead of the main body.

Hand weapons
• pike
• rapier

Missile weapons
• musket

Defenses
• hand-guards

Clothing
• cabasset
• cuirass
• gorget
• lamellar
• sash
• tasset

Warriors
• musketeer
• pikeman

Concepts & Tactics
• political ideologies and religious warfare

Buildings & Transport

Military costumes

The mid-17th-century costumes worn by officers and others included long coats similar to the type sometimes termed a cassock. On the left is a pikeman performing the part of the drill called "advance your pike"; next to him is a junior officer of pikemen, wearing the sash sometimes used as a mark of rank.

Musketeers

The figures second left and second right are wearing bandoliers with single-shot measures of powder—a new development. Musketeers still carried flasks to charge their muskets when the tubes were emptied, however. The soldier at far right is filling his priming-pan from his flask, holding his match away from the gunpowder.

Swords

As carried by the men engaged here in hand-to-hand combat, the sword remained a universal weapon. The classic rapier, a straight-bladed sword designed for the thrust, usually had an elaborate hand-guard. Swords of plainer construction, with a simpler guard or knucklebow, were very common. The man at the far left is a musketeer, as is evident from his bandolier of powder-tubes.

War in Europe

The Thirty Years War

The terrible Thirty Years War devastated much of Europe; cities were destroyed or plundered and populations decimated. Military methods were refined by the necessities of war, armies became truly professional, including many mercenaries, and the ongoing conflicts led to technological and tactical developments. The war produced a number of outstanding commanders, including the Flemish Johann Tserclaes, Graf von Tilly, a loyal Imperial general; Albrecht von Wallenstein, a general driven by ambition, whose relationship with the Imperial cause was somewhat ambiguous and who exercised almost independent powers until murdered by his own officers; Gottfried, Graf zu Pappenheim, a mercenary cavalry commander of noted ability; and one of the greatest of commanders, Swedish King Gustavus Adolphus, whose tactical developments were of immense significance.

Officers

Two versions of cavalry uniform are illustrated here, worn by senior officers. One has his protective equipment limited to a sleeveless buff-coat and cuirass; the close helmet with visor could be worn with such limited armor. The other officer wears full cuirassier armor, without armor on the lower leg, which was often protected instead by a sturdy leather boot.

Typical costumes, earlier 17th century

These figures include a musketeer whose firearm is sufficiently heavy to require a rest, two armored pikemen, two officers, and a man with a lighter caliver. Second from right is a cavalryman with arquebusier equipment, including a lobster-tailed helmet and bandolier of powder-tubes. Although musketeers usually carried swords, some advocated that the musket butt used as a club was more effective.

See also

Matchlock and wheel-lock,
pages 156–7

The Thirty Years War, *pages 170–1*

Buff-coat, *page 181*

Handheld firearms, *pages 298–9*

Cavalry firearms

An important part of cavalry equipment, firearms usually comprised pistols for heavier troops and light muskets for arquebusiers. The mounted figure is equipped as the latter, his musket attached to a shoulder belt for security. The soldier below left wears half-armor with a lobster-tail helmet with sliding nasal-bar. He is spanning, or cocking, his wheel-lock pistol.

Officers in buff-coats

Officers of the mid-17th century often wore the buff-coat. This thick leather garment was made of hide sufficiently strong to turn a sword cut, and was often cut low enough to cover the upper leg to the point where it met the high top of the riding-boot. The buff-coat could be worn alone or beneath armor.

Arquebusier

Taken from John Cruso's *Militarie Instructions for the Cavallerie* (1632), one of the earlier English manuals, this shows typical arquebusier equipment: breast-and-back plates probably worn over a short buff-coat, a burgonet-style helmet, and a light arquebus or carbine carried on a shoulder belt, with a firelock or snaphaunce mechanism, an early flintlock easier to use on horseback.

Anatomy of an Army

By the early 16th century armies were no longer the feudal assemblies typical of the Middle Ages but more precisely formed, disciplined bodies composed of contingents with specified duties. The increase in professional military service was exemplified by the publication of many manuals and books of instruction, sometimes embellished with very detailed engravings. These covered almost all aspects of military service, including weapons-handling and pike and musket drill as well as artillery, fortification, horsemanship, tactical formations, and methods of deploying troops on the battlefield.

This very detailed view of a military deployment is derived from the work of Ludovico Melzo, whose writings were translated into a number of European languages. A noted Italian edition, *Regnole militari sopra il governo e servitio particolare della cavalleria*, was published in 1611. An English edition of 1632 was entitled *Military Rules*.

1 The central features of the mode of deployment shown are the infantry contingents, three large divisions of pikemen supported by musketeers. A regiment could be split into three divisions, each of pikemen with musketeers on the flanks; latterly they might be assembled six or eight deep, the actual formation depending upon whether the commanding officer preferred Dutch or Swedish theories.

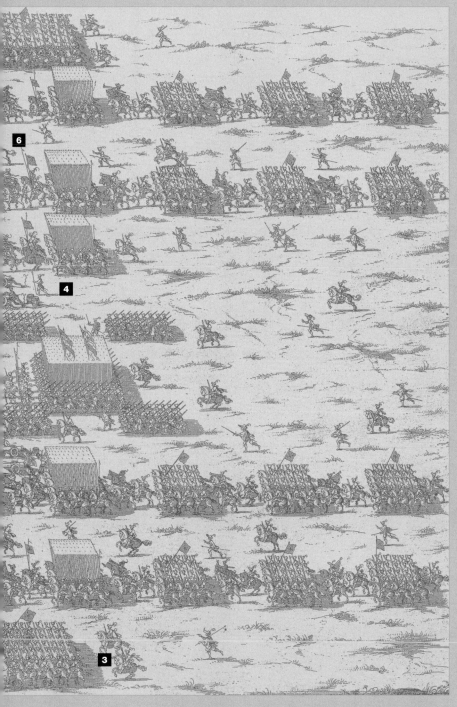

2 Files might be about a yard/meter apart, giving each man room to handle his weapons with ease, although the distance could be much less or even more. In the formation illustrated, each stand of pikes forms the center of a unit, with musketeers around the faces and in a body at each corner.

3 Troops of cavalry are arrayed on the flanks of the infantry; the majority carry firearms, but among them are bodies armed with lances.

4 Artillery is positioned in front of the infantry to give the guns an unrestricted field of fire; some artillery is held in reserve.

5 Some cavalry have been sent forward as skirmishers, and they are discharging their pistols in the direction of the enemy.

6 Note the large number of flags. Each infantry company might have its own color, or flag, and each cavalry troop its own standard, the latter carried by a cornet, or junior officer, in front of the troops armed with lances, but within the ranks of the other cavalry formations. The infantry's colors are carried within the center of each stand of pikes.

War in Europe

The development of the cavalry

Despite the increasing use of firearms, older cavalry weapons and the tactics they employed still remained in use. John Cruso's manual of 1632 described why the heavily armored lancer was introduced—"to pierce and divide a grosse body, and therefore requires force and velocitie for the shock"—but then explained why the lance had fallen out of use. It was, he stated, partly because of the difficulty of providing horses of sufficient quality in the numbers required, but mostly because of the training needed to produce a proficient lancer, "it being a thing of much labor and industry to learn," implying that it was much easier to train a horseman to fight with pistols and sword. Contemporary instruction manuals show that in addition to weapons-handling a considerable degree of discipline was required for units armed with lances.

See also
Arquebusier, *page 173*
Cavalry tactics, *pages 178–9*
Weapons of reach, *pages 284–5*

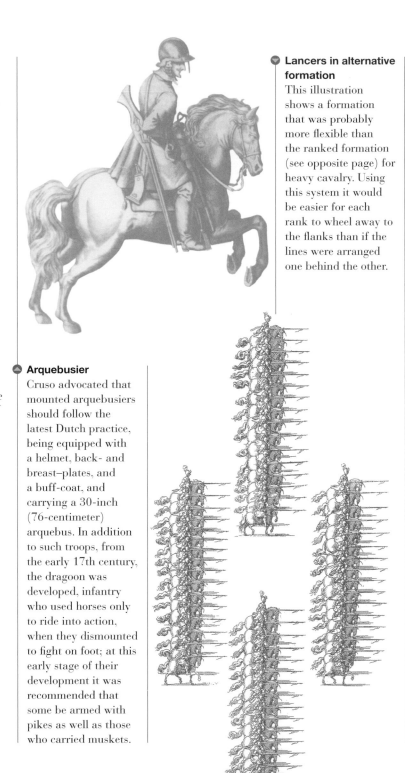

Arquebusier
Cruso advocated that mounted arquebusiers should follow the latest Dutch practice, being equipped with a helmet, back- and breast–plates, and a buff-coat, and carrying a 30-inch (76-centimeter) arquebus. In addition to such troops, from the early 17th century, the dragoon was developed, infantry who used horses only to ride into action, when they dismounted to fight on foot; at this early stage of their development it was recommended that some be armed with pikes as well as those who carried muskets.

Lancers in alternative formation
This illustration shows a formation that was probably more flexible than the ranked formation (see opposite page) for heavy cavalry. Using this system it would be easier for each rank to wheel away to the flanks than if the lines were arranged one behind the other.

Cavalry in defensive posture

In this diagram a body of lancers has formed in two ranks, facing outward in a defensive posture. Such a formation might have held off an attack by cavalry but would have been vulnerable to firearms.

Lancers in ranked formation

The tactical illustrations here are taken from Hermanus Hugo's *De militia equestri antique et nova ad regnem Phillipum IV* (1630). They show a troop of heavy cavalry, armed with lances, arrayed four ranks deep; in practice the formation might have been more successful in combat conditions had there been a wider gap between the ranks.

Lancers attacking an enemy

This illustration shows a method of surrounding and attacking an enemy formation. A determined defense by a body of pikemen, supported by the fire of musketeers protected by the pikes, would have made the task of the cavalry extremely difficult unless they used their own firearms to unsteady the enemy ranks before closing with the lance.

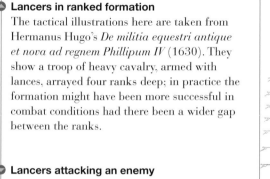

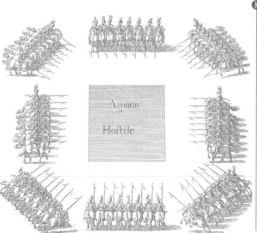

Pikeman

The most secure defense against cavalry was a hedge of pikes. In this pose the pike is angled and braced against the pikeman's foot. The illustration is derived from Henry Hexham's *The Principles of the Art Militarie; Practised in the Warres of the United Netherlands* (1637). Many military developments arose out of the long wars between the Spanish and Dutch in the 16th and 17th centuries, and these were copied elsewhere.

Hand weapons
• lance

Missile weapons
• arquebus
• musket

Defenses

Clothing
• back- and breast-plates
• buff-coat

Warriors
• arquebusier
• cavalry
• pikeman

Concepts & Tactics
• cavalry formations

Buildings & Transport

War in Europe

Cavalry tactics

The tactic that most depended upon cavalry firearms was that employed by the German reiters, and which for a period predominated: the caracole. In this, cavalry advanced at a trot in a compact body several ranks deep. Having approached the enemy, the front rank fired their pistols then broke off toward the flanks and reassembled at the rear of the column to reload. This was repeated by each rank in turn until the enemy formation might be sufficiently weakened to be vulnerable to a charge. The caracole was difficult to perform effectively, requiring considerable discipline, and it negated the cavalry's ability to make a rapid attack. But it remained in use for some time and led to a demand for German mercenary reiters schooled in the tactic. The caracole fell from use when the traditional charge with the sword was reasserted as an effective cavalry tactic.

Pikeman

A pikeman in the pose "charge your pike," derived from Hexham's manual (*see page 177*). Although a hedge of pikes could hold off a cavalry attack, it could be made vulnerable by a fusillade from the caracole. This emphasized the advantage of having the pikemen supported by musketeers, who were able to return the fire of the caracoling horsemen.

Cuirassier firing

A cuirassier firing his pistol, as he might during the caracole maneuver (see opposite page). The long sash shown in such illustrations was not always merely a decoration; in the period before the development of recognizable national uniforms, so-called field-signs had to be used to distinguish friend from foe amid the confusion of the battlefield, one method being the color of the sash.

Cuirassier loading

The caracole depended upon the ability of the cavalryman to reload on horseback. In this illustration, derived from Cruso's manual (*see page 176*), the cuirassier has rammed home the projectile and propellant and is ready to fire again.

See also
Arquebusier, *page 173*
Anatomy of an army, *pages 174–5*
Development of the cavalry, *pages 176–7*

Cavalry in opposition

Shown here are opposing bodies of cavalry, all armed with light muskets or carbines, the gaps between ranks allowing greater scope for maneuver.

Cavalry formations

Cavalry in offensive and defensive formations: for the attack, in ranks arrayed in echelon at either side of the leading troop, whose attack could be seconded by succeeding waves; and for defense in a compact body. The reiter tactic's emphasis on firearms was replaced by the revival of the rapid charge, notably in Gustavus Adolphus's Swedish system, when the cavalry would be supported by musketeers.

The caracole

This illustrates the caracole, here apparently delivered from the flank of a cavalry formation. The horsemen are shown peeling away in ranks, firing at the enemy, then wheeling away to reload as the next rank in succession repeats the procedure.

War in Europe

The English Civil War

The English Civil War was a defining event in Britain, and its effects were felt more widely than the name implies, as it involved Scotland, Wales, and Ireland in equal measure. The war began as a struggle for supremacy in government between King Charles I and his Parliament, although other factors came into play as the conflict progressed. At the outset in 1642 the troops on both sides were largely amateurs. There was no standing army and the only individuals with any military experience were those who had served abroad or in the trained bands, the existing local militia who had some experience of weapons-handling and drill but not of actual combat. The campaigns of 1642–45, 1648, and 1650–51 raised the level of military professionalism enormously and involved the use of tactics and methods that had been perfected in mainland Europe.

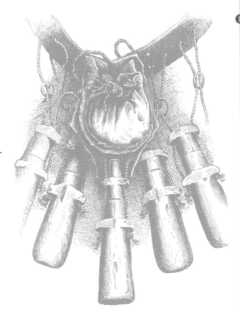

◗ Musketeer's bandolier

This bandolier has powder tubes, a bullet bag, and a flask of priming-powder. This was sometimes nicknamed a Twelve Apostles bandolier, because of the number of tubes often carried, and it was in common use throughout the 17th century, only being supplanted by the introduction of cartridges—paper tubes containing the powder and ball for one shot.

◗ Pikeman

The complete armor originally worn by pikemen consisted of breast- and back-plates, gorget, helmet, and tassets, but during the English Civil War gorget and tassets were often discarded as not being worth the burden of their weight. Further protection often came from a single buff-leather glove on the left hand, with an ordinary wrist-length glove on the right, the latter being easier to use when handling a sword.

Buff-coat

This shows the buff-coat reputedly worn by Thomas Fairfax at the Battle of Naseby in 1645. A stout hide garment that saw very widespread use throughout the 17th century, even as a form of civilian dress, it might have sleeves of thinner or more supple leather to facilitate movement.

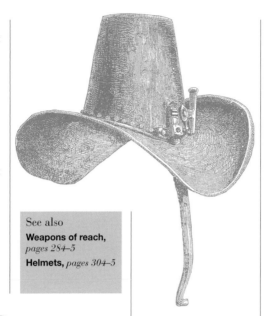

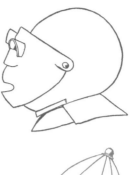

See also
Weapons of reach,
pages 284–5
Helmets, *pages 304–5*

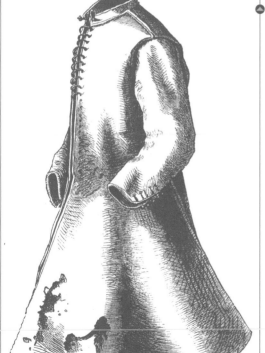

Iron hat

Copied directly from a civilian style of hat, this uncommon iron headdress combines a fashionable shape with a sliding nasal or face bar, as carried on many cavalry helmets. The use of helmets declined during the English Civil War, having fallen from use among musketeers by the beginning of the 17th century.

Helmets, early- to mid-17th century

Top, a close helmet with a hinged visor. Center, a helmet with a barred facemask and a peak similar to that on a burgonet; more common in the English Civil War was the lobster-tailed pot helmet with facebars attached to a movable peak and flaps to protect the ears. Bottom, the style of pikeman's helmet that developed from the morion, a combed headdress and a wide brim, commonly used during the Civil War.

War in Europe

The English Civil War

The military abilities of both sides in the English Civil War were enhanced as armies and their leaders became more experienced. A number of commanders achieved great prominence in the war. On the Parliamentary side was Thomas, Baron Fairfax, an experienced soldier and skilled organizer, and, notably, Oliver Cromwell. At first Cromwell was an amateur leader of cavalry whose "Ironsides" became among the best-known of the Parliamentary forces; later he became not only an effective general but also led the government after the execution of the king. On the Royalist side was the king's nephew, Prince Rupert of the Rhine, who had gained much experience in Europe; his cavalry skills made him one of the outstanding leaders of the war. Fairfax's New Model Army, formed in 1645, created a professional force that had a profound effect in the later years of the conflict.

English Civil War military costumes
This shows various troops from the time of the English Civil War and the Commonwealth. Included (left) are seamen, cavalry (including an arquebusier with his musket on his back), and infantry (right). The musketeer carries a matchlock and rest, although a new firearm was coming into use, the firelock, or flintlock, which dominated warfare until the mid-19th century.

See also
Cavalry tactics,
pages 178–9

First Battle of Newbury, September 20, 1643
Although full cuirassier armor was used during the English Civil War, it was restricted to some officers and two Parliamentary units. Otherwise cavalry armor usually consisted of breast-and-back plates and sometimes an armored gauntlet and a helmet. This illustration shows the death of the secretary of state, Lord Falkland; note the civilian hats preferred by many to helmets.

Hand weapons

Missile weapons
• flintlock
• matchlock

Defenses

Clothing
• armored gauntlet
• breast-and-back plates
• helmet

Warriors
• arquebusier
• cavalry
• musketeer
• seaman

Concepts & Tactics
• New Model Army

Buildings & Transport

Battle of Naseby, June 14, 1645

This later illustration of hand-to-hand combat supposedly shows the Battle of Naseby, in which the army of King Charles I was defeated decisively by the Parliamentarian forces of Sir Thomas Fairfax. Cromwell's cavalry played an important role in this victory.

Military costumes, 1650s

This illustration shows costumes from the period around the end of the English Civil War. Left to right: a "cavalier" in the civilian dress of a gentleman with the addition of breast-and-back plates over a short buff-coat; a musketeer in a full-skirted coat, sometimes styled a cassock, equipped with a Twelve Apostles bandolier; an officer wearing a breast-and-back plate over a buff-coat, that has wings, or projections, at the shoulder and hoops of lace on the sleeve, a quite fashionable decoration.

The Flintlock at War
1650–1815

The period from the end of the 17th century to the beginning of the 19th century might be termed the era of the flintlock. Europe was convulsed by a succession of major conflicts during this time, which accelerated the evolution of military theory. Dynastic rivalries, territorial disputes, and the maintenance of spheres of influence gave rise to most of the major conflicts, including the War of the Grand Alliance (1688–97), the War of the Spanish Succession (1701–14), the War of the Austrian Succession (1740–48), and the Seven Years War (1756–63), the latter in particular spreading to include the overseas colonies of the major European nations. At the end of the 18th century the French Revolution developed into the greatest and most prolonged conflict of the era, the French Revolutionary and Napoleonic Wars of 1792 to 1815. Some of the greatest commanders in history exercised their skills between the mid-17th and early 19th centuries, including the French Vicomte de Turenne, the English Duke of Marlborough, the Imperial general Eugene of Savoy, King Frederick II "the Great" of Prussia and, at the end of the period, the French Emperor Napoleon Bonaparte (arguably the greatest of all) and his nemesis, Arthur Wellesley, Duke of Wellington.

Technological advances led to tactical developments. The flintlock's improved rate of fire permitted a reduction in the depth of infantry units, so that linear formations became common. The pike fell from use as the bayonet enabled the soldier to turn his musket into what was, in effect, a short pike. Artillery became increasingly potent and mobile, while cavalry evolved into a fighting force most suited to exploiting a breakthrough or conducting a pursuit. During the 17th century fortification, became an increasingly sophisticated science, the greatest theorist and builder of fortresses being the 17th-century French engineer Sébastien de Vauban.

During the flintlock era, and prior to the evolution of the "citizen army" of the French Revolutionary period, armies became professional, permanently and regularly organized, embracing a wider social base.

The Flintlock

The weapon that defined the age

Developed originally as a sporting weapon in the early 17th century, the flintlock increasingly came into use as a military weapon in the second half of that century. Although lighter and easier to use than the matchlock, it was more expensive to produce, and its adoption suffered from the conservatism of military authorities satisfied with the performance of the matchlock. The flintlock consisted of a cock, or hammer, holding a piece of flint in its jaws, connected to the trigger. This, when pressed, caused the flint to strike a spark against a hinged steel plate, or frizzen, which was forced back to uncover a small amount of gunpowder in the priming-pan. This was ignited by the spark and the resulting flame communicated into the musket barrel via the touch-hole, setting off the propellant charge that sent the projectile on its course.

Fixing bayonets
This illustration from 1798, depicting a member of the Oxford Loyal Volunteers, a British volunteer corps, shows how the bayonet was fixed on to the end of the musket barrel by a half-turn to the lug.

Shoulder Arms
Drill—known in Britain as the Manual Exercise—was based upon the handling of the musket; the flintlock was easier to handle than the more unwieldy earlier matchlock. This is the "Shoulder Arms" position, showing the British infantry uniform of the mid-1790s.

Pistol with shoulder stock
Despite its very restricted range the flintlock pistol was carried by virtually all cavalry. A development was the provision of a detachable shoulder stock to permit the pistol to be fired with greater steadiness, as on this early 19th-century example.

Plug bayonet
Originating in the late 16th century, its name derived from the French town of Bayonne, which had a reputation for the manufacture of cutlery, the bayonet gave the musket one of the attributes of the pike. Initially it was simply a form of dagger that could be jammed into the barrel—the musket could not be fired when the bayonet was in place— hence the name plug bayonet. This is a typical dagger-shaped English example, dated 1686.

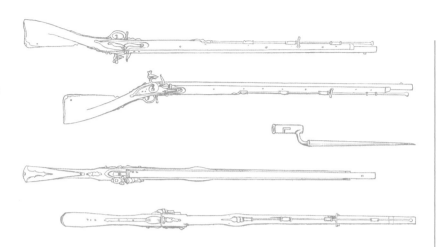

"Brown Bess" flintlock

Arguably the most famous of all flintlock muskets was the British "Brown Bess." This name was a term of endearment probably derived from the German *Büchse*, gun, and the browning applied to the barrel to remove the shine. The name was applied, albeit unofficially, to a number of models from the early 18th century until the flintlock was replaced by the percussion lock from the late 1830s. As was standard, the lock is carried on the right-hand side of the stock.

Combined flint and matchlock

A very uncommon lock from the mid-17th century combined the new flintlock mechanism with the earlier matchlock. At the left is the flintlock, the flint held in the jaws of the cock, and in the center the frizzen and pan cover; at the right is the serpentine, or match-holder, of the matchlock. The pan cover was perforated to permit the match to ignite the gunpowder in the priming-pan.

French socket bayonet

To enable the musket to be fired while the bayonet was fixed, an early expedient was to affix a plug bayonet to the end of the musket barrel by means of rings. However, this was very insecure. The next development was the socket bayonet, which consisted of a tube, or socket, that slid over the end of the musket barrel, with a blade offset to one side of the socket, as shown in this early French model.

See also
Anatomy of the flintlock, *pages 188–9*
The musket, *page 193*
Handheld firearms, *pages 298–9*

Mold for a ball

Until the 1820s, the projectile used by all military firearms was a simple, spherical lead ball. It could be manufactured in the field simply by melting lead and pouring it into a hinged steel mold. Despite its simplicity, the musket ball could inflict the most dreadful injuries.

Anatomy of the Flintlock

Although tactics were determined to a considerable extent by the characteristics of the musket, in one sense it was an extremely inefficient weapon. Although its maximum range was much longer than its effective range, it was generally thought that on the battlefield the maximum practical range was about 300 yards (275 meters), and often fire was delivered at 100 yards (90 meters) or less. Even at this range the musket was very inaccurate; one British writer of the period stated that no man was ever killed at 200 yards by the person who aimed at him. However, because of the prevailing tactical system it was not necessary to hit a single figure but merely to register a hit at any point in the large blocks of troops in which armies maneuvered.

1 A musket lock-and-trigger mechanism, *c.* 1800. The cock is drawn back into the firing position but the pan is open. The flintlock was prone to misfiring—the flint would become worn after a number of shots and cease to strike a spark effectively, and the touch-hole could become blocked with burned powder so that the spark might not communicate to the charge in the barrel, producing only a "flash in the pan."

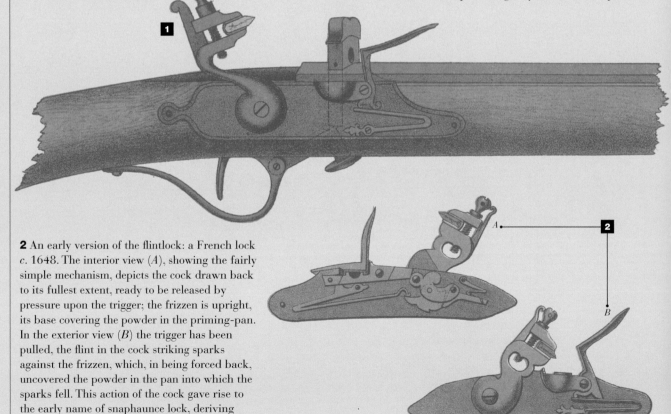

2 An early version of the flintlock: a French lock *c.* 1648. The interior view (*A*), showing the fairly simple mechanism, depicts the cock drawn back to its fullest extent, ready to be released by pressure upon the trigger; the frizzen is upright, its base covering the powder in the priming-pan. In the exterior view (*B*) the trigger has been pulled, the flint in the cock striking sparks against the frizzen, which, in being forced back, uncovered the powder in the pan into which the sparks fell. This action of the cock gave rise to the early name of snaphaunce lock, deriving from the Dutch *snaphaan*, a snapping hen.

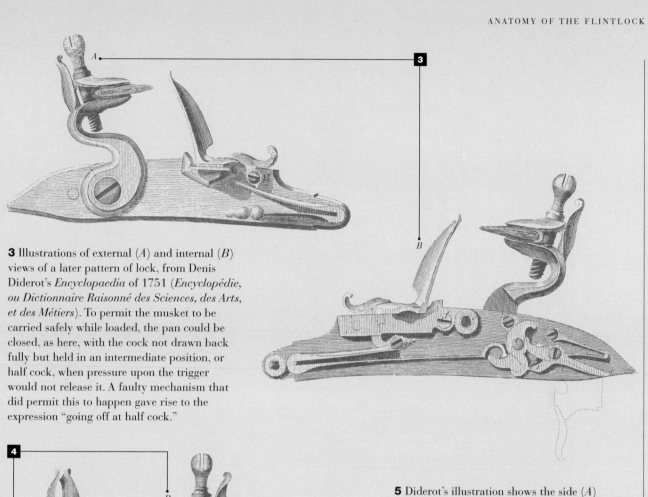

3 Illustrations of external (*A*) and internal (*B*) views of a later pattern of lock, from Denis Diderot's *Encyclopaedia* of 1751 (*Encyclopédie, ou Dictionnaire Raisonné des Sciences, des Arts, et des Métiers*). To permit the musket to be carried safely while loaded, the pan could be closed, as here, with the cock not drawn back fully but held in an intermediate position, or half cock, when pressure upon the trigger would not release it. A faulty mechanism that did permit this to happen gave rise to the expression "going off at half cock."

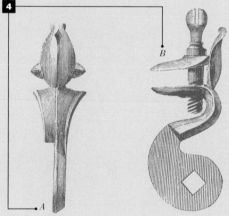

4 Diderot's illustration of a flintlock cock, or hammer, shows the rear (*A*) and internal side view (*B*). This cock is of the S-shaped style; the other principal design was reinforced and rather more robust, as shown in the earlier example (*2*). The flint was held within the screw-operated jaws of the cock, usually with a padding of leather or lead to hold it more firmly.

5 Diderot's illustration shows the side (*A*) and front (*B*) views of a frizzen; its rear face was perfectly flat to facilitate the striking of sparks when hit by the flint. The pan cover was the segment at right-angles to the plate struck by the flint.

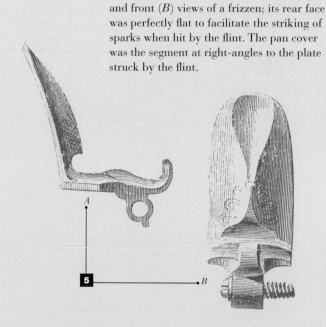

The Flintlock

The arms drill

Tactics of the 18th and early 19th centuries relied, perhaps to an even greater extent than before, upon precise drill and maneuvers. The foundation of infantry training was the arms drill, which attained its greatest complexity in the 18th century and continued into the 19th. The various movements were choreographed into a sequence that was instilled into the soldier by continuous practice, incorporating all the features of weapons-handling that were required to be performed in combat as well as some that were used primarily for ceremonial occasions. Some of the movements might appear unnecessary for the practicalities of service on the battlefield, but they helped inculcate the sense of discipline required for a battalion to act upon the word of command even under the dreadful conditions of close-quarter combat. Each nation had its own drill—sometimes with regimental variations until a universal, regulated drill was introduced—but all covered the basic movements required to produce an efficient unit.

See also
Battlefield tactics, *pages 192–3*
Tactics and technology, *pages 198–9*

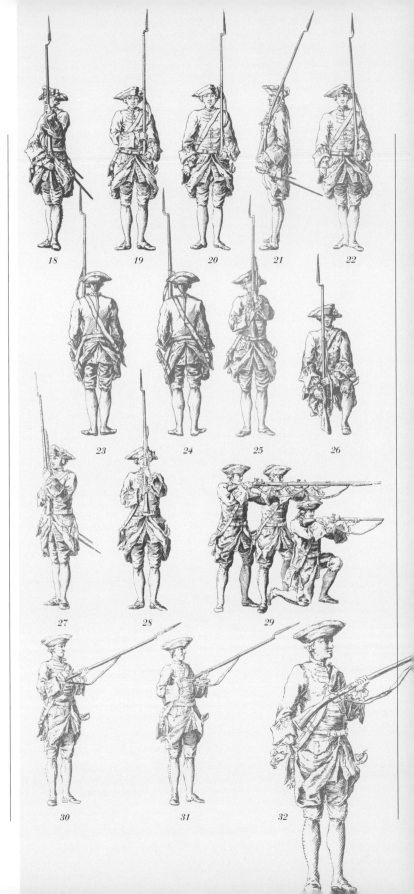

33, 34, 35, 36, 37, 38, 39, 40, 41

Arms drill: twenty-four figures

This extract from the French infantry arms drill is taken from Diderot's *Encyclopaedia* and depicts members of the Gardes Françaises, the elite infantry of the royal guard, who were distinguished from the ordinary white-coated French infantry by wearing blue coats with red facings and white lace. The beginning of the drill that preceded the movements shown included the fixing of the bayonet and the drawing and sheathing of the sword. The latter was one of the least important parts of the drill in terms of combat effectiveness, as the sword was rarely used in action. The parts of the drill illustrated here, identified by numbers, are as follows: *18–20* shoulder arms; *21–24* right turn (seen from front and rear); *25* port arms; *26–28* ready arms, positions for first to third ranks respectively (this prepares for firing, the cock on the musket lock being drawn back to full cock); *29* is the position for firing, showing how three ranks could fire together, the front rank kneeling and the third or rear rank firing through the intervals in the second or middle rank. Then follows the reloading sequence: *30–31* pulls the cock to half cock; *32* extracts a cartridge from the ammunition pouch on the shoulder belt; *33–34* bites off the end of the cartridge with the teeth (a part of the drill that helped account for the great thirst often experienced by troops in combat, as morsels of gunpowder could be introduced into the mouth); *35* pours some powder from the cartridge into the priming-pan; *36* closes the pan; *37–40* grounds the musket butt and inserts the remainder of the powder, musket ball, and cartridge paper into the barrel, following which the ramrod was extracted and used to ram the cartridge to the bottom of the barrel; *41* present arms.

The Flintlock

Battlefield tactics

Troops maneuvered on the battlefield in solid blocks and serried ranks, the whole operation of an army at this period depending upon formations remaining steady in their ranks. Discipline was of paramount importance, for only by maintaining their formations and alignments could units operate effectively and move by marching and counter-marching; once broken, with formation lost, a unit could neither fight effectively nor resist the onset of an enemy advance. Drill and maneuvers were inculcated into the soldier by continuous training, so that he could march, load, and fire almost as an automaton and became so used to standing in the ranks that he could perform his duties without flinching when surrounded by the smoke, noise, confusion, and danger of the battlefield.

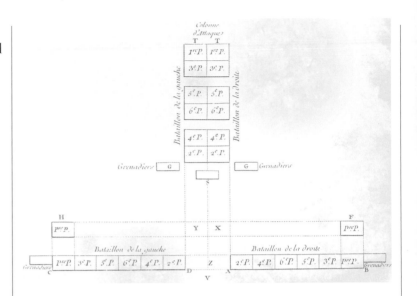

Line and column

The primary maneuver element of the infantry was the battalion, composed of a number of companies. This diagram from Diderot's *Encyclopaedia* depicts two French battalions, each of six line companies, identified as pelotons, or platoons, and a company of grenadiers, the battalion's elite element. In the formation A–B they are arrayed in line and changing formation into a column of attack. The first company of each battalion, identified here as Pre(mier) P(eloton), advances and takes position in front of the center of the line Y–X. The other companies follow, and the formation advances in three bodies, each of four companies, with a reserve including the two grenadier companies. This was typical of the method of maneuver employed in this period.

See also

The flintlock,
pages 186–7

Anatomy of the flintlock, *pages 188–9*

Arms drill, *pages 190–1*

War in Europe 1688–1763, *pages 194–5*

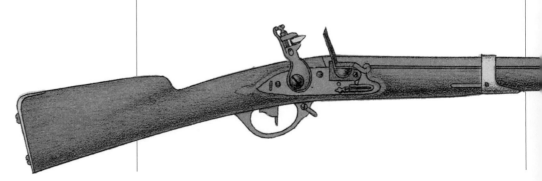

Hand weapons

Missile weapons
• flintlock musket

Defenses

Clothing

Warriors
• infantry
• tirailleurs

Concepts & Tactics
• troop maneuvers

Buildings & Transport

Illustration of line and column tactics

The column of attack in Diderot's plan is illustrated here, demonstrating the compact nature of infantry formations. This reflects the discipline that was an essential factor in maneuvers of the time, as such a column would move with much greater cohesion than was possible for troops in line. The French regulations of 1755 allowed for lines three or four ranks deep, double lines of six or eight ranks, and the close-order column. Light infantry and sharpshooters, as used at an earlier period, had declined in importance. A number of authorities still recognized the significance of such troops, however, and some use was made of them during the War of the Austrian Succession. Experiments conducted before the Seven Years War were subsequently put into practice, introducing an element of light-infantry tactics and aimed fire by *tirailleurs*, sharpshooters, as distinct from the massed volley fire utilized by troops in close-order formations.

The musket

The flintlock musket was the foundation of military tactics, and it is represented here by the French pattern of 1777, from which developed that used during the Napoleonic Wars. Muskets were predominantly smoothbored and muzzle-loading; breech-loaders did exist but were hardly ever used in a military context. This musket had a length of 59¾ inches (1.52 meters) and a bore of 0.69 inch (1.75 centimeters), the latter slightly less than that of the corresponding British musket, which fired a ball of 14 to the pound (454 grams), the French having 20 balls to the pound. Some commentators at the time believed that the heavier ball was more effective, but the difference cannot have been great.

War in Europe, *1688–1763*

The 18th-century soldier

Military equipment and tactics, always interrelated, continued to evolve from the late 17th century into the 18th. The pike, so dominant earlier, fell from use almost entirely, although it lingered on as the spontoon, or half-pike, carried by British infantry sergeants until 1830. The compact blocks and precise discipline by which troops continued to maneuver could inhibit speed of movement on the battlefield, but developments continued to be made. King Frederick the Great of Prussia, the most influential commander of the period, while emphasizing the crucial importance of precision drill, added an extra dimension with increased speed and maneuverability, creating a most formidable force, aspects of which were emulated throughout Europe. Infantry tended to dominate the battlefield; cavalry and artillery, although very significant, often acted rather more as support to the infantry.

See also
Battlefield tactics,
pages 192–3
War in Europe,
pages 196–7
Tactics and technology, *pages 198–9*

French troops, 1724
From left to right: Company of the Provost-General of the Marechaussée (*gendarmerie*) of the Île-de-France; Marechaussée; Provost-General; infantry field officer wearing the characteristic white coat of the 18th-century French infantry; grenadier sergeant of the Régiment du Dauphin carrying a *fourche à croc*, an archaic pole-arm carried as a regimental tradition; a cavalry quartermaster of Régiment Colonel Général; a Marshal of France, the highest-ranking military appointment; and a drum-major of Régiment de Linck.

Troops of the early 18th century
The military costume of the first half of the 18th century was a development from that worn in previous years and reflected prevailing civilian styles. From left to right: a senior officer wearing a late 17th-century uniform, including body armor and a decorated coat and carrying the baton that served as an indication of rank; a drummer; a junior officer wearing an armored gorget to protect his throat and carrying a half-pike; and soldiers of the middle of the century, with the cocked hats and tailcoats that were a style universal throughout Europe.

▼ Cavalry uniforms and equipment of the French army of the reign of King Louis XV

From left to right: a trooper of the Royal Regiment of Carabiniers, 1724, showing how the carbine was carried suspended from a shoulder belt; Colonel-General of Carabiniers, 1724; Chevau-léger of the Maison du Roi, the king's household troops, 1745; a dragoon from 1724, the period when these troops were becoming as much cavalry as their original role of infantry who rode into action; a member of the 2nd Company of Musketeers (*Mousquetaires*) of the Maison du Roi, 1745, wearing the distinctive cross-emblazoned tabard of that corps; and an officer of the Gendarmes, literally "armed men," in 1724, the elite cavalry that ranked alongside the Maison du Roi.

● Battle of Culloden

The Battle of Culloden, fought on 16 April 1746 and depicted here in a print published in that year, was the decisive encounter of the Jacobite Rebellion of 1745–46. Here, the army of Prince Charles Edward Stuart, whose father was claimant to the British throne, was defeated by the forces of King George II, led by William Augustus, Duke of Cumberland. The illustration shows a common style of deployment, with infantry arrayed in lines, artillery in the front line and cavalry on the flanks or in reserve.

War in Europe

The early 18th century

The system of tactics and weaponry that had evolved by the beginning of the 18th century formed the foundation for the conduct of operations until the technological developments of the mid-19th century. Troops continued to maneuver in compact formations and fired on command; not until the mid-18th century and later was there much recognition of the merits of units designated for specific tasks. These included light infantry, who were adept at skirmishing; cavalry, divided into heavy units, best suited to shock action on the battlefield; and light troops for reconnaissance, pursuit, and raiding—although dragoons, originally mounted infantry, had existed from the 17th century. Among the most notable of the early specialized corps were the Austro-Hungarian light troops drawn from the borders adjoining the Ottoman Empire, and the Hungarian hussars, the most efficient light cavalry of the time.

See also
Battlefield tactics,
pages 192–3
**War in Europe
1688–1763,** *pages 194–5*
**Tactics and
technology,** *pages
198–9*

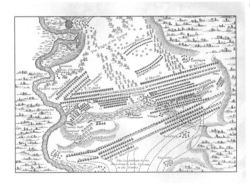

Battle of Blenheim
The Battle of Blenheim was the culmination of an audacious march from the Netherlands to the Danube by Marlborough's army of British, Dutch, and other allied contingents, which united with Eugene of Savoy's Imperial forces. On August 13, 1704 they shattered the Franco-Bavarian forces of the French Marshals Tallard and Marsin and the Elector of Bavaria. This plan illustrates the linear formations employed universally at the time.

Blenheim
The first great conflict of the 18th century was the War of the Spanish Succession, arising from conflicting French and Austrian claims to the Spanish throne. Two of the greatest generals of the time collaborated in leading the Imperial-Anglo-Dutch forces at Blenheim: the English Duke of Marlborough and the Imperial General Eugene of Savoy. This interpretation of the Battle of Blenheim gives a good idea of troops of the period. They are pictured on the approach march before deploying for combat.

Hand weapons
• saber

Missile weapons
• musket
• pistol

Defenses
• fieldworks

Clothing
• cocked hat
• long boots
• long-skirted coat

Warriors
• Austro-Hungarian
  light troops
• dragoons
• Hungarian hussars

Concepts & Tactics
• assaulting the
  enemy's flank
• linear formations

Buildings & Transport

Ramillies

Marlborough's second great victory occurred over the French Marshal Villeroy at Ramillies, between Brussels and Namur, on May 23, 1706. This plan illustrates Marlborough's approach march on the French, who were drawn up defensively upon rising ground, before deploying for battle. Marlborough feinted against the enemy's left, drawing in French reserves, before making his main attack against their weakened right. Marlborough's attack overwhelmed the opposition, exemplifying the efficacy of the tactic of assaulting an enemy's flank.

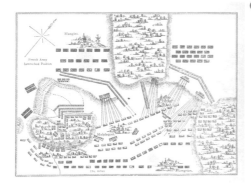

Malplaquet

Marlborough and Eugene again took on the French at Malplaquet on September 11, 1709. The French were protected by field-works so Marlborough first attacked their flanks then launched his main assault through the center. It succeeded, but at heavy cost; the French retired in good order.

John Churchill, 1st Duke of Marlborough, 1650–1722

Marlborough was one of the greatest commanders of the age. Other than a gift for diplomacy he possessed two attributes essential for successful war leaders: military skill and the ability to motivate his subordinates. His nickname, "Corporal John," indicates the affection held for him by his men.

Typical cavalryman, mid-18th century

This British trooper wears the cocked hat, long-skirted coat, and protective long boots common in European armies. He is armed not only with a saber, the principal cavalry weapon, but also a carbine and pistols concealed beneath the decorated housings at the front of the saddle.

War in Europe

Tactics and technology

By the beginning of the 18th century, many armies had developed into relatively small but professional formations of a permanent nature, standing armies that continued in peacetime and provided a nucleus of trained troops that could be augmented by vigorous recruiting when hostilities commenced. To some extent these formations could be almost mercenary in character, sometimes exhibiting little enthusiasm for the dynastic causes for which they fought, although in some countries this was to change toward the later 18th century. While the higher ranks were often occupied by members of the aristocracy and gentry, there was also the emergence of what might be described as a professional officer class, although this was more evident in some armies than others.

French infantry of the late 17th century

The equipment shown here reflects the changes that occurred during this period. The use of pikes was reduced in the last third of the 17th century and abolished in 1703, and the last matchlock muskets were replaced by flintlocks in 1699. One major innovation was the cartridge, a paper tube containing a measured charge of powder and musket ball, that replaced the unwieldy powder-tubes as carried by the figure second from left. A grenadier is shown second from right.

Grenadier of the British 1st Foot Guards

This figure is taken from a drill book of 1735. The grenade was an iron sphere filled with gunpowder. It was officially introduced by the British Army in 1677 and was popular between the later 17th and the mid-18th centuries. This pose is "Blow your match": the grenadier has a smoldering match in his left hand with which to light the grenade's fuse. Here it is held at arm's length to prevent premature ignition.

See also
Warfare in Europe 1688–1763,
pages 194–5

British infantryman of the early 18th century

This infantryman is carrying equipment typical of the period, including a sword and bayonet carried in a frog on the waistbelt and a leather belt over the shoulder supporting a large cartridge box, or pouch, in which the ammunition was carried. The pose shown is part of the musket drill, "Club your firelock," in which the musket could be rested upon the shoulder, butt uppermost.

European uniforms of the early 18th century

Styles common across Europe at the time and shown here include a cavalry kettle-drummer (rear left) and a mounted general (right) with his baton. The elite grenadiers (far right) are distinguished by their tall brimless caps, adopted originally because a brim could impede the arm when throwing a grenade.

British infantry officer

This figure is derived from one of the earliest British drill books, *A Plan of Discipline Composed for the Use of the Militia of the County of Norfolk* of 1759. It shows a typical uniform of the period, and exemplifies the practice adopted by some officers of carrying light muskets with the cartridge box carried at the front of the waist. The sash over the shoulder and the metal gorget at the throat, the last vestige of armor, were indicators of rank.

Member of the British Royal Horse Guards, 1742

Cavalry were often armed with carbines (short-barrelled muskets) and almost always with pistols. The Royal Horse Guards were formed in 1661 and became part of the Household Cavalry in 1820. It was the only regiment of heavy cavalry to wear blue coats, from which they took their sobriquet The Blues.

Hand weapons
- bayonet
- pike
- sword

Missile weapons
- carbine
- cartridge
- flintlock musket
- grenade
- matchlock musket
- pistol

Defenses

Clothing
- blue coats
- brimless cap
- gorget
- sash

Warriors
- cavalry
- grenadier
- infantry

Concepts & Tactics
- permanent professional armies

Buildings & Transport

The American War of Independence, *1775–1783*

The colonies in revolt

The American War of Independence (1775–83) was the conflict that forged the United States in a rebellion against the British colonial administration in North America. It was somewhat unusual in that it involved, on the British side, a regular army operating to some extent in isolation, separated from Britain by the breadth of the Atlantic—albeit with the assistance of locally raised loyalist forces—and, on the "rebel" side, an army that grew from existing militia that, latterly, had significant assistance from France. Although the American forces were mostly organized and equipped on conventional European lines, there was considerable irregular warfare that included troops armed with rifled muskets, who were capable of considerable feats of marksmanship. The British countered by developing effective light-infantry tactics.

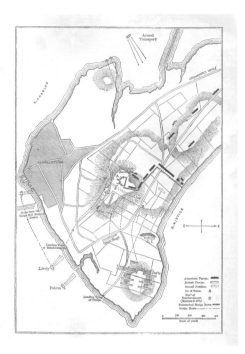

The Battle of Bennington, August 16, 1777
Britain supplemented its forces with German mercenaries. At Bennington, a small detachment composed largely of Brunswickers and provincial troops was defeated by American militia, a noted success against professional soldiers. There was hand-to-hand fighting after the Brunswickers ran out of ammunition, but it ended after their commander was mortally wounded.

Battle of Bunker's Hill
Fought on June 17, 1775, this battle was one of the earliest engagements of the war, when a British force drove a body of rebel militia from their entrenchments near Boston. The attack was mounted in conventional European style, the British arrayed in three lines, led by composite battalions of grenadiers and light infantry detached from their battalions. The British suffered severe losses and were twice checked before their third attack succeeded.

British light infantryman

Light infantry was formed by the British Army in North America during the Seven Years War, and from 1770 each battalion had one light-infantry company. Their uniform and equipment was modified to be suitable for skirmishing, with short jackets and practical headwear. Although rifled muskets were used by the Americans, British regular troops only adopted the rifle during the Napoleonic Wars.

Charles Cornwallis, 1st Marquess Cornwallis

Cornwallis was one of the most prominent British commanders during the American War; his surrender at Yorktown on October 19, 1781 virtually ended the conflict. This image illustrates a characteristic uniform of the period, including the long-skirted coat. Some adjustments were made in America to produce a more practical campaign dress.

British light dragoon

From the mid-18th century, there was an increasing use of light troops trained for skirmishing and reconnaissance. Such tactics were especially useful in the North American terrain, where they were developed by the British. Light troops were added to British cavalry regiments from 1756, and whole regiments of light dragoons were formed from 1759. Their distinctive crested helmets contrasted with the usual tricorn hat. Two such regiments, the 16th and 17th Light Dragoons, served in the American War.

See also
Battlefield tactics,
pages 192–3

Lieutenant-Colonel Banastre Tarleton

A number of 18th-century armies formed specialized units. Among the provincial corps created by the British in America was the British Legion, a unit of light cavalry and infantry, which wore green uniforms rather than the traditional British red. Their commander, Lieutenant-Colonel Tarleton, was a skilled cavalry leader with a reputation for ruthlessness. In this print he wears the fur-crested leather helmet that was to bear his name.

The French Revolutionary Wars, *1792–1802*

The citizen army

The warfare that arose as a direct consequence of the French Revolution of 1789 engulfed the whole of Europe for a quarter of a century and involved considerable changes in both the composition of armies and their tactics. In France the social upheaval virtually destroyed the old royal army, replacing it with a "citizen" army recruited by conscription and often inspired by patriotic motives. This led to some of the principal tactical changes. Initially, there was little time to train the new recruits beyond basic weapons-handling and maneuvers, which led to a simplification of tactics. These included the attack in column, preceded by a horde of skirmishers whose fire both unsettled the enemy and partially concealed from view the advance of the main body, thus increasing the significance of light-infantry tactics. This proved extremely successful against the more formalized maneuvers still employed by the opponents of the French.

French observation balloon

The first manned balloon flight had taken place in November 1783, and the technology was utilized by the French military in the early Revolutionary Wars. Probably the most famous use of a reconnaissance balloon at the time occurred at the Battle of Fleurus on June 26, 1794, where information provided by balloon observers had a significant effect on the outcome. The French formed a balloon corps with four balloons, but the unit was disbanded by Napoleon, ending military aerial observation for some seventy years.

Thionville, October 16, 1792
In the early Revolutionary Wars, the French created an effective combination by uniting the discipline of more experienced units with the fervor of the new battalions. In this illustration of the action at Thionville, Austrian infantry (right) are defeated by the combination of a French charge (left) and the disciplined musketry of a French unit in line.

French cavalry

The French cavalry comprised heavy and light regiments, the latter represented (as illustrated here) by the Chasseurs à Cheval and hussars. Despite the upheaval of the Revolution some regiments retained traces of their previous identity. Shown here is an officer (center) wearing the classic hussar uniform of braided jacket, or dolman, and fur-edged over-jacket, or pelisse, and the cylindrical mirliton cap. One of the troopers is using his short carbine to fire from horseback, a form of skirmishing at which the light regiments excelled. At far right is a dragoon officer, wearing the green coat and brass helmet associated with those troops throughout the period.

French infantry

The French Army suffered greatly in the early Revolutionary period from the emigration or dismissal of many officers, whose aristocratic backgrounds were deemed unacceptable. The infantry was reorganized into "demi-brigades," and the white coat of the French infantry replaced by Republican blue. Seen here is a mounted officer and (fifth from left) a grenadier, each battalion having one company of these elite troops. Second from the right is a drum-major, and at the extreme right a sapeur, or regimental pioneer. The new national *tricolore* flag is shown on the left.

Hand weapons

Missile weapons
• carbine musket

Defenses

Clothing
• dolman
• mirliton cap
• pelisse

Warriors
• cavalry
• Chasseurs à Cheval
• dragoon
• grenadier
• hussars
• light infantry

Concepts & Tactics
• attack in column
• citizen army

Buildings & Transport
• air balloon

See also
Cavalry: tactics and technology, *pages 204–5*
Infantry: column and line, *pages 206–7*
Light infantry, *pages 208–9*

The Napoleonic Wars, *1803–1815*

Cavalry: tactics and technology

Despite the fact that they usually represented only the smaller parts of armies, which numerically were dominated by infantry, cavalry played a vital role in the Napoleonic Wars. Although usually classified as either heavy or light, the distinction was often blurred. The heaviest regiments were the cuirassiers, equipped with armored front- and backplates, although this equipment was not universal—for much of the period Prussian and Russian cuirassiers wore no armor, for example. Designed to execute charges on the battlefield, the heaviest cavalry was not suited to skirmishing, and such duties were performed best by the lighter regiments—Chasseurs à Cheval, hussars, light dragoons, and lancers—which were also most useful for reconnaissance and pursuits. Dragoons, often classed as heavy cavalry, were usually versatile and able to execute all cavalry tactics.

See also
Light infantry,
pages 208–9

The great redoubt at Borodino
At times Napoleon used his cavalry as a primary offensive weapon rather than holding them back to exploit the efforts of infantry and artillery. Examples of this tactic include the huge cavalry charges at Eylau (February 8, 1807) and Waterloo (June 18, 1815). Illustrated here is the attack by French cuirassiers on the Russian "great redoubt" at Borodino on September 7, 1812.

French military uniforms, 1811
Cavalry formed an important element of Napoleon's armies, three categories of which are illustrated here. From left to right: a member of the Carabiniers, two heavy regiments equipped in cuirassier style with combed helmets and armor; a hussar, wearing the classic uniform derived from that of the first Hungarian hussars; a cuirassier; and two infantrymen, including a Grenadier à Pied of the Imperial Guard in his characteristic bearskin cap.

Cavalry sabers
Opinions varied about the most effective design for a cavalry saber. Some held that a thrust with a straight, pointed blade was most lethal; others favored a wider blade for executing a chopping blow. This hand-to-hand combat features a French cuirassier (left) and Captain Edward Kelly of the British 1st Life Guards at Waterloo.

Spanish hussar Regiment Maria Luisa

While heavy cavalry usually carried straight-bladed sabers, light cavalry commonly used curved sabers, as shown here, which were designed primarily for delivering a slash rather than a thrust. The Spanish hussar regiment Maria Luisa wore a typical hussar uniform, including braided dolman and laced breeches.

Chasseurs à Cheval of the French Imperial Guard

Among the most prominent light-cavalry regiments was the Chasseurs à Cheval of Napoleon's Imperial Guard, depicted here in hussar-style full dress (right) and undress coat (left), which was also used on campaign. The regiment provided Napoleon's personal escort, and he usually wore its uniform.

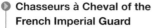

Battle of Albuera

A traditional Polish weapon, the lance had largely fallen from use but was adopted by a number of armies during the Napoleonic Wars, notably by Polish troops in the French Army. It could be devastating against infantry. During the Peninsular War, at the Battle of Albuera in May 1811, French lancers annihilated a British brigade before it could form the protective square formation.

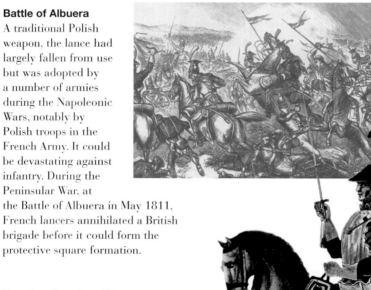

French cuirassier officer

In 1802–3 Napoleon converted existing heavy cavalry into twelve, later fifteen, regiments of cuirassiers. They had iron breast-and-back plates and helmets—as worn by the officer here—which defended against sword cuts and, at longer ranges, musketry. However, it could be hard to procure sufficient horses strong enough to carry the weight of an armored trooper.

The Napoleonic Wars

Infantry: column and line

Although infantry drill and maneuvers continued to be extremely complex, two principal formations were utilized on the battlefield: column and line. Columns were used for maneuver, as the best formation for maintaining good order and the cohesion necessary to operate effectively. In column, however, only the first two or three ranks could use their muskets, whereas troops arrayed in a two- or three-deep line could bring every musket to bear. Consequently, having advanced in column, units would attempt to deploy into line before contact with the enemy, although in some cases the French might attempt to batter through the enemy without deploying. This tactic notably failed against the disciplined musketry of the British in the Peninsular War, whose lines could concentrate a much greater weight of fire.

French Gendarme d'Elite and sapeur of the Grenadiers à Pied of the Imperial Guard
All armies had engineers to perform the more skilled tasks of construction and fortification. Infantry battalions usually included a small section of pioneers, styled *sapeurs* by the French. The *sapeur* (right) of the Grenadiers à Pied of Napoleon's Imperial Guard carries an ax and wears the beard, apron, and crossed-axes sleeve-badge that distinguished them. The mounted man is a member of the Gendarmerie d'Elite of the Guard, an escort and provost unit.

Austrian infantry
The Austro-Hungarian Empire opposed Napoleon, notably in the campaigns of 1805, 1809, and 1813–14. This illustration dates from somewhat later, but the uniform of the grenadiers (center), with their white coats and peaked fur caps, had not changed much. Austrian regiments wore white breeches and Hungarian regiments light-blue pantaloons.

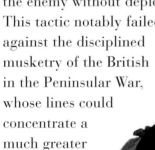

See also
Light infantry,
pages 208–9

British troops, 1812, in uniforms worn during the Peninsular War
From left to right: a private of the 4th (King's Own) Regiment, wearing the 1800 shako known as the "stovepipe" and the classic British red coat; a trooper of the 1st (Royal) Dragoons in typical heavy-cavalry uniform; a sergeant wearing the Highland version of the infantry uniform, with feathered bonnet and kilt and armed with the broadsword carried by sergeants.

Grenadier à Pied, French Imperial Guard
Arguably the most famous military unit of the era, Napoleon's Imperial Guard grew to become the most elite element of the French Army. Its senior infantry units were the Grenadiers and Chasseurs à Pied, whose bearskin caps became an iconic symbol. The Grenadier à Pied illustrated wears typical campaign dress, in which practicality took precedence over adornment.

Fusilier-Grenadier of the Imperial Guard
From 1806 Napoleon augmented the original, or Old Guard, units of his Imperial Guard with the Middle and Young Guards. The Fusiliers were associated with the Grenadiers and Chasseurs à Pied, and this Fusilier-Grenadier wears a version of the classic French infantry uniform and equipment.

French Imperial Guard Dragoon
Formed in 1806, the Dragoons of Napoleon's Imperial Guard wore a version of the characteristic dragoon uniform, including a green coat and brass helmet. Although cavalry, French dragoons retained the traditional ability to fight on foot and were armed with the dragoon musket, a weapon much more effective than the short carbines carried by other cavalry.

Hand weapons
- ax
- broadsword

Missile weapons
- carbine
- dragoon musket
- musket

Defenses

Clothing
- apron
- bearskin cap
- brass helmet
- kilt
- pantaloons
- stovepipe

Warriors
- 1st Royal Dragoons
- 4th (King's Own) Regiment
- Gendarmerie d'Elite
- Grenadiers à Pied
- *sapeurs*

Concepts & Tactics
- column and line maneuvers

Buildings & Transport

The Napoleonic Wars

Light infantry

While most maneuvers were conducted in fairly close-order formation, light infantry played an increasingly important role, reaching a height of efficiency in armies such as those of France and Britain. Many armies formed entire regiments of light infantry, and each ordinary infantry unit usually contained an element of light troops trained in skirmishing and fighting in open order rather than in dense formation. They scattered to take advantage of natural cover and fired aimed shots rather than by volley. Light troops preceded an advance, harassing the enemy before the main body came into action, and covered withdrawals. Most light troops used conventional smoothbored muskets, but more accurate rifled muskets were carried by a number of units—for example, the British 95th Rifles and the rifle battalions of the 60th (Royal American) Regiment and by various Austrian and Prussian Jäger corps.

Typical French infantry advance in column
This exemplifies the nature of a combat column. For example, a French column of divisions, according to the establishment of six companies per battalion used from 1808, comprised two companies side-by-side in three waves, so that if each company numbered 120 men in three ranks, a column would have a frontage of eighty men and a depth of nine.

Battle of Maida
The effect of the bayonet was largely psychological, and it was rare for bayonet fights to occur in the open field. Bayonet charges were usually used only against troops already weakened, and such troops would almost always give way before bayonets were crossed. Here, French troops are about to break before a British charge at the Battle of Maida in Calabria, July 4, 1806.

Bergen-op-Zoom
This illustration of the British attack on Bergen-op-Zoom in March 1814 portrays an example of a regiment's colors: flags served not only as a symbol of regimental pride and identity but also as a rallying point amid the smoke and confusion of battle. The capture of an enemy color was the greatest triumph and its loss the greatest blow to pride and morale.

Battle of Waterloo

The final great battle of the Napoleonic Wars, Waterloo, on June 18, 1815, was Napoleon's decisive defeat by Wellington's Anglo-Netherlands-German army and Field Marshal Gebhardt von Blücher's Prussians. This plan shows the linear deployment of armies, the use of fortified strongpoints —as used to secure points on Wellington's front (top)—and, along Napoleon's front line (bottom), how artillery could be concentrated to facilitate the bombardment of particular points on the enemy line.

French Consular Guard at Marengo, June 1800

The formation that protected infantry from cavalry attack was the square, a rectangular formation several ranks deep. Here, the French Consular Guard are in square formation, with an impenetrable hedge of bayonets on every side. As cavalry approached, the outer ranks could kneel, their bayonets presented at horse's breast height.

French grenadiers in action

In addition to firing by volley, firing at will—file firing—could be employed. This scene of French grenadiers shows various stages of the firing drill, including a man in the foreground biting off the end of his cartridge, and also the practice of men in the rear ranks passing loaded muskets to the firers in the front ranks.

French lancers at Waterloo

Cavalry had a greater chance of success against steady infantry if their actions were coordinated with other arms. The French charges against Wellington's line at Waterloo, like that by lancers of Napoleon's Imperial Guard illustrated, were thrown in with almost no support and foundered against the defense of the Anglo-Allied infantry and artillery.

Hand weapons
• bayonet

Missile weapons
• rifled musket
• smoothbored musket

Defenses
• fortified strongpoints

Clothing

Warriors
• 60th (Royal American) Regiment
• 95th Rifles
• Consular Guard
• grenadiers
• lancers

Concepts & Tactics
• aimed shots
• firing at will
• open-order fighting
• square formation

Buildings & Transport

See also
The flintlock,
pages 186–7

Infantry: column and line, *pages 206–7*

The evolution of firearms, *pages 216–17*

The Napoleonic Wars

The evolution of artillery

Artillery pieces were generally identified by the weight of the projectile they fired: for field service these included 3- and 4-pounders (light support weapons), 6- and 9-pounders (medium field artillery), and 12-pounders (the heaviest, most effective fieldguns). The larger 18- and 24-pounders were generally restricted to siege or garrison duties. Artillery units were generally organized in companies or batteries of six or eight guns, usually of the same calibre but also including one or two howitzers. During this period artillery theory shifted from piecemeal deployment along a line of battle to the assembly of larger concentrations of guns, so-called massed-battery fire being regarded as more effective than the sum of its parts. In concentrating a heavy bombardment upon a specific section of the enemy positions, the function of artillery shifted from a supporting to a more offensive role.

Napoleon at Montereau, February 18, 1814
Napoleon trained as a gunner and retained his faith in the power of artillery. Here, at Montereau, he uses his old skills to aim a shot. This gun team of the Imperial Guard shows the various duties of the crew: the gunner on Napoleon's right holds a portfire, or match-holder; the gunner far right holds the rammer, used to insert the propellant and projectile into the gun and to swab out the barrel with water.

Artillery team
Artillery consisted of foot companies, in which the gunners mostly marched alongside the guns, and horse artillery, with the gunners mounted and thus sufficiently mobile to support the cavalry. This shows a typical heavy field gun with limber, horse team, and gunners on foot, wearing the distinctive leather helmets used by Bavaria and some other German states.

A field gun
As shown by this print published in 1802, artillery could be manhandled on the battlefield, pulled by gunners hauling on leather straps or ropes known as bricoles.

Hand weapons

Missile weapons
• cannon
• howitzer

Defenses

Clothing
• leather helmet

Warriors
• gunners
• Imperial Guard

Concepts & Tactics
• heavy bombardment

Buildings & Transport
• ammunition wagon
• wooden carriage

Howitzer

Howitzers were short-barreled guns that fired projectiles with a high trajectory, and thus were the only ordnance capable of effective indirect fire—that is, over the heads of obstacles or friendly troops. They were usually classified not by weight of projectile but by diameter of bore—5½-inch (14 centimeter), for example. Visible at the rear of the barrel is the screw-elevator, used for all artillery to adjust the angle of fire.

See also
Fortification and siege warfare, *pages 212–13*
Anatomy of a cannon, *pages 224–5*
Artillery, *pages 296–7*

Mortar

Mortars were similar to howitzers in comprising a short barrel, as shown, fixed upon a static carriage or "bed"; they were used almost exclusively for firing explosive shells upon fortifications, using a very high trajectory.

Ammunition wagon

Each gun was accompanied in the field by one or more wagons carrying ammunition, generally four-wheeled carts with a hinged top.

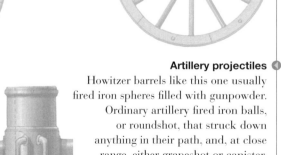

Cannon barrel

A cannon barrel of typical construction, the barrel widening toward the muzzle, with a rounded knob, or cascabel, at the sealed end near the touch-hole, projecting lugs, or trunnions, at the sides—which supported the gun upon its carriage—and dolphins, or lifting handles, on top of the barrel.

Artillery projectiles

Howitzer barrels like this one usually fired iron spheres filled with gunpowder. Ordinary artillery fired iron balls, or roundshot, that struck down anything in their path, and, at close range, either grapeshot or canister, packages of smaller balls that ruptured on firing, turning the cannon into a giant shotgun. Unique to the British was spherical caseshot, or shrapnel, shells filled with musket balls that exploded in the air, showering the balls on the enemy.

The Napoleonic Wars

Fortification and siege warfare

Partly as a consequence of Napoleon's preferred system of warfare, which sought the destruction of the enemy's field army in preference to the mere occupation of territory, the significance of fortifications was less marked in the Napoleonic Wars than during the 18th century. Strategically placed fortresses still retained great importance, however, and featured prominently in a number of campaigns. For example, much of Napoleon's Italian campaign of 1796–97 concerned Austrian attempts to raise the siege of Mantua; the Lines of Torres Vedras during the Peninsular War proved an insurmountable barrier to French attempts to attack Wellington's base; and, in the same war, possession of the fortresses of Ciudad Rodrigo and Badajoz led to some of the bitterest actions of the period.

▶ Siege of Badajoz

The border fortress of Badajoz was the subject of two sieges by Wellington's Anglo-Portuguese forces during the Peninsular War, eventually falling to an assault on the night of April 6–7, 1812, in one of the bloodiest engagements of the war. This plan illustrates how, in the standard manner of siegecraft, lines of siege trenches and artillery emplacements were pushed increasingly close to the fortress until a breach was battered in the wall, through which the attackers would try to penetrate.

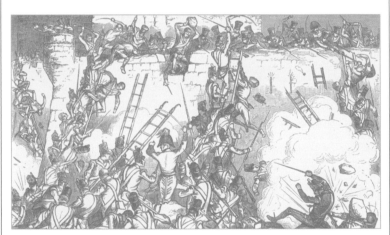

▶ Torres Vedras

The Lines of Torres Vedras were mutually supportive forts constructed under Wellington's direction to defend the Anglo-Portuguese base of Lisbon; they took advantage of the nature of the terrain and proved to be unassailable by the French. This plan of the main fortification shows how three strongpoints were connected by entrenchments. This position had twenty-four cannon and could accommodate 1,720 troops.

Storm of Badajoz ▲

When Badajoz was stormed in April 1812, the main assault was mounted against the breaches between the Santa Maria and Trinidad bastions, but these were so well defended that no penetration could be made. Instead, a diversionary attack succeeded, made by escalade, or scaling-ladder, against the castle walls, shown here. Ladders were used to descend into the fortress ditch and to mount the walls.

Hand weapons

Missile weapons
• mortar

Defenses
• bastions
• enceinte
• trenches

Clothing

Warriors

Concepts & Tactics
• escalade
• siegecraft
• strategically placed fortresses

Buildings & Transport
• Lines of Torres Vedras

Storm of a fortification

Fortifications varied in construction from ancient walled enclosures with a continuous enceinte, or outer wall, to more modern, bastioned fortifications of considerable complexity that involved geometrical plans and features such as artillery emplacements and protected magazines. Similar temporary fortifications were constructed to shield the besiegers, with trenches to allow troops to approach the defenses under cover and gun emplacements of sandbags and gabions, wickerwork baskets filled with earth. This illustration shows a breaching battery, with troops storming the gap battered in the walls, while a second wave of infantry shelters behind the artillery emplacement.

Artillery

For fortress and siege warfare the artillery was often considerably different from that used in the field, the guns being larger to fire the heavier shot required. Guns used in fortresses often had distinctive carriages, as illustrated below, and among the ordnance used were mortars such as that illustrated (right), with its bed and barrel transported upon a wagon. The ammunition expended in a siege could be enormous: in Wellington's siege of Badajoz more than 35,000 projectiles were used, in all about 970,000 pounds (440,000 kilograms) of munitions.

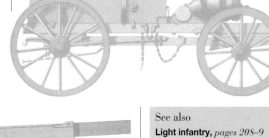

See also
Light infantry, *pages 208–9*
Mortar, *page 211*

Storm of Ciudad Rodrigo

The storm of a defended breach, as at Badajoz or, as here, at Ciudad Rodrigo on January 19, 1812, was one of the most hazardous undertakings in all warfare, as the defenders hurled missiles and shot against the attackers as they endeavored to clamber over the rubble of the collapsed wall. John Kincaid, who survived the slaughter to write about the unavailing attack on the breaches of Badajoz, was accurate in his description of the action as being "as respectable a representation of hell itself as fire, and sword, and human sacrifices could make it."

The Harbinger of the Modern Battlefield 1841–1865

A major revolution in the development of weaponry and tactics took place between 1841 and 1865. The introduction of the rifle-musket in the USA in 1841 initiated the development of a series of small arms that led to the production of the Springfield Rifle Musket in 1861. The range and accuracy of this new weapon type had a devastating effect on troops deployed in the close-order formations required by outdated tactics from the Napoleonic era.

The Crimean War (1853–56) between Russia and the Alliance of Britain, France, Sardinia, Italy, and Turkey, was the beginning of the end of this style of battle, being largely conducted in the same manner and with almost the same uniforms, weapons, and equipment as at Waterloo forty years earlier. However, advancements in science and technology were beginning to alter the face of warfare. The Crimean War saw the first tactical use of the electric telegraph, railroads, chloroform, and blind artillery fire. The introduction of the Minié ball and the rifling of barrels greatly increased range and accuracy for the Allied infantryman. As a result of both deadly weaponry and disease, the Crimean War caused over a million casualties compared with approximately 625,000 in the American Civil War, which began five years later.

The War Between the States (1861–65) was the key turning point in the history of 19th-century warfare. Although the opening stages saw scenes reminiscent of the Napoleonic era, developments in weapons technology and the use of field fortifications rapidly transformed the conflict into the first modern war. The deadly impact of the rifle-musket, the introduction of breech-loading weapons and widespread use of rifled cannon reduced the role of cavalry to raiding and reconnaissance, and commanders deployed their armies behind breastworks whenever possible. The miles of trenches and bomb shelters constructed during the sieges of Vicksburg and Petersburg foresaw the horrors of the First World War. The American Civil War allowed strategy and tactics to catch up with and surpass technology, paving the way for the warfare of the 20th century.

The Evolution of Firearms

The rifle-musket

Military establishments realized the benefits of weapons advancements in the 1840s and 1850s. In 1823, Englishman Captain John Norton had developed a muzzle-loaded projectile that expanded when fired, so engaging the rifling in the barrel, and English gunsmith William Greener invented a similar bullet in 1836. These were at first ignored by the British Army, who considered the manufacture too complicated. A .54-caliber "rifle-musket" with a percussion system and a round ball was produced in the USA in 1841. By 1847 experiments in France by Colonel Louis-Etienne de Thouvenin and Captain Claude-Etienne Minié established the shape of the bullet. The British had developed their pattern of 1853 rifle-musket, and in 1855 the USA developed a .58-caliber rifled musket and shorter "rifle" designed to use the Minié ball.

The Enfield in Crimea

The British Army was in the midst of changing from smoothbore muskets to rifled muskets on the eve of the Crimean War in 1853. By the end of that year the Enfield rifled musket was approved by the War Department and issued in increasing numbers throughout the conflict. This contemporary engraving depicts British infantrymen commanded by Major-General Ashe Windham defending a redan in 1855.

BALL FOR ALTERED MUSKET.

Weight of ball, 730 grains; weight of powder, 70 grains.

BALLS FOR NEW RIFLE-MUSKET AND PISTOL-CARBINE.
No. 1.   No. 2.

Weight of No. 1, 500 grains. Weight of No. 2, 450 grains.
Weight of powder, 60 grains. Weight of powder, 40 grains.
No. 1, section of musket ball.
No. 2, section of pistol-carbine ball.
Both balls have the same exterior.

The Minié ball

French Army Captain Claude-Etienne Minié is credited with developing the cylindro-conoidal musket projectile called the Minié ball. This had a hollow base and three ring bands that expanded into the rifling inside the musket barrel upon firing. These diagrams from an 1856 publication entitled *Reports of Experiments with Small Arms* show three types of ball based on this pattern.

Claude-Etienne Minié

Claude Etienne Minié was born in 1804 and served with the French Army in North Africa. As a reward for his contribution to the arms industry, the French government awarded him 20,000 francs and installed him as a member of the staff at the Vincennes military school. Retiring with the rank of colonel in 1858, he later served as a military instructor for the Khedive of Egypt and as manager at the Remington Arms Company in the USA.

British Legion

The Legion raised in Britain in 1860 to join Giuseppe Garibaldi in the fight for Italian independence from Austrian rule was armed with the "long Enfield [rifle-musket] of the government pattern of 1853." Based on a sketch by Thomas Nast, this detail from an *Illustrated London News* engraving depicts them marching in triumph along the Via Toledo in Naples during October of that year.

Springfield Rifled Musket

Harper's Ferry Rifled Musket

Austrian Rifle

Belgian Rifle

Enfield Rifle

Jaeger Rifle

Rifled weapons of the American Civil War

This detail from a plate in the *Official Military Atlas of the Civil War* shows some of the rifled weapons that had the greatest impact during the American Civil War. A total of 265,129 Springfield rifle-muskets were produced between 1861 and 1863. The shorter Model 1855 rifle is incorrectly labelled a "rifled musket." The other weapons shown were imported from European manufacturers, those used by the Confederacy being run through the Union naval blockade.

Range and accuracy

Most infantrymen on both sides in the American Civil War carried .58- or .577-caliber rifle-muskets. The rifling—spiral grooves etched inside the barrel—greatly increased the accuracy of these weapons by spinning and stabilizing the bullet as it sped toward its target. A trained marksman could hit his mark as far as 600 yards (550 meters) away, and even an average shot could expect to strike the target at 250 yards (230 meters).

See also
Anatomy of a Model 1863 Springfield rifle-musket, *pages 218–19*
The American Civil War, *pages 226–47*

Anatomy of a Model 1863 Springfield Rifle-Musket

On May 18, 1860 the US Ordnance Board adopted the new, improved .58-caliber rifle-musket. The Model 1861 Springfield rifle-musket was manufactured from 1861 to 1863. Two slightly modified models were introduced in 1863 and 1864. The Springfield increased the effectiveness of infantrymen fivefold during the American Civil War. Not only was the effective range 500 yards (460 meters) but the rate of fire was slightly greater because of the development of paper cartridges, the percussion cap, and the ease of loading the Minié ball, which was slightly under bore size.

1

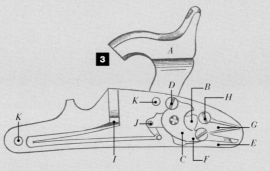

2

3

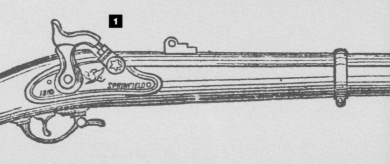

2 The lock-plate of the Model 1863 Springfield was secured from the other side of the black walnut stock by three screws; it accommodated the percussion hammer that pivoted on the tumbler-screw. The mark "US SPRINGFIELD," year of model, and eagle logo was always included on the lock-plate.

3 This interior view behind the lock-plate shows the working parts at half cock. The various parts labeled are the hammer (A), tumbler (B), bridle (C), bridle-screw (D), sear (E), sear-screw (F), sear-spring (G), sear-spring screw (H), mainspring (I), swivel (J), and side-screws (K).

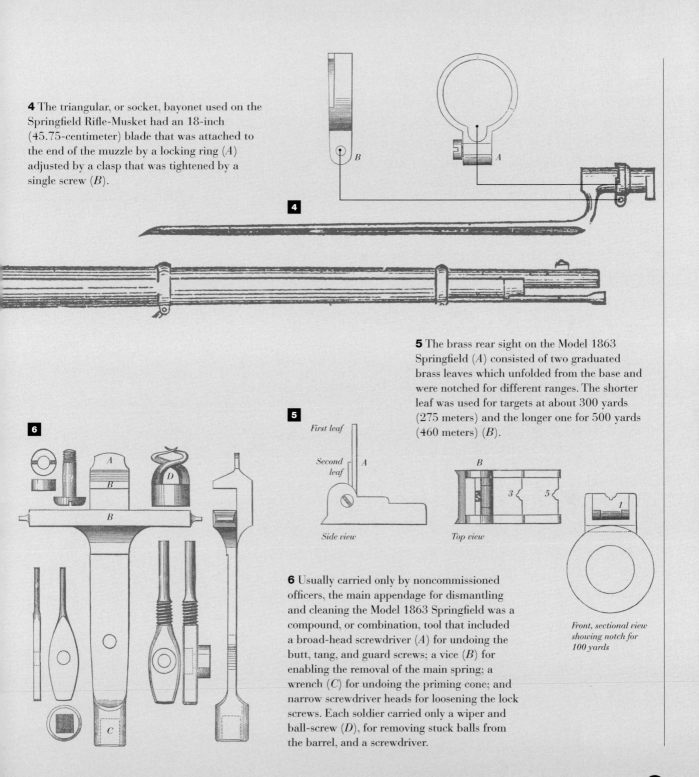

4 The triangular, or socket, bayonet used on the Springfield Rifle-Musket had an 18-inch (45.75-centimeter) blade that was attached to the end of the muzzle by a locking ring (*A*) adjusted by a clasp that was tightened by a single screw (*B*).

5 The brass rear sight on the Model 1863 Springfield (*A*) consisted of two graduated brass leaves which unfolded from the base and were notched for different ranges. The shorter leaf was used for targets at about 300 yards (275 meters) and the longer one for 500 yards (460 meters) (*B*).

First leaf

Second leaf

Side view

Top view

Front, sectional view showing notch for 100 yards

6 Usually carried only by noncommissioned officers, the main appendage for dismantling and cleaning the Model 1863 Springfield was a compound, or combination, tool that included a broad-head screwdriver (*A*) for undoing the butt, tang, and guard screws; a vice (*B*) for enabling the removal of the main spring; a wrench (*C*) for undoing the priming cone; and narrow screwdriver heads for loosening the lock screws. Each soldier carried only a wiper and ball-screw (*D*), for removing stuck balls from the barrel, and a screwdriver.

The Crimean War, *1853–1856*

Tactics

The Crimean War was especially noted for the hardship endured by the soldiers of all armies in the inhospitable Russian climate and terrain. The armies of Britain, France, and Turkey were racked with cholera and dysentery. Storms, heat, and freezing winters also took their toll. The breakdown in supply systems meant soldiers often went without food, clothing, ammunition, and medical help. At the same time, cavalry, infantry, and artillery tactics did not keep up with the technological innovations of the first half of the 19th century. Cavalry continued to be used in the grand style of the Napoleonic Wars, as evidenced by the disastrous Charge of the Light Brigade. Infantry armed with the new rifle-musket continued to advance in close-order formation. Artillery went into action in neat rows with limbers and caissons to the rear, making them easy targets for Russian guns.

Cossacks

This Donskoi, or Cossack, wears what one eyewitness called a "handsome and becoming" uniform consisting of "a scarlet tunic, with belt studded with cartridge cases, loose trousers reaching to the knee, and a broad flat cap of white or black sheepskin." He is armed with a plain lance, a sword without guard, and "brace of pistols" tucked into his belt.

Into the Valley of Death

Both sides used cavalry extensively during the Crimean War. The ill-fated Charge of the Light Brigade, led by Lord Cardigan during the Battle of Balaclava on October 25, 1854, resulted in 118 men killed, 127 wounded, and 335 horses killed in action or destroyed afterward because of their wounds.

See also
Cavalry: tactics and technology,
pages 204–5
Light infantry,
pages 208–9

Highlanders
Brightly colored uniforms made easy targets during the Crimean conflict. Wearing their bearskin bonnets, scarlet doublets, and kilts of black and green tartan, the Black Watch, or 42nd Highlanders, part of the Highland Brigade under General Sir Colin Campbell, are depicted capturing the slopes of the hills overlooking the River Alma on September 20, 1854.

Naval forces
After the fall of Sebastopol in September 1855, British troops and Royal Navy seamen inspect the Russian redoubts composed of gabions, wicker baskets filled with earth and rubble. The Russians had to scuttle their ships, and used the naval cannon as additional artillery and the ships' crews as marines during this action.

Zouaves
Originally formed in 1831 by the French Army in North Africa, the Zouaves served with distinction in the Crimea during the battles of Alma, Inkermann, Balaclava, and the final siege of Sebastopol. Regarded as the finest light infantry in the world, they wore a colorful Arabic-style uniform consisting of a red stocking cap, or *calotte*, short blue jacket, and baggy red pantaloons, or *serouel*.

Hand weapons
• lance
• sword

Missile weapons
• cannon
• pistol
• rifle-musket

Defenses
• gabions

Clothing
• Arab-style uniform
• Black Watch uniform
• Cossack uniform

Warriors
• Cossacks
• Highland Brigade
• Zouaves

Concepts & Tactics
• outdated cavalry, infantry, and artillery tactics

Buildings & Transport

The Crimean War

Technology

The Crimean War saw the first large-scale tactical use of trench warfare; blind, or indirect, artillery fire; telegraph; and the railroad. Blind fire was introduced so that artillery could fire from behind cover. Balloons had first been used for reconnaissance by the French Revolutionary armies in 1794, but their use in locating concealed batteries came to the fore in the Crimea. A submarine electrical telegraph cable was laid between Varna and Balaclava, and a land cable linked, for the first time in history, a commander in the field with the War Office in London. Newspaper reporters used this new technology to communicate the fortunes of the Allies in the Crimea. In January 1855 a railroad was constructed by civilian contractors under Royal Engineers supervision to carry stores from Balaclava to the front.

Mining and countermining

Both Allied and Russian armies engaged in mining and countermining operations during the prolonged eleven-month siege of Sebastopol. The Engineer Corps of the British Army deployed numerous companies of sappers and miners who were skilled at digging tunnels and destroying enemy positions by igniting explosive charges under their defenses.

Embuscades

In response to the development of the more accurate rifle-musket, both Allies and Russians used pits known as embuscades during the siege of Sebastopol of 1854–55. These were usually composed of a pit burrowed into the ground with a few stones heaped up before it, and a loophole through which the occupant could fire without exposing himself to enemy fire in return.

Sappers and miners

British troops in the siege works before Sebastopol dig and repair trenches protected by gabions, while sharpshooters in the rear man the earthen platform known as a banquette tread. As the Pioneer Corps was not established in the British Army until the First World War, sappers and miners, supplemented by nonspecialized troops, were usually assigned to this type of duty.

Nursing

Known as the "Lady With the Lamp," Florence Nightingale, and her staff of thirty-eight women volunteer nurses pioneered battlefield medicine during the Crimean War at her hospital at Scutari. There, chloroform was used for the first time as an anesthetic in the treatment of casualties of war. In the aftermath of the conflict, the importance of public health and hygiene was better understood and the status of nursing as a vocation for women was elevated.

See also
French observation balloon, *page 202*
Sending telegraphic messages, *page 239*

Cacolets

As their ambulance wagons were too cumbersome for the rough terrain of the Crimea, the British Army was grateful to the French for the use of their *cacolets*, which consisted of a type of litter sling hung on each side of a strong mule. With these, wounded troops could be transported from field dressing stations to the hospital in Scutari with relative ease.

News correspondents

Sent by the London *Times* newspaper to cover the Crimean War, William H. Russell wrote—uncensored at this time—about the privations suffered by the soldiers and praised the devotion and courage of Mary Seacole, the black Jamaican nurse who had been rejected by Nightingale and had established a hospital at her own expense. Such news was conveyed back to Britain via the new electrical telegraph.

Anatomy of a Cannon

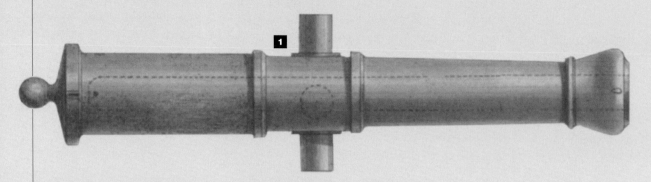

1 Part of a cannon used extensively by the USA during the Mexican–American War of 1846–48, this 6-pounder gun tube shows the last vestiges of decoration that had prevailed until the beginning of the 19th century, including the curved muzzle, fillet, and roundel at the throat, wider breech band, and cascable fillet.

2 By the early 19th century artillerists in most Western countries had settled on a standard method of categorizing cannon that was based on the weight of the solid shot it fired. All shot at this time was spherical and typically made of iron, and its weight corresponded with the bore size of the piece. So, a cannon with a $3^2/_3$-inch (9.32-centimeter) bore used shot weighing 6 pounds and was thus called a 6-pounder. This size of gun was chiefly used by horse artillery.

3 Suspended underneath the cannon was the sponge bucket. Made of sheet iron, it had a wooden lid and a toggle fastened to the top of the handle by two links and a swivel, which was used to attach it to an eye under the axle on the gun carriage. This bucket held water in which a sponge was dipped when washing out the cannon barrel after firing.

4 The gun was attached to the wooden field carriage by trunnions, which were an integral part of the tube. These enabled the gun tube to be elevated to adjust the range and trajectory of the shot fired. A typical Model 1841 6-pounder had a range of about 1,520 yards (1,390 meters).

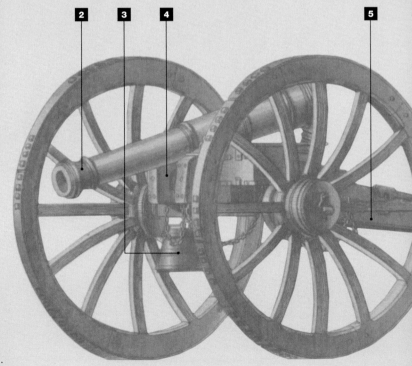

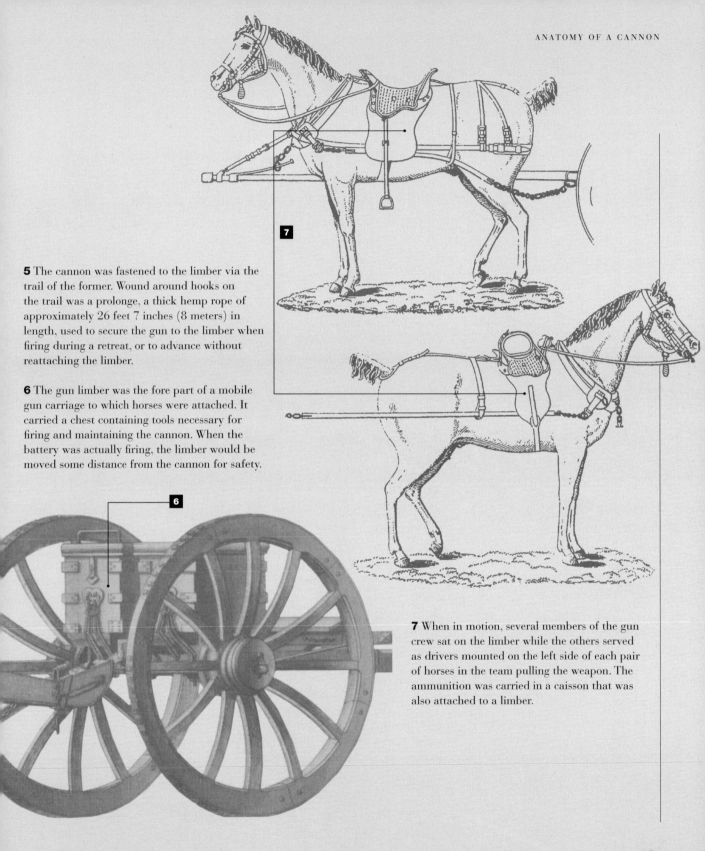

5 The cannon was fastened to the limber via the trail of the former. Wound around hooks on the trail was a prolonge, a thick hemp rope of approximately 26 feet 7 inches (8 meters) in length, used to secure the gun to the limber when firing during a retreat, or to advance without reattaching the limber.

6 The gun limber was the fore part of a mobile gun carriage to which horses were attached. It carried a chest containing tools necessary for firing and maintaining the cannon. When the battery was actually firing, the limber would be moved some distance from the cannon for safety.

7 When in motion, several members of the gun crew sat on the limber while the others served as drivers mounted on the left side of each pair of horses in the team pulling the weapon. The ammunition was carried in a caisson that was also attached to a limber.

The American Civil War, *1861–1865*

Infantry tactics

Devised by Lieutenant Colonel William J. Hardee, who served in the US Army from 1838 to 1861, *Hardee's Rifle and Light Infantry Tactics* was adopted for use by the Army and Militia of the United States on March 29, 1855. Designed to make full use of the advantages of the improved rifle and rifle-musket of the day, it was mainly based on *L'Exercise et Maneuvres des Bataillons de Chasseurs à Pied*, a French military manual translated by Lieutenant Stephen V. Benet of the US Ordnance Department. It became the best-known drill manual at the beginning of the American Civil War, but it was superseded by the *Infantry Tactics* of General Silas Casey, published in 1862. As a native of Georgia, Hardee supported the South during that conflict and produced a slightly amended version of his manual for the Confederacy during the same year.

HARDEE'S
RIFLE AND LIGHT INFANTRY
TACTICS,
FOR THE INSTRUCTION, EXERCISES AND MANŒUVRES OF
RIFLEMEN AND LIGHT INFANTRY.
INCLUDING
SCHOOL OF THE SOLDIER AND SCHOOL OF THE COMPANY.
BY BREVET LIEUT. W. J. HARDEE.
To which is added,
DUTIES OF NON-COMMISSIONED OFFICERS.
MILITARY HONORS TO BE PAID BY TROOPS.
THE ARTICLES OF WAR,
Containing Rules by which the Armies of the United States are governed;
Relating to Courts-Martial; Suppressing Mutiny or Sedition;
Granting Furloughs, Commissary of Musters; Accepting a
Challenge; Chaplains; Sutlers; To whom any Officer
may apply for Redress; Sentinels; False
Alarms; Misbehaviour; Making Known
the Watchword; Engineers; Spies;
How Courts-Martial must be
Authenticated, Etc.;
———
NEW YORK.
J. O. KANE, PUBLISHER, 126 NASSAU STREET,
1862.

Drill manual

The title page of *Hardee's Rifle and Light Infantry Tactics*, published by J.O. Kane of New York in 1862.

Shoulder arms

Lesson one concerned the "Principles of Shouldered Arms," in which the soldier held the rifle-musket at his right side with his arm nearly at full length and with the trigger guard to the front. Before passing to the second lesson, the positions "eyes right, left, and front, and the facings" were learned.

Support arms

Lesson two contained the multipart "Manual of Arms," the first of which was "Support—Arms," in which the soldier transferred the rifle-musket to his left shoulder and supported the cock, or hammer, against his left forearm with his left hand resting on his chest. He could then bring his weapon to "Shoulder—Arms" from this position.

Present arms

This involved bringing the rifle-musket from the right shoulder to an erect position before the center of the body with the rammer to the front, and the left hand grasping the weapon halfway between the sight and lower band, while the right hand held the small of the stock against the trigger guard.

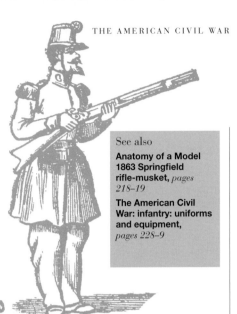

Prime

At the command "Prime" the soldier brought the rifle-musket to waist height with his left hand, with the butt below the right forearm and the muzzle at eye level. The hammer was half cocked with the thumb of the right hand, and a copper percussion cap was taken from the pouch and pressed on to the nipple on top of the lock of the gun.

See also

Anatomy of a Model 1863 Springfield rifle-musket, *pages 218–19*

The American Civil War: infantry: uniforms and equipment, *pages 228–9*

Order arms

At the command "Order—Arms" the rifle-musket was brought to rest on the ground by the right foot with the muzzle about two inches from the shoulder, the rammer in front and the "beak" of the butt "against, and in line with the toe of the right foot, the barrel perpendicular." At "Rest" the soldier was not required to "preserve silence or steadiness."

Fire

On the command "Fire" the soldier squeezed the trigger with his forefinger and the rifle-musket discharged its Minié ball. The soldier remained in the firing position "without lowering or turning the head," and remained in this position until ordered otherwise.

Load

The rifle-musket was loaded through a series of commands. At "Load" the butt was placed between the feet and the rifle-musket was grasped with the left hand while the right hand drew the cartridge box to the front to obtain a cartridge. The remaining commands consisted of "Handle—Cartridge"; "Tear—Cartridge", by biting through the cartridge paper; "Charge—Cartridge", which involved pouring the black powder into the barrel followed by the ball; "Draw—Rammer"; "Ram—Cartridge"; and "Return—Rammer."

Ready—aim

Given the commands "Ready" and "Aim" the right foot was drawn to the rear, the rifle-musket was raised to eye level, the soldier took aim using the sight on the barrel, and the hammer was pulled back to cock the weapon fully with a finger on the trigger.

The American Civil War

Infantry: uniforms and equipment

Both Union and Confederate armies wore a profusion of brightly colored uniforms during the first few months of the American Civil War, and it was not until 1862 that it may truly have been regarded as a conflict between "the Blue and the Gray." While the small US Army had worn dark blue since 1851, gray uniforms had been adopted for the militia of many northern and southern states. Furthermore, many state militia regiments permitted variations in uniforms within the companies of regiments. The uniform chosen in June 1861 for the small Regular Army of the Confederate States included a "cadet gray" frockcoat with facings of branch color on the collar and cuffs. The most colorful units were those that adopted the zouave-style uniform, based on that worn by the Zouaves of the French Army.

Union infantryman

From a plate published in the *Official Atlas of the Civil War*, this figure is uniformed and equipped as most Union infantrymen would have been from 1862 onward. He wears a dark-blue 1859-pattern forage cap and four-button sack coat with sky-blue trousers. He holds a Model 1861 Springfield Rifle-Musket, and his equipment consists of a US regulation black rubberized knapsack with blanket roll, oblate spheroid canteen, and black-painted canvas haversack.

Ellsworth's Zouave Cadets

This detail from an engraving of the United States Zouave Cadets, published in *Frank Leslie's Illustrated Newspaper* in July 1860, provides an example of the elaborate uniforms influenced by the popular zouave military fashions that were worn by some militia companies. Organized in Chicago, Illinois by Elmer Ellsworth, a friend of Abraham Lincoln, the US Zouave Cadets gave drill displays when they toured many states in 1860.

Militia knapsack

Many state militia regiments carried spare clothing and other military essentials in rigid-box knapsacks with a wooden frame covered with black painted canvas. A British Army-style mess tin was attached to the retaining straps on this example carried by the 7th New York State Militia, one of the most prestigious regiments of that state.

Hand weapons

Missile weapons
• rifle-musket

Defenses

Clothing
• chasseur uniform
• blue Union uniform
• gray Confederate uniform
• hunting shirt
• zouave-style uniform

Warriors
• 1st Massachusetts
• 7th and 14th New York State Militias
• US Zouave Cadets
• infantrymen

Concepts & Tactics

Buildings & Transport

Chasseurs

The 14th New York State Militia was recruited in Brooklyn, New York, and wore a French-style chasseur uniform consisting of "red pants, dark blue jacket with two rows of bell [round] buttons, and red breast piece having also a row of bell buttons and a red cap." Unlike most Civil War regiments, the 14th New York continued to wear various versions of their chasseur uniform until its men were mustered out in 1864.

Confederate infantrymen

The clothing and equipment of Confederate infantrymen was far less uniform. Most wore short gray or "butternut" shell jackets and trousers, with various types of headgear, while blanket rolls and overcoat slings replaced knapsacks. Much of the rest of their equipment was similar to their Northern counterparts, although it was manufactured in the South.

See also
Zouaves, *page 221*

Unionist in gray

A Northern regiment, the 1st Massachusetts, wore gray uniforms edged with red cord around the collar and shoulder straps. Changing this for Union blue soon after, this unit enlisted for three years in 1861 and went on to fight throughout all the major campaigns of the Eastern Theater of the war until it was mustered out in 1864.

Hunting shirts

Most Confederate infantrymen were farmers and backwoodsmen who, at the beginning of the Civil War, wore fanciful uniforms. Representing a volunteer from Kentucky, this man wears a fringed hunting shirt reminiscent of clothing dating back to the Revolutionary War of 1775–83.

The American Civil War

Cavalry

The role of cavalry was in a stage of transition when the Civil War began. Used very effectively in mass charges against infantry squares during the Napoleonic period, the advent of the rifle-musket with its greater range and accuracy put an end to this. Both Union and Confederate cavalry were deployed in smaller numbers as couriers and escorts, as well as for reconnaissance. They also served as an effective rearguard in defensive actions, pursued and harassed a retreating enemy and guarded the flanks of offensive actions. The greatest tactical use of cavalry was in long-distance raids behind enemy lines, when they destroyed valuable communications, supply depots, and railroads. Nineteen Confederate and fifteen Union cavalry raids were conducted during the war.

Union cavalry trooper

Also from the *Official Atlas*, this Union corporal wears the full dress prescribed for the US cavalry in 1861. His headgear consists of the 1858 Pattern Hardee hat, and his dark-blue shell jacket is trimmed with yellow cord on collar and cuffs. Adorning his shoulders are brass scales, which were originally designed to offer protection against saber cuts.

The saber

The saber carried by many cavalrymen, both North and South, was the Model 1840 Heavy Cavalry (Dragoon) saber. Based on the French pattern, this had a curved blade, brass pommel with Phrygian helmet molding and half-basket guard, and a wooden grip covered with leather and wound with twisted brass wire. The iron scabbard had two rings and a drag.

Saber drill

A major drill manual for Civil War cavalry was *Cavalry Tactics*, published in 1861 and written by Brigadier-General Philip St. George Cooke, a Union Army officer and father-in-law of General "Jeb" Stuart, commander of the Confederate cavalry of the Army of Northern Virginia. These engravings accompany the sections describing "Right—Parry" and "Left—Parry" with the saber.

Confederate cavalry trooper

From the *Official Atlas of the Civil War*, this Confederate cavalryman wears the uniform prescribed for the small Regular Army in June 1861. Believed to have been designed by Nicola Marschall, a German artist who immigrated to America, it was probably based on the uniform worn by Austrian *feldjaeger* troops. The yellow facings on collar and cuffs were the branch service color for cavalry in the USA.

The McClellan saddle

The McClellan saddle was designed by George B. McClellan, a career officer in the US Army, after a tour of Europe as a member of a commission charged with studying the latest military developments. Based on the Prussian cavalry saddle, which incorporated the Hungarian tree, the McClellan saddle was selected as the regulation issue for the US Army in 1859, being used extensively during the Civil War and beyond.

Couriers and escorts

Union Regular Army cavalry often served as couriers and escorts for commanding officers. This resulted in many regiments being broken up into smaller units on detached service. The escort for Lieutenant-General Ulysses S. Grant, General-in-Chief of the Armies of the United States, in 1864–65 was Companies B, F, and K of the 5th US Cavalry.

Guerrillas

Confederate cavalry often operated at its best when serving as a guerrilla force. Quantrill's Raiders was a loosely organized unit of pro-Confederate bushwhackers who fought under the leadership of William Clarke Quantrill on either side of the Kansas–Missouri border. John S. Mosby led an equally effective guerrilla cavalry force behind Union lines in Virginia.

The American Civil War

Artillery

Civil War artillery can be divided into several categories according to their basic design, weight, barrel length, and type of projectiles used. The lighter 6- and 12-pounder field artillery mainly consisted of guns and howitzers. A gun was a long-barreled heavy weapon that fired solid shot at long range with a low degree of elevation, using a large powder charge. A howitzer had a shorter barrel and could throw shot and shell at a shorter range but higher elevation with smaller powder charges. Rifled guns, such as the Parrott and Whitworth, had exceptional ranges and accuracy. For siege and garrison use 18- and 24-pounders were employed, while larger-caliber guns called Columbiads were used for coastal defense and by the navies. Short, stubby-barreled weapons called mortars fired heavy projectiles in a high arc. Only a small powder charge was needed for a mortar to project shot or shell to its maximum elevation.

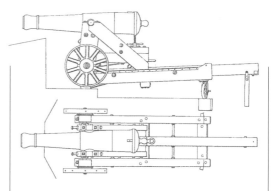

Siege guns

This detail from the 1861 *Ordnance Manual* shows a 24-pounder siege gun mounted on a wooden barbette carriage, which elevated the piece so that it could be fired over a parapet. This type of heavy gun was most often located in fortifications such as those surrounding Washington, DC, from 1861 to 1865.

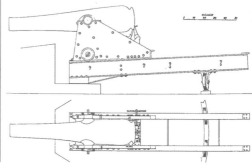

Field artillery

Commanded by a captain, a battery of Civil War field artillery usually consisted of between six and eight guns. Each section, or pair of guns, was the responsibility of a lieutenant. Each gun was under the command of a sergeant, plus two corporals and about four cannoneers.

Coastal batteries

Heavy cannon, such as this 10-inch (25-centimeter) Rodman gun, were often mounted in coastal batteries on iron barbette carriages with front pintles. These enabled them to be swiveled around as well as elevated. Note the circular rail in the platform around which the gun was pivoted.

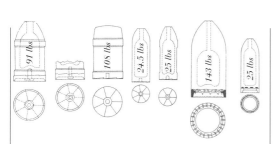

Shells and sabots

Shells fired by rifled weapons such as the 100-pounder Parrott gun employed a sabot made of wrought iron, brass, lead, or copper that was attached to the shell base. When the projectile was fired the sabot expanded into the rifling of the tube, which spun the shell out with far greater accuracy and range than that of smoothbore cannon. These drawings from the *Official Atlas* show projectiles with copper sabots that screwed on to the base of the shell.

Garrison guns

Based on an original photograph, this engraving shows officers and crew of the 3rd Massachusetts Heavy Artillery with a 100-pounder Parrott gun placed on an iron barbette with a center pintle at Fort Totten, Washington, DC, in August 1865. Invented by Robert Parker Parrott, a West Point graduate, the Parrott gun had a wrought-iron reinforcing band overlaid around the breech for additional strength.

Mountain howitzers

Designed for use in mountain combat, small-caliber mountain howitzers were dismantled and strapped to pack horses or mules, or the gun remained on its carriage and was drawn by animals harnessed to it, as seen above. One animal (right) has ammunition or tool chests strapped to it.

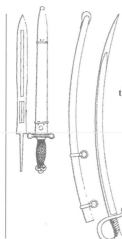

Swords and sabers

Both Union and Confederate cannoneers were usually armed with edged weapons for use if their battery or gun position was overrun by the enemy. The Model 1833 foot artillery sword was carried by those manning heavier artillery pieces, such as 24-pounders, while mounted, or flying, artillery crews carried the Model 1840 light artillery saber.

Railroad batteries

One of the first uses of armored trains in the Civil War took place on the Baltimore and Ohio Railroad east of Cumberland, Maryland, in August 1864. Manned by Union troops, it consisted of "iron-clad railroad batteries containing three guns each, and four musket-proof boxcars with loopholes for riflemen." Improved armored trains would be used later during the siege of Paris in 1870.

See also
The evolution of artillery, *pages 210–11*
Anatomy of a cannon, *pages 224–5*
Artillery, *pages 296–7*

The American Civil War

Tactics: forts and sieges

The American Civil War saw a massive development in the use of field fortifications. Many of the officers in both Union and Confederate armies had learned their profession at West Point, where they were taught military engineering and the art of fortification by Dennis Hart Mahan. Believing in the preeminence of the spade in combat, Mahan drew inspiration from the works of the 17th-century French military engineer Sebastien Le Prestre, Seigneur de Vauban, and the 19th-century Swiss military theorist General Baron Antoine Henri de Jomini. His *Complete Treatise on Field Fortification* was first published in 1836, and it was reprinted in New York in 1861 and 1863 and in the Confederacy in 1862. This volume became the standard manual on the subject, and it contained complete and detailed instructions for planning, constructing, defending, and attacking field fortifications and entrenchments.

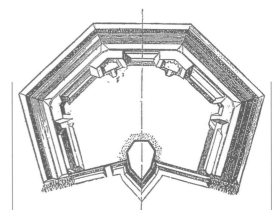

Lunettes
A common form of fortification in the Civil War was a detached field fortification called a lunette. Containing emplacements for large guns, these earthworks were protected by deep ditches on all but the gorge, or rear, which in this case is enclosed by a stockade from which projects a small two-sided bastion called a redan.

Flying saps
This engraving depicting the siege of Vicksburg in 1863 shows Union sharpshooters firing behind a flying sap, consisting of a gabion revetment, a protective wall composed of large baskets filled with soil. Others rest in a deep trench protected by a parados, or bank of earth, piled on its rear side.

Hand weapons

Missile weapons

Defenses
• Friesland horse
• gabion revetment
• lunettes
• parados
• redan
• wolf traps

Clothing

Warriors

Concepts & Tactics
• field fortifications
• military engineering

Buildings & Transport
• blockhouse
• star fort

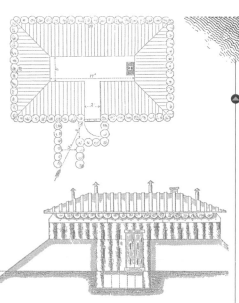

Profile of parapet and ditch

The main features of the parapet and ditch of a fort were the interior, superior, and exterior slopes of the parapet. The side of the ditch facing the enemy was often pierced with a fraise of sharpened stakes, while the bottom of the ditch might also contain a sharpened palisade. The area enclosed within the parapet was called the terreplein.

Outer-field obstacles

Various obstacles were used as outer-field fortifications, including the *cheval de frise*, or Friesland horse. Possibly invented by the Dutch during the siege of Groningen in 1594, this consisted of a horizontal beam, 9–10 feet (2.75– 3 meters) long, with two diagonal rows of 10-foot (3-meter) sharpened lances. Other obstacles shown here are square and round *trous-de-loup*, or wolf traps, with sharpened stakes at their base, and wire entanglements.

Star forts

A star, or tenaille, fort was surrounded on the exterior with projecting angles, or salients, and was categorized by the number of salients it contained. This octagonal star fort is surrounded by a wide ditch and has a traverse or barrier across its terreplein that offered additional protection from flying shell fragments.

Blockhouses

Larger field works often contained blockhouses that served as a place of refuge if the outer defenses were breached. Small garrisons posted in isolated locations were also reliant on blockhouses for protection from attack by a larger force. Based on Mahan's principles of fortification, this example is built with a single thickness of vertical logs and has a gallery protecting its doorway and soil piled halfway up its walls for additional protection.

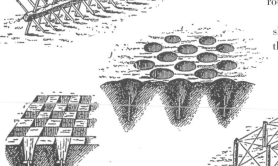

Anatomy of a Repeating Rifle and Carbine

1 The American Civil War saw the first mass use of breech-loading repeating rifles and carbines. The introduction of the seven-shot Model 1860 Spencer rifle contributed greatly to the Union victory. Nicknamed "the horizontal shot tower," this was a manually operated lever-action weapon fed with rimfire cartridges from a tube magazine in the buttstock. It was adopted by the Union Army, especially by the cavalry, which used the shorter and lighter Spencer carbine. Versions of the rifle were produced for compatibility with either the triangular or sword bayonet.

3 The hammer was then manually cocked and the weapon was ready for firing. The tubular magazine for feeding the rimfire cartridge to the receiver was located in the buttstock. This magazine held seven rimfire cartridges and worked with a coiled spring. An expert marksman could release seven aimed shots in less than ten seconds.

4 The accuracy of the Spencer was assisted by a single folding-leaf sight seated on a curved-spring base 3⅜ inches (8.6 centimeters) from the breech and a front sight on the muzzle.

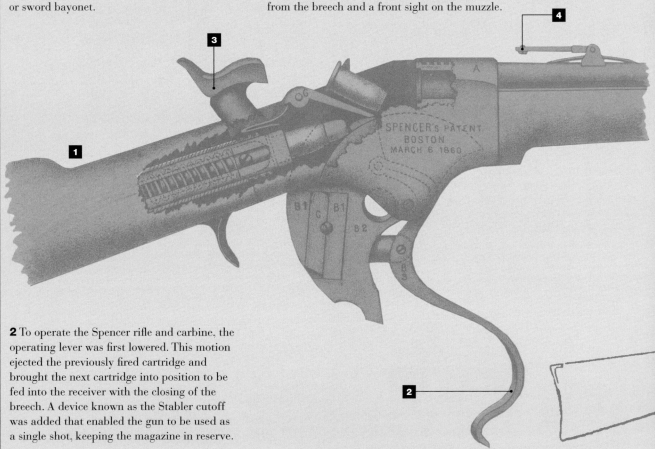

2 To operate the Spencer rifle and carbine, the operating lever was first lowered. This motion ejected the previously fired cartridge and brought the next cartridge into position to be fed into the receiver with the closing of the breech. A device known as the Stabler cutoff was added that enabled the gun to be used as a single shot, keeping the magazine in reserve.

5 With the introduction late in the Civil War of Blakeslee cartridge boxes—known as "quick-loaders" by the troops—the Spencer-carrying soldier had extra ammunition at his disposal. The cavalry version carried ten magazine tubes, while the infantry version contained thirteen. This meant they had either seventy or ninety-one extra rounds at their disposal.

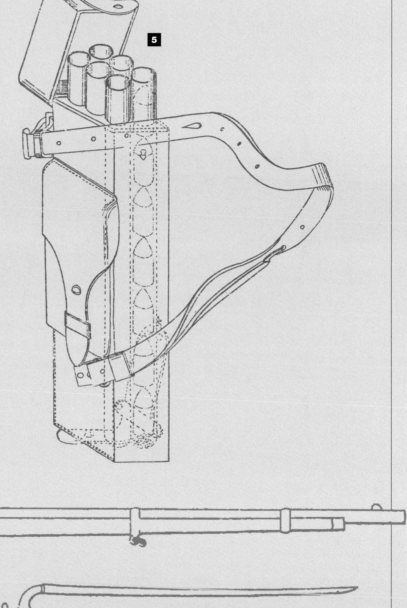

6 The largest Union procurement of breech-loading rifles during the Civil War was for 11,472 .52-caliber Spencer rifles. This weapon weighed 10 pounds (4.5 kilograms) and had an overall length of 47 inches (119 centimeters). Its 30-inch (76-centimeter) barrel was equipped to take the angular bayonet. In this inaccurate drawing from the *Official Atlas* only two of the actual three barrel bands are shown.

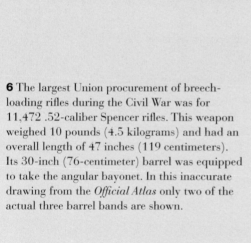

The American Civil War

Technology—communications

Both the Union and Confederate armies relied on signal corps for communications. The Union organization began when Major Albert J. Myer was appointed as its first signal officer just prior to the conflict. The Confederate equivalent, begun by Colonel William Norris and Myer's former Regular Army assistant, Edward Porter Alexander, consisted of a much smaller group but used similar methods as the Union. Both accomplished tactical and strategic communications using electromagnetic or aerial telegraphy and "wig-wag" signaling. Both sides also used balloons for aerial observation.

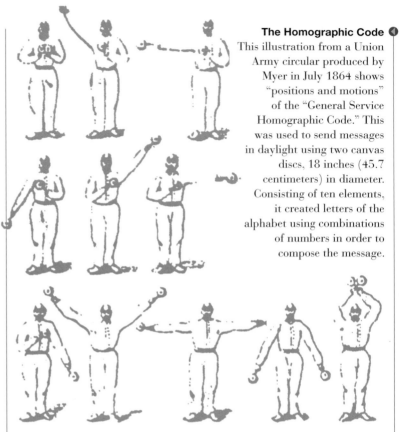

The Homographic Code
This illustration from a Union Army circular produced by Myer in July 1864 shows "positions and motions" of the "General Service Homographic Code." This was used to send messages in daylight using two canvas discs, 18 inches (45.7 centimeters) in diameter. Consisting of ten elements, it created letters of the alphabet using combinations of numbers in order to compose the message.

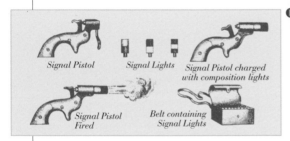

Signal Pistol   *Signal Lights*   *Signal Pistol charged with composition lights*

Signal Pistol Fired   *Belt containing Signal Lights*

Signal pistols

Signals were conveyed at night using pistols that fired single- and multicolored cylindrical "light" cartridges that were produced by B.T. Coston. Under good conditions the Coston system had a practical working range of about 5 miles (8 kilometers). A single-light signal burned for about 8 seconds, the double and triple signals lasted around 17 and 26 seconds respectively.

Signal mortars

The Union Signal Corps also provided nighttime signals to begin military operations. This involved using a signal mortar that fired a candle bomb with cartridge attached, which was ignited by a lighted match. The signaler here is shown carrying the mortar and the bomb suspended from shoulder straps. A pack animal was used to transport his full equipment greater distances.

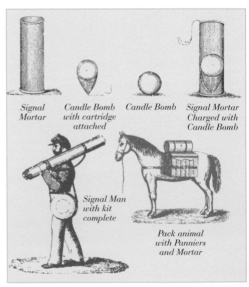

Signal Mortar   *Candle Bomb with cartridge attached*   *Candle Bomb*   *Signal Mortar Charged with Candle Bomb*

Signal Man with kit complete

Pack animal with Panniers and Mortar

Hand weapons

Missile weapons

Defenses

Clothing

Nighttime signals

This engraving of a Union signaling station shows a signaler holding a torch at the first position, or "Ready." A daytime signal flag is suspended from his platform, while to his right a signals officer peers through a night telescope.

Telegraphic wire

These signalers are shown setting up a telegraph wire during battle. The wire used was of insulated copper, and it was raised on light poles, suspended on convenient trees, or trailed along fences. The equipment was transported in a cart from which the wire was unwound. When a connection was made the cart became the telegraph office. The men on the left are making holes for the telegraph poles.

Warriors
• Confederate Signal Corps
• Union Balloon Corps
• Union Signal Corps

Concepts & Tactics
• electromagnetic signaling
• "wig-wag" signaling

Buildings & Transport
• hot-air balloon
• pack animals

Sending telegraphic messages

The electromagnetic device for sending messages was worked by a handle, which was passed around a dial-plate marked with numerals and the alphabet. By stopping at the required letters a message was spelled out on the instrument at the other end of the line. According to one contemporary account, "The whole thing is so simple that any man able to read and write can work it with facility."

Observation balloons

Both the Union and Confederate armies used balloons for reconnaissance as well as for telegraphing messages from the balloon to the field commanders below. Hydrogen-filled balloons such as the *Intrepid*, developed by Thaddeus Lowe, were employed by the Union Balloon Corps, a civilian organization under the authority of the Bureau of Topographical Engineers. The Confederacy used *montgolfière*-style hot-air balloons for similar purposes.

Anatomy of a Colt Revolver

1 Born in Hartford, Connecticut, in 1814, Samuel Colt was intrigued by guns and how they worked from an early age. While serving aboard a merchant ship on a voyage to India, he developed a concept for a handgun with a simple revolving ammunition cylinder based on the mechanism of the ship's wheel, the spokes of which aligned with a clutch as it was turned.

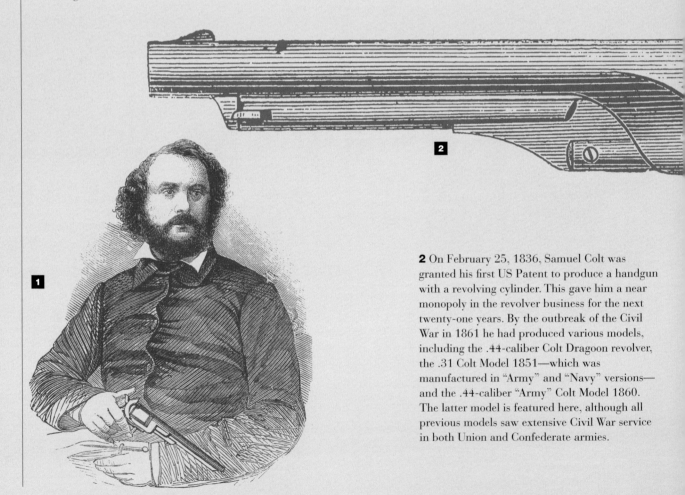

2 On February 25, 1836, Samuel Colt was granted his first US Patent to produce a handgun with a revolving cylinder. This gave him a near monopoly in the revolver business for the next twenty-one years. By the outbreak of the Civil War in 1861 he had produced various models, including the .44-caliber Colt Dragoon revolver, the .31 Colt Model 1851—which was manufactured in "Army" and "Navy" versions— and the .44-caliber "Army" Colt Model 1860. The latter model is featured here, although all previous models saw extensive Civil War service in both Union and Confederate armies.

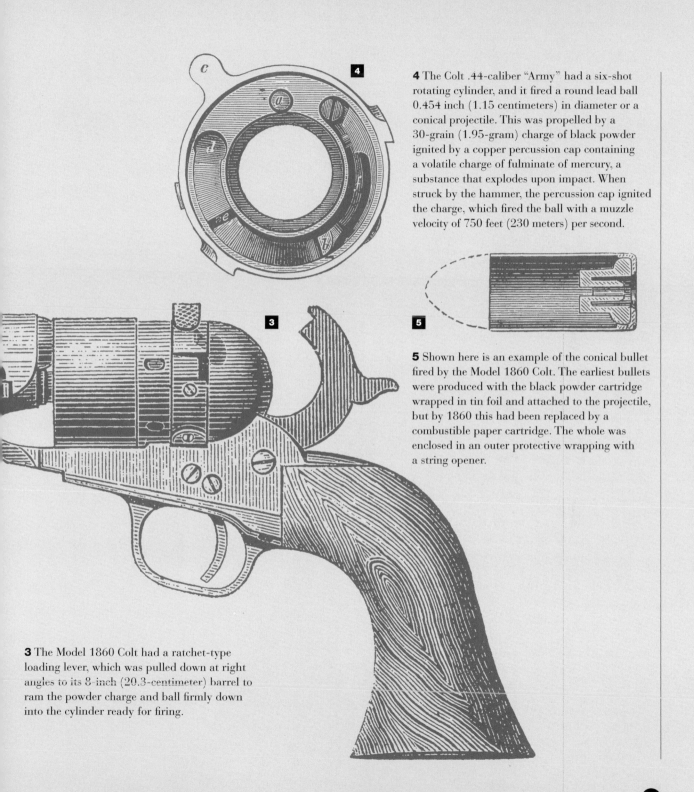

4 The Colt .44-caliber "Army" had a six-shot rotating cylinder, and it fired a round lead ball 0.454 inch (1.15 centimeters) in diameter or a conical projectile. This was propelled by a 30-grain (1.95-gram) charge of black powder ignited by a copper percussion cap containing a volatile charge of fulminate of mercury, a substance that explodes upon impact. When struck by the hammer, the percussion cap ignited the charge, which fired the ball with a muzzle velocity of 750 feet (230 meters) per second.

5 Shown here is an example of the conical bullet fired by the Model 1860 Colt. The earliest bullets were produced with the black powder cartridge wrapped in tin foil and attached to the projectile, but by 1860 this had been replaced by a combustible paper cartridge. The whole was enclosed in an outer protective wrapping with a string opener.

3 The Model 1860 Colt had a ratchet-type loading lever, which was pulled down at right angles to its 8-inch (20.3-centimeter) barrel to ram the powder charge and ball firmly down into the cylinder ready for firing.

The American Civil War

Camp life

The Union Army used tents of different kinds in semipermanent camps as well as on campaign. The size of the tents tended to decrease as the war went on. Because of lack of availability the Confederate army used tents less frequently, except for officers, who had ordinary wall tents of the same pattern—often captured—as those produced for the Union Army. Both armies also constructed shebangs or shanties covered with materials such as milled lumber, fence rails, cornstalks, or straw. More comfortable log cabins were built for winter quarters. Larger iron camp stoves were used in camps in the rear echelons, while soldiers on campaign resorted to the more portable skillet. Each soldier carried his own utensils, which included cup, mess plate, knife, spoon, and three-tang fork.

The Sibley tent

The Sibley, or Bell, tent was invented by West Point graduate Henry H. Sibley in 1857. Based on the Native American tepee, it was 18 feet (5.5 meters) in height and 12 feet (3.7 meters) in diameter and was supported by a single pole which rested on an iron tripod, by means of which the tent could be tightened or slackened. These tents were comfortable for twelve men.

Dog tents

Also known as a dog tent, pup tent, or *tente d'abri*, this shelter was invented in late 1861 or early 1862 and was made of cotton drilling, light canvas, or rubber. Each soldier carried a half shelter, which he combined with another man. Their two muskets with fixed bayonets were stuck erect in the ground the width of a half shelter apart. A guy rope supplied with every half shelter was stretched between the trigger guards of the muskets, and the tent was pitched over this as a ridge pole.

See also

The American Civil War: infantry: uniforms and equipment,

pages 228–9

The Hope stove

As soldiers spent much of their time fighting, living and sleeping in trenches toward the end of the Civil War, the Hope camp stove was designed to be placed over a trench or rifle pit. Patented in January 1863, it consisted of a box top of sheet metal, provided with holes for the chimney and for a kettle.

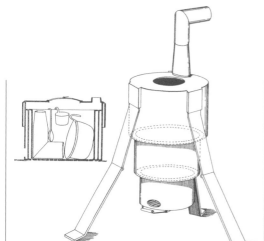

🔵 Wooden shelters

Brush arbors were constructed by both Union and Confederate soldiers when tents were unavailable. These were makeshift structures with a wooden framework over which was placed brushwood, leafy tree branches, and anything else the soldier could scavenge or find. This provided only very limited shelter from the elements in both summer and winter.

🔵 The Smith stove

Patented in March 1863 by Lowell H. Smith of Owensville, Ohio, the Smith camp stove was made of sections that fitted into each other. When the outer section was raised and supported on logs, the other sections slipped out in telescope fashion. The cooking equipment was contained within the stove in transit.

🔵 Spooning

The wedge tent usually held four men but was often occupied by five or sometimes six when tents were in limited supply. In such a case it was necessary that all the occupants "spooned" together while sleeping.

The American Civil War

Technology—medicine

Whether Union or Confederate, the Civil War soldier was exposed to the devastating effects of new weapons technology at a time when the science of medicine was woefully inadequate and only beginning to respond to the new demands. If seriously wounded in battle he was almost certain to be permanently maimed or impaired. When languishing in camp he lived under conditions that were very likely to make him sick with disease. In either case he had very little chance of receiving the kind of medical treatment that would be considered routine a generation or so later. Both governments did their best to provide proper medical care for their soldiers, and by the middle part of the war improved provision was made in the form of ambulance and medicine wagons and litters plus hospital trains and ships.

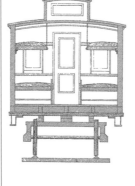

Hospital railroad cars
Several types of improvised hospital railroad cars were used, but one of the best was created late in 1862 by the Philadelphia Railroad Company. The internal layout was similar to a sleeping car except that the berths slid in and out. Each berth with its patient could be carried by two men like a stretcher. Each hospital car had fifty-one berths and a seat at each end for an attendant. It was also provided with a simple cooking stove, a water tank, and a toilet.

The "Rocker" ambulance
The allotment of field ambulances within the Union Army in 1863 was three per regiment of infantry, two per cavalry regiment, and one per artillery battery. The padded leather seating in a "Rocker" ambulance could be rearranged to accommodate four recumbent wounded.

Panniers and cases
Medicine panniers were used by hospital orderlies to carry essential medicines and appliances from the medicine wagon to the field. From 1863 the leather field case, or companion (bottom), containing, among other things, chloroform, whisky, opium, and isinglass plaster, was carried by the surgeon.

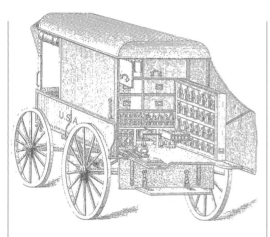

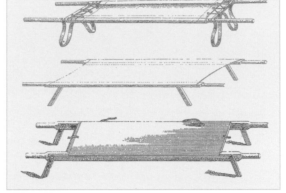

Medicine wagons

One of various medicine wagons used by the Union Army, the Autenrieth wagon was adopted during the last year of the war. Constructed at the government shops, it carried instruments intended for surgeons and assistant surgeons for use in major operations, which were performed on a table close by. The medicines were arranged in convenient slides; the hospital stores, dressings, furniture, and utensils were arranged in drawers or on shelves.

Litters

At the beginning of the Civil War the canvas Satterlee (top), the US regulation litter, was used by the Union Army. With a wrought-iron frame, the bearers supported the additional weight with leather shoulder straps. The Halstead litter (middle), a stretcher of lighter and more compact pattern, soon superseded it, and the Confederate Army developed a similar wood-and-canvas litter (bottom).

Hospital ships

Converted from a Confederate steamer captured in April 1862, the USS *Red Rover* was the US Navy's first hospital ship. Serving as a floating hospital on the Mississippi River, it was commanded by Captain McDaniel, with thirty surgeons and male nurses as well as four nuns under the charge of Surgeon George H. Bixby. It housed 2,947 patients, both Union and Confederate, over a three-year period.

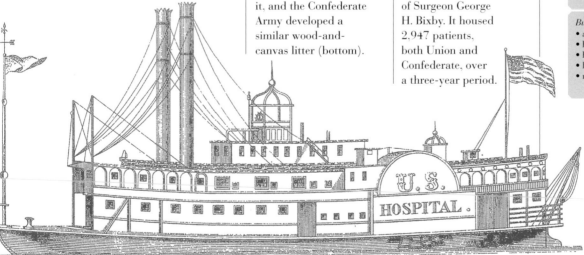

The American Civil War

Legacy

The wars following the American Civil War saw the development of even more deadly weapons, including rapid-fire machine guns and breech-loading and bolt-action rifles using metal-cased bullets as well as huge rifled cannon. Realizing that the further use of such devastating weapons was going to make future warfare even more brutal, Swiss businessman and social activist Jean Henri Dunant campaigned to make wars more humane. With the help of others he organized a meeting of thirteen nations at Geneva in 1863, and during the following year a diplomatic conference organized by the Swiss Parliament led to the signing of the first Geneva Convention by twelve states. The agreement provided for the neutrality of ambulance and military hospitals during wartime; nonbelligerent status of persons aiding the wounded plus the same status for sick soldiers of any nationality; repatriation of prisoners incapable of serving; and the adoption of a white flag with a red cross for use on hospitals, ambulances, and evacuation centers in order that their neutrality might be observed.

The Gatling gun

A hand-cranked weapon with six barrels revolving around a central shaft, the Gatling gun was designed by the American inventor Dr. Richard J. Gatling in 1861 and patented in 1862. Although it saw only very limited Civil War service, a later version with ten barrels firing 320 rounds per minute became an essential part of the arsenal of most major armies in Europe as well as the USA.

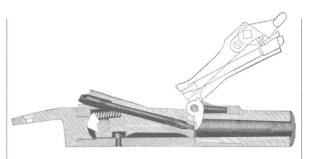

Breech-loading rifles

The Model 1873 was the last of a series of single-shot, breech-loading "trapdoor" Springfield rifles issued to the US infantryman. The lift-up trapdoor breech block gave this weapon its nickname. The fall of the external hammer initiated the action of a firing pin rather than detonating the separate percussion cap of the pre-1866 muzzle-loader.

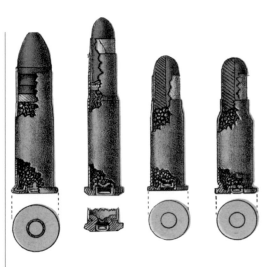

Metal-cased cartridges

Metal-cased rim-fire cartridges were used with breech-loading and bolt-action rifles. The copper or brass casing contained the primer and powder, while the lead ball or bullet was crimped to the end of the case. In operation, the hammer or firing pin of the weapon struck the rim of the cartridge, which inflamed the primer, or fulminate, that in turn exploded the powder and fired the ball.

Krupp's cannon

Large guns made at the factory of "Cannon King" Alfred Krupp in Essen, Germany, helped Prussia to defeat Austria in 1866 and France in 1871. By 1887 Krupp had sold 24,567 big guns to twenty-one nations.

Jean Henri Dunant

The International Committee of the Red Cross was founded following the publication of *A Memory of Solferino*, a book by Jean Henri Dunant describing the suffering he witnessed following the Battle of Solferino in 1860. The 1864 Geneva Convention was also based on Dunant's ideas, and in 1901 he received the first Nobel Peace Prize together with Frédéric Passy, who campaigned for international conflict arbitration.

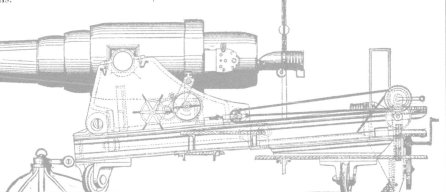

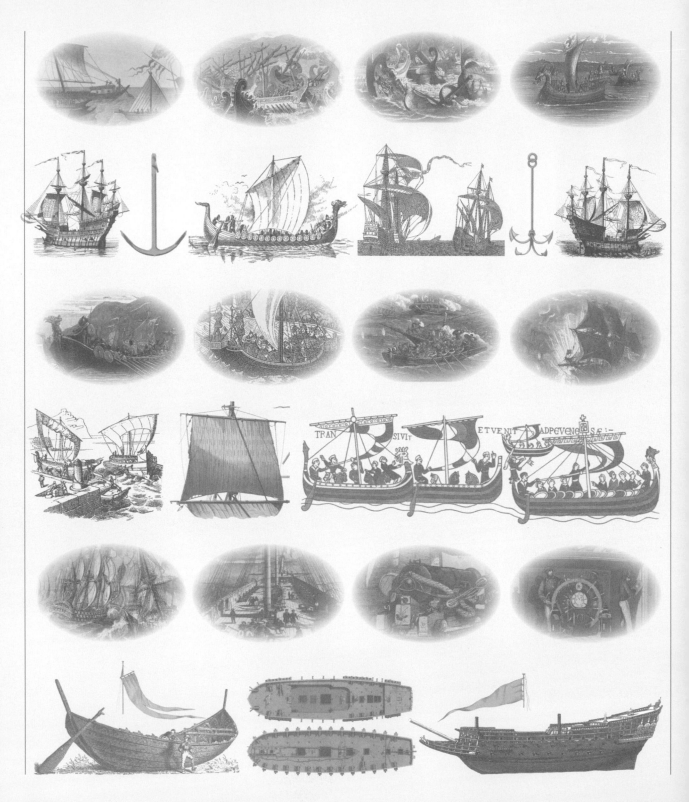

War at Sea
500 BCE to 1865 CE

The first vessels used for river and sea warfare were the multidecked *lou chuan*, or tower ships, of the ancient Chinese. The development of Chinese warships peaked during the Qin (221–210 BCE) and Han (206 BCE–220 CE) dynasties, when a variety of vessels were used, including the *xian deng*, an assault ship; the *meng chong*, for ramming; and the *ben ma*, described as being "as fast as a galloping horse."

In the Mediterranean, the Phoenicians, Greeks, and Romans used the single-decked galley propelled by oars (many also had sails for when the winds were favorable) and galleys dominated naval warfare there until the fall of the Western Roman Empire during the 5th century. They remained in use to a lesser extent with the Byzantine Navy and other successors of Rome as well as with the Muslim states. The Italian maritime republics, including Venice, Pisa, and Genoa, continued to use galleys until oceangoing wind-powered cogs and carracks rendered them obsolete.

The galleon was a multidecked wind-powered warship with three to five masts. Famously used by the Spanish to bring American gold to Europe during the 16th century, in 1588 the principal warships of the Spanish Armada and the opposing English fleet under Sir Francis Drake were also galleons. The modified English "race built" galleon proved decisive against the larger Spanish vessels. The square-rigged galleon was the prototype of all warships for the next 250 years.

The 17th century saw the development of the ship of the line, which had three and sometimes even four gun decks and could carry up to ninety guns. This type of vessel reached its zenith in 1805 at the Battle of Trafalgar, when the British fleet under Vice-Admiral Horatio Lord Nelson defeated a combined French and Spanish fleet off Cape Trafalgar.

By 1850 the development of steam power led to the construction of propeller-driven, wooden-hulled ships of the line. The introduction of the ironclad frigate by 1860 led to the decline of such steam-assisted ships, and the ironclad warship of the American Civil War heralded the age of the modern battleship.

The Chinese, Egyptians, and Phoenicians

The age of galleys

The first ships designed for river and sea warfare were developed by the forefathers of the Chinese during the late Neolithic period, between roughly 10,000 and 4,000 years ago. By the time of the Han Dynasty "floating fortresses," known as tower ships, carried huge catapults manned by hundreds of soldiers and crew. Ancient Egyptian sea power peaked in the 15th century BCE, during the New Kingdom, when Queen Hatshepsut ordered naval expeditions along the eastern coast of Africa and the maritime operations of Thotmos III brought the eastern Mediterranean coast under Egyptian rule. Phoenician sea power was at its greatest from 1200 to 800 BCE. The founders of Carthage and many other colonies, the prows of their warships had sharp beaks or spikes to ram and sink the enemy.

Chinese tower ship
The use of Chinese *lou chuan*, or tower ships, reached a peak during the Qin (221–10 BCE) and Han (206 BCE to 220 CE) dynasties. Made up of these multidecked vessels, the fleet of Qin Emperor Qin Shi Huang was used to conquer the Chu state during the unification of China.

Square-rigged Egyptian galley
Egyptian warships of the late period had a single mast with square-rigged sails. They could accommodate up to thirty oarsmen and were steered by long oars attached to a raised "stern castle." High bulwarks protected the crew from enemy missiles. They had no keel but derived their structural strength from a gangway connecting bow to stern.

Egyptian first-dynasty galleys
This Egyptian vessel is similar to the archaeological remains of First Dynasty boats found at Tarkhan and Abydos in 1991. About 82 feet (25 meters) long and 10 feet (3 meters) wide, they could seat as many as thirty rowers and had a rising prow and stern. As shown in this engraving, sails on Egyptian boats were often triangular.

Cleopatra's show ship

Egyptian royal barges and river boats had no sails and were either towed by other vessels or propelled by oarsmen. They often had several decks with cabins, kitchens, and luxurious living accommodation. Originally known as "Cleopatra's show ship," the vessel in this engraving has elaborate masts and banners, plus a canopy covering the upper deck.

Tessarakonteres

The pharaoh Ptolemy IV Philopator (reigned 221–205 BCE) is said to have built a giant galley known as the tessarakonteres, or forty, because of the legendary number of its banks of oars. It is now thought to have been a catamaran galley similar to a Chinese tower ship, 50 feet (15 meters) wide, 400 feet (122 meters) long, with 4,000 oars, and 3,250 marines and crew.

Tower ship

The *Syracusia* was probably the largest ship of antiquity. Designed by Archimedes and built *c.* 240 BCE by Archias of Corinth for Hieron II, King of Syracuse, it was later gifted to Ptolemy III Euergetes of Alexandria and renamed the *Alexandria*. It could carry 400 soldiers and had eight deck towers and a catapult capable of hurling an 18-foot (5.5-meter) arrow or a 180-pound (82-kilogram) boulder.

Hand weapons

Missile weapons
• catapult

Defenses

Clothing

Warriors
• Chinese
• Egyptian
• Phoenician

Concepts & Tactics

Buildings & Transport
• Chinese tower ship
• Egyptian galley
• Egyptian royal barge
• tessarakonteres

See also
**Ancient Egypt at war:
New Kingdom tactics
and technology,**
pages 16–17
**The Greeks:
warships and rams,**
pages 252–3
The Roman navy,
pages 254–5

The Greeks

Warships and rams

The earliest Greek warship was known as a pentekonter, which had a single bank of twenty-five oarsmen on each side. During the Archaic Period, *c.* 500 BCE, faster vessels were developed, impelled by multiple banks of oars—called biremes, triremes, and quadriremes depending on the number—with a bronze ram, or *embolos*, on the prow. Archaeologists believe the three-banked vessels could reach 14 knots when being rowed effectively. By the Classical Period, *c.* 400 BCE, the Greeks were also using the three-decked quinquireme, a heavier type of warship with five men to an oar. Harder to blow off course, some of these vessels were the forerunners of the ironclad warships of the 19th century CE, having lead cladding below the waterline to protect against ramming by enemy vessels.

Sea power

Because of warships like these, Greek sea power led to control of the eastern Mediterranean by the time of Alexander the Great (reigned 356–23 BCE). As a result, the Greek city-states held sway over the Persian Empire, including Egypt, plus lands as far east as the fringes of India.

See also
Rams and figureheads,
page 254

The Argo

Named after its builder Argus, the *Argo* was the mythological Greek warship that carried Jason and the Argonauts to Colchis (modern Georgia) in their quest to find the Golden Fleece. According to other legends its prow consisted of a magical piece of timber from the sacred forest of Dodona, which could speak and render prophecies. Although no crew are depicted, this engraving shows the shape of early Greek warships.

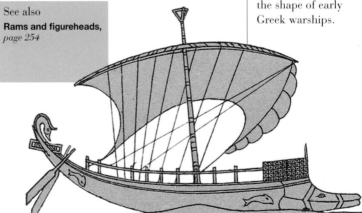

Triremes with rams

As shown in this detail of a prow, Greek triremes were powered by three sets of oars a side. As a result, these vessels were fast and agile, becoming the dominant warship in the Mediterranean between the 7th and 4th centuries BCE, after which they were mostly superseded by the larger quadriremes and quinquiremes. Note the sharp bronze ram, called an *embolos*, attached to the prow at water level.

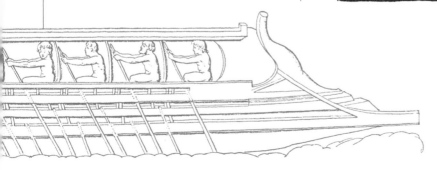

A pentekonter
This two-masted Greek pentekonter-type warship features the high forecastle designed to protect the crew. With a sharp ram attached to its prow, such a vessel was designed for fighting a sea battle rather than fulfilling the troop-carrying role of earlier ancient warships.

The influence of Archimedes
Ancient wooden warships were always susceptible to fire. The Greek scientist and mathematician Archimedes is believed to have invented a device that used an array of mirrors to set enemy galleys ablaze, and it was used by the Greeks to defend the city of Syracuse against Roman attack in 212 BCE.

The Battle of Salamis
The naval power of the Greek city-states reached its peak in 480 BCE with the defeat of the Persian fleet under Xerxes I by Themistocles during a sea battle off the Island of Salamis. Lured into the Gulf of Corinth by the retreating Greek fleet, the aim of the archers aboard the tall-masted Persian galleys was spoiled by a brisk early morning wind. Meanwhile the Greek hoplites were lethal in hand-to-hand fighting as the Greek vessels closed on them.

The Romans

The Roman navy

Founded *c.* 311 BCE and massively expanded during the course of the First Punic War against Carthage (264–241 BCE), the Roman Navy played a vital role in the early stages of expansion of the Roman Republic. However, it was gradually reduced in size and importance under the Empire, undertaking mainly policing duties and coastal patrols. In the 4th century CE the bulk of the fleet was moved to the Eastern Roman Empire and continued to serve as the Byzantine Navy. With their high curved sterns and sharp reinforced rams, Roman warships were adapted from Greek triremes and quinquiremes, but they also had fighting towers, stronger gunwales, and a hooked gangplank called the raven, Latin *corvus*, for boarding enemy vessels.

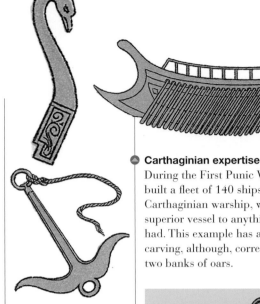

Carthaginian expertise

During the First Punic War the Romans built a fleet of 140 ships based on a captured Carthaginian warship, which was a far superior vessel to anything that the Romans had. This example has an elaborate stern carving, although, correctly, it should have two banks of oars.

Prows and anchors

An important feature of a Roman warship was the tall, swanlike carving attached to the stern of the vessel. The earliest form of ship's anchor consisted of a basket filled with stones, but by Graeco-Roman times anchors were made from lead-covered wood.

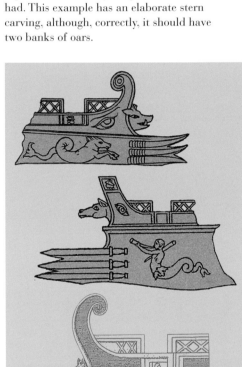

Rams and figureheads

Some Roman galleys had three-pronged rams attached to their prows, which were elaborately painted and carved with mythological symbols and imagery. These examples have the carved heads of animals (wild hogs and a horse) as figureheads.

The bireme

This Roman bireme is inaccurately shown with a topsail and bowsprit in addition to the large mainsail. Roman ships were commonly named after gods such as Mars and were often distinguished by their figureheads, which in this case is a ram. The rudders projecting from the stern helped steer and stabilize the huge vessel.

Navis lusoria

The navy of the Roman Empire used smaller-oared ships with lighter drafts in order to police the Mediterranean waterways and rivers. This type of vessel was succeeded during the latter years of the Empire by the *navis lusoria*, or playful ship, which was extensively used for patrols and raids by the legionary flotillas of the Rhine and Danube frontiers.

Sea battle

After being defeated at sea during the First Punic War by the more experienced Carthaginian Navy, the Romans developed a much stronger force. In this depiction of a sea battle, the second vessel on the left has a *corvus* poised to be used, while rams and forecastles are much in evidence.

Catapults

This Roman war galley of the period of the First Punic War has a catapult erected on its forecastle. The larger the ship, the more stable it was as a firing platform. The use of catapults largely replaced the *corvus* by the end of the Republic, as an accurately aimed catapult could destroy an enemy ship long before it was close enough to board.

Corvus

In the original Roman relief sculpture on which this engraving is based, the beam protruding from the galley bows represented a *corvus*, or assault bridge, and the marines were preparing to use it to grapple on to an enemy vessel before boarding. This has been mistaken for a fishing pole in the engraving.

The fortified turret, or forecastle, has been more faithfully represented.

The Vikings

Snekkes and *drakkar*

Long, narrow ships packed with warriors made the Vikings and their descendants the dominant power in Europe from about 800 CE until toward the end of the 11th century. Smaller vessels, called *snekkes*, with up to twenty pairs of oarsmen, were maintained by Danish communities for royal service and answered the call whenever the king sent around the symbolic war arrow. Larger longships, called *drakkar*, or dragon ships, of up to thirty rowing benches, were the pride of Viking kings and earls and displayed craftsmanship of superb quality. The great ships with more than thirty rowing benches were about 120 feet (36 meters) long and served only in the dynastic wars of the late Viking Age.

See also
Viking invaders,
pages 76–7
The Normans,
pages 78–9

Removable mast
Snekkes were one of the most common types of Viking longship. According to Viking lore, the fleet of Cnut the Great consisted of 1,400 of these vessels in 1028, and William the Conqueror had about 600 built for the invasion of Britain in 1066. Sails and masts were lowered to make their coastal approach less obvious.

Dragon ships
Viking dragon ships had crews of twenty to thirty oarsmen, who rowed to the beat of a drum when their vessel was becalmed. As their lives depended on their shields, they probably stored them safely aboard during rough seas, although they may have suspended them on the sides of their ships for protection when going into action in calmer weather.

Shallow draft
The hulls of Viking warships were tarred and coated with animal fur to seal them against water. Most *snekkes* were so light and had such a shallow draft that the crew could beach them without need of a port or harbor. Viking raiders would simply pull them up on to the beach and wade through the surf to reach their victims on dry land.

Hand weapons

Missile weapons

Defenses
• shields

Clothing

Warriors
• Vikings
• William the Conqueror

Concepts & Tactics
• raiding
• shallow-draft ships

Buildings & Transport
• drakkar
• longships
• snekkes

Deep draft

Most Norwegian longships were designed for deep fjords and Atlantic weather and typically had more draft than Danish vessels, which were designed for low coasts and beaches. As Norwegian vessels approached the shore, a lookout in the prow would watch for rocks in shallow waters.

Raiding and plundering

Used by those who went raiding and plundering, dragon ships were described as having prows carved with menacing beasts such as dragons and snakes to ward off the terrible sea monsters of Norse mythology as well as to frighten their enemies. Fore and aft castles were probably not included on this type of war vessel.

The Norman invasion of England, 1066

The grandnephew of Queen Emma of Normandy—wife of English King Ethelred the Unready and later of Danish Cnut the Great—William of Normandy was of Viking descent. He gathered a fleet of *snekke*-type longships at Saint-Valery-sur-Somme for use in his invasion of England in 1066. William's flagship was called the *Mora*.

Medieval Warships

Cogs and carracks

Bulky ships, called cogs, with two or three masts and square, as well as lateen rigged sails, were developed during the Middle Ages, although the Viking-style longship continued to see some use well into the 15th century. An oceangoing vessel with tall stern and stable deck offering an effective gun platform, the carrack was developed toward the end of the period. As ramming was impractical for these vessels, their main military purpose before the introduction of the cannon was to transport soldiers to fight on the decks of enemy ships. When the cannon appeared in the 14th century, heavier guns were placed in the waist of the vessel to be fired over or through the bulwarks and lighter pieces were in the castles at either end. The recoil caused when these weapons were fired could destabilize medieval men-of-war.

14th-century galleys

There is little difference between the warships used by Crusaders and Islamic forces in this Mediterranean sea battle of the 14th century. While cog-style vessels predominated in northern European waters, the Christian countries surrounding the Mediterranean continued to develop the Roman galley impelled by oar, assisted by the triangular lateen sail that had long been used by Arab craft. Like northern warships, they were often fitted out with castles.

Fighting platforms

When, during the Seventh Crusade in 1249, the Crusaders under Louis IX captured the city of Damietta, an important Arab commercial center in the Nile Delta, they used their warships as platforms for scaling ladders. In this engraving from the Victorian period, a chain has been stretched across the harbor entrance to prevent invading vessels passing.

See also
Artillery, *pages 296–7*

Floating castles

The hull of a medieval cog was more rounded than that of a longship or a galley, and it was slower and less maneuverable. The dominant vessel in the waters of northern Europe, they were used extensively as cargo carriers but could be fitted out with castles for self-defense or offensive purposes.

The Great Harry

The *Henri Grâce à Dieu*, or *Great Harry*, was one of the first ships of war to carry guns that fired through ports along her sides. A carrack-style vessel, she was built by order of Henry VIII at Woolwich, near London, in 1514 and was accidentally burnt in 1553. Although originally armed with 186 guns, most of these were of small caliber, although they also included a number of iron great guns.

Mary Rose ordnance

One of several pieces of ordnance recovered from the wreck of the *Mary Rose* by diver John Deane in 1836, the iron gun shown in this engraving is held today in the Tower of London collection.

Early breech-loading cannon

Cannon came into use aboard warships toward the end of the Middle Ages. Shot was rammed into the barrel while gunpowder was placed in a chamber in the breech, making these weapons predecessors of the breech-loading gun of the 19th century. The difficulty at the time of heating iron sufficiently to pour into molds resulted in gun barrels made of longitudinal wrought-iron strips that were welded together and strengthened with numerous iron rings.

Mary Rose

A firm favorite in the fleet of Henry VIII, the *Mary Rose* was built between 1509 and 1511 and was one of the first cannon-mounted ships able to fire a broadside. After long and successful service at sea she sank accidentally during an engagement with the French fleet in 1545. Her rediscovery in 1971 and raising in 1982 were seminal events in the history of nautical archaeology.

Galleons and the Armada

Race-built revolution

The galleon was a large, multidecked ship developed primarily by the English, Dutch, and Spanish between the 16th and 18th centuries. Superseding the clumsier carrack, their lower forecastle and more elongated, race-built hull made them more stable and maneuverable. They also had a squarer stern than earlier warships and a snout or head projecting forward from the bows below the forecastle. The principal warships of the English and Spanish fleets in the Armada battles of 1588 were galleons. The lighter English vessels—developed by Sir John Hawkins, Treasurer of the Queen's ships— outmaneuvered the more cumbersome Spanish carracks and larger galleons designed primarily as transports for long voyages.

▶ Sir Francis Drake

The first race-built English galleon was HMS *Revenge*, built by Matthew Baker at a cost of £4,000 at the Royal Dockyard at Deptford, near London, in 1577. A comparatively small vessel weighing about 500 tons (450 metric tons), she carried 46 guns ranged along both sides of a single gun deck. This vessel served as the flagship of Sir Francis Drake, Vice-Admiral of the English fleet during the defeat of the Spanish Armada in 1588.

● 16th-century galleons

The main features of a 16th-century galleon were a longer, narrower hull, a forecastle moved behind the protruding bowsprit, and an overhanging stern castle. This allowed vessels to sail closer to the wind. The emphasis was now on ships' improved sailing qualities, so instead of marines taking charge of the fighting, seamen sailed the ship and manned the guns, and success in battle now depended on seamanship rather than medieval naval tactics.

● Spanish Armada in crescent formation

Commanding the Spanish Armada in 1588, the Duke of Medina Sidonia formed his ships into a tightly packed, crescent-shaped formation that would enable them to mutually defend one another. Faced with superior cannon fire from the faster and more agile English galleons, this tactic was severely disrupted as the Spanish proceeded into the English Channel.

Dutch naval power

Only fifty years after becoming a free republic in 1609, the Dutch reached their golden age as a naval power with a vast trading empire in the Far East to protect. This engraving of a Dutch galleon under construction (below left) shows the high squared-tucked stern and snout, or head, projecting forward from the bows. Full-rigged vessels with square sails and bowsprit, they still carried a lateen-rigged mizzen mast. Armament consisted of two and sometimes three decks of guns.

Fireships

The threat of fire was one of the greatest hazards aboard a wooden warship, and fireships had been used with great success since ancient times. On July 28, 1588 the English sea captains ignited eight fireships and sent them downwind toward the Armada at anchor off Calais. Fearful that their vessels would be destroyed by fire, many of the Spanish captains cut their anchor cables and scattered.

See also
Artillery, *pages 296–7*

Changing shape of galleons

This vessel under construction shows the ornately carved, overhanging stern of galleons. As the tactic of boarding enemy ships was outmoded by the use of cannon, the forecastle became reduced in height and the stern castle less pronounced.

Ships of the Line

Line-of-battle tactics

The age of the ship of the line began in the 17th century with the development of warships carrying many guns capable of firing a broadside. With two, three, and even four decks carrying as many as 140 guns, these vessels were the culmination of a naval tactic known as the line of battle, in which two columns of opposing warships would bring the greatest weight of broadside guns to bear on each other. The most effective ship of the line was known as the 74, based on the number of guns it carried. Lighter and easier to maneuver in battle, it was originally developed by the French in the 1730s and was later adopted by all the great maritime powers. Larger warships with more guns were still built to serve as command ships, but they were slower to respond to the helm and were more effective in battle when they could sail in close proximity to an enemy.

HMS Ocean

The second of two Royal Navy vessels with this name, HMS *Ocean* was a 98-gun second-rate ship of the line launched at Woolwich Dockyard on October 24, 1805. Designed by Sir John Henslow, Surveyor to the Navy between 1774 and 1806, the ship was typical of the vessels that gained British supremacy at sea during the Napoleonic Wars.

Flagship of the Sun King

The *Soleil Royal* (Royal Sun) was a 104-gun ship of the line that served as the flagship of the French Navy from 1688 to 1692, when it was destroyed by English and Dutch fireships. Named after King Louis XIV, who was known as the Sun King, her decorations were among the most beautiful and elaborate of all flagships of the baroque period.

Sovereign of the Seas

The *Sovereign of the Seas* was the most magnificent ship of her era when she was launched in 1637. She carried 102 guns by order of King Charles I and was the first warship to have three full gun decks. All her guns were made from bronze instead of cast iron, which meant they were lighter but more expensive.

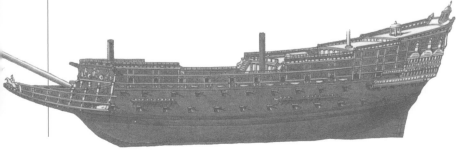

Hand weapons

Missile weapons

Defenses

Clothing

Siege of Gibraltar

In 1779 the military forces of both France and Spain laid siege to the British garrison at Gibraltar. The British endured bombardment and blockade for over three years. The most serious action of the siege took place on September 13, 1782 when an assault involving 100,000 men and numerous ships of the line was repulsed by the determined defenders.

Battle of Quiberon Bay

The Battle of Quiberon Bay took place off the coast of France near St Nazaire on November 20, 1759 during the Seven Years War. The British Admiral Sir Edward Hawke, with twenty-three ships of the line, caught up with a French fleet of twenty-one ships under Marshal de Conflans. After a short battle lasting about an hour and a half most of the French vessels were either sunk, captured, or forced aground, giving the Royal Navy one of its greatest victories.

Warriors
• French Navy
• Royal Navy

Concepts & Tactics
• blockade
• line of battle

Structure of a mast

This full-rigged French ship of the line of the Napoleonic period illustrates how masts on larger war vessels were built up to the required height using up to four sections. These were known, in order of rising height above the sea, as the lower, top, topgallant, and royal masts.

Buildings & Transport
• 74
• HMS Ocean
• Soleil Royal
• Sovereign of the Seas

See also
Anatomy of a Man-of-War,
pages 264–7

Anatomy of a Man-of-War

1 The classic man-of-war was the frigate. Designed to scout for the battle fleet and protect merchant shipping, these warships were originally developed by the French Navy but were quickly adopted by other nations. This plan of the upper gun, or spar, deck shows the layout of the vessel, with hatches and gangways either side at the ship's waist.

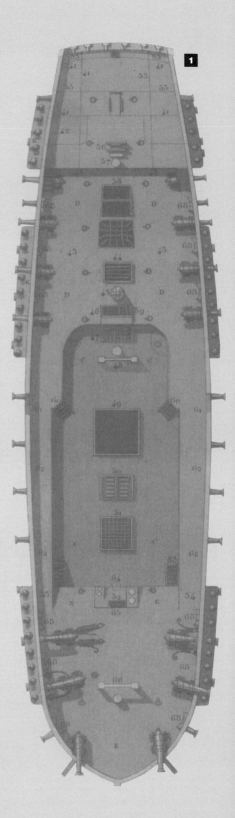

A

B

2 The various anchors used included: the grapnel anchor (*A*), which was more suitable for hard, rocky seabeds and for grappling on to an enemy vessel for boarding purposes; the mushroom anchor (*B*), which was better for a muddy seabed; and the kedge anchor (*C*), used for out-maneuvering opponents when the wind had dropped by warping, which involved throwing the anchor into the water in the direction the commander wished the vessel to steer, then all hands hauling on the rope to move the ship.

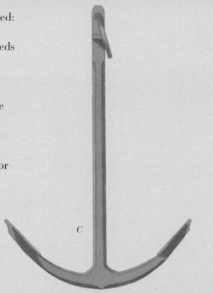

C

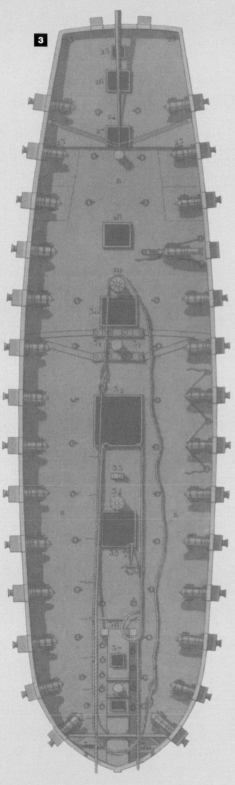

4 Part of the sails and rigging of a frigate: a topgallant sail on a topsail yardarm is seen in the center, with a gaff, or fore-and-aft sail called a spanker, either side, and pennants beneath, which were flown from the mast tops.

5 Probably invented by the Chinese in medieval times, the windlass was a winding apparatus used to raise the ship's anchor.

3 This plan of the lower, or main, gun deck illustrates the powerful broadside these vessels were capable of delivering. The cannon at the bows were known as bow-chasers because they were the only guns capable of being fired when the frigate was in pursuit of another vessel. When the vessel was being pursued, the last two cannon either side were wheeled into position in the empty gun ports as stern-chasers.

Anatomy of a Man-of-War

Key

1 Sailors on the main top	**7** The captain's cabin	**15** Hospital	**23** Prison	**A** Boats hanging in their scantlets
2 Men drying the sails	**8** The dining room	**16** Drilling the marines	**24** Shot and rigging room	**B** The stern galleries
3 Hoisting the signal flags	**9** The galley	**17** The sailors at dinner	**25** Wine and spirits room	**C** The rudder
4 Tarring the bowsprit	**10** Midshipmen's cabin	**18** Repairing the sails	**26** Powder magazine	**D** The poop
5 Lowering the water-casks through the main hatch	**11** The sailors' quarters	**19** Provision room	**27** Tackle room	**E** The hammocks
6 The surgeon examining the sick	**12** Drilling at the guns	**20** Sick-bay	**28** General store room	**F** The first battery
	13 Officers' cabin	**21** Small boat	**29** Cattle steerage	**G** The second battery
	14 Officers' mess-room	**22** Sail and rigging room		**H** The third (half) battery

17 For eating, the crew was divided into messes of twelve to fifteen individuals. The mess-cook collected each man's ration from the purser and took this to the galley in the forecastle where it was prepared by the ship's cook. Meals were then served up around the mess chest in the berth deck. Officers were allowed to stop their rations and take the value in money with which to stock their own larder.

29 The steerage contained the quarters and mess of the midshipmen, purser, and ship's clerk. The purser's stores held the ship's provisions and clothing. When ready for sea a man-of-war was supposed to have six months' supply of provisions and water, together with sails and rigging to last a lengthy cruise. Also, some vessels carried livestock for slaughter and other animals. All of this was contained in the ship's hold.

12 Seamen drilled with small arms in order to prepare to repel boarders or take part in shore expeditions. Others are at their quarters exercising the great guns of the ship.

20 The sick bay was the realm of the ship's surgeon and three assistants. Although shown here in beds, most sick sailors were expected to swing in hammocks like the rest of the crew. An open space amidships was used as a surgeon's room, or cockpit, when the ship was cleared for action.

25, 26 The ship's gunner was in charge of the powder magazine, plus shot and shell. This was usually located close to the water tanks, or "wet" stores, and was only accessible through small hatches draped with dampened canvas to reduce the danger from sparks.

7 This cross section shows the cramped layout aboard a ship of the line of the 1840s. The captain's quarters contained a cabin and pantry, and the ship's clock was usually hung above the doorway. Beneath this area was the wardroom and cabins where the other officers ate, socialized, and slept.

Ships of the Line

Life aboard a man-of-war

Daily routine aboard an early 19th-century man-of-war began with "turn to." British and American seamen awakened to the boatswain's whistle and bugle, while the French Navy used the drum and bugle. Within five minutes every man had his hammock stowed and was scrubbing the spar deck. Time aboard a warship was divided into watches and reckoned by bells, with five watches of four hours and two of two hours, called dog watches. General muster occurred once or twice a week around the capstan, when the whole crew turned out in full dress for inspection. Assembling at the guns and calling the roll took place twice a day. The crew was thoroughly exercised at the guns by division twice a week, while the whole ship was called to general quarters once a week, when the ship was cleared for action.

The view aft

Abaft, or behind, the main mast was the raised quarterdeck, where only the officers were allowed to congregate. Seen in the foreground is the ship's bell, which measured the five watches that made up a day aboard ship. A ship's cutter, or small boat, used by shore parties is mounted behind this.

The view forward

The forecastle and bowsprit with the *tricolore* can be seen at the prow of this forward-facing view on a French frigate. In the foreground, seamen can be seen manning the capstan to raise the anchor, while others are holystoning and cleaning the deck.

Carronades

The carronade was an important innovation in naval ordnance during the 18th century. Invented by the Carron Company of Scotland in 1776, it was a short, light gun capable of being mounted on the poop or forecastle, where the weight of heavier guns could not be withstood. When it was fired the recoil pushed the wooden bed back along a slide and against the breeching ropes.

Broadside gun

This 36-pounder broadside gun on a wooden truck carriage aboard a French ship of the line shows the side tackle and breeching, or stout rope, designed to absorb the recoil when the piece was fired. In practice, breeching did not pass around the gun on French ships, but went through holes in the middle of the carriage cheeks.

Ship's wheel

When under way the ship's wheel was manned by the helmsman. He was watched constantly by a petty officer known as the quartermaster, who was one of the most experienced members of the crew. The ship's compass and barometer are seen standing in front of the wheel.

Ships of the Line

The Battle of Trafalgar

The Battle of Trafalgar, fought on October 21, 1805, saw a Royal Navy fleet of twenty-seven ships of the line commanded by Admiral Lord Nelson defeat a combined French and Spanish fleet of thirty-three men-of-war under French Admiral Pierre Villeneuve. During this most decisive naval engagement of the Napoleonic Wars the French and Spanish had twenty-two ships sunk, while the British lost none, although Nelson was mortally wounded by a French sharpshooter late in the battle. Despite the fact that the British mourned the death of a national hero, this spectacular victory confirmed the supremacy established by the Royal Navy during the 18th century, and it was also a vindication of the naval tactics developed by Nelson.

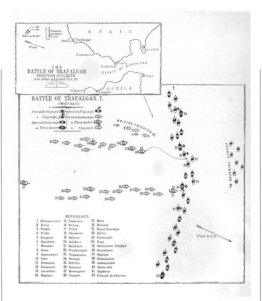

Nelson

A brilliant naval strategist who understood the practicalities of sea warfare, Nelson had already won a resounding naval victory against the French during the Battle of the Nile in 1798. His fleet fired on enemy vessels after maneuvering between their shoreward side and dangerous sand shoals.

French line of battle

The prevailing French naval tactics of the Napoleonic wars involved approaching the enemy fleet in a single line of battle and engaging in parallel lines. This was based on the late 17th-century writings of Paul Hoste, a Jesuit priest and mathematician who served as chaplain to Vice-Admiral de Tourville.

Nelson's tactics

At Trafalgar, Nelson's fleet attacked in two columns, which broke up the enemy formation and enabled the British to capture or sink the French and Spanish vessels in separate actions.

See also
**Anatomy of a
Man-of-War,** *pages
264–7*

HMS Victory
Over an hour after the enemy battle line was cut, Nelson's flagship, HMS *Victory*, seen here in the foreground on the right, locked masts with the French ship *Redoutable*, and Nelson was fatally wounded. As a French boarding party prepared to storm the *Victory*, HMS *Téméraire* approached *Redoutable* and fired on her crew, soon after which the French vessel surrendered.

Death of a hero
Although the great guns caused the most death and destruction at Trafalgar, sharpshooters aboard all vessels were also lethal once the ships closed with one another. Wearing his glittering full uniform, Nelson was easily spotted by a French sniper aboard the *Redoutable* and was mortally wounded during the closing stages of the battle.

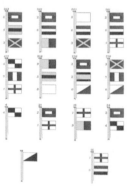

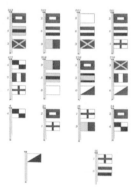

Signal flags
The ability of ships of the line to communicate clearly was essential to success in naval engagements, and much attention was paid in the late 18th century to improving systems of signaling in the Royal Navy. Codes that used the hoisting of colored flags had been used since the 16th century. The four upper columns of flags here spell out: "England expects that every man will do his duty."

The Age of Steam

The first steam ships

Although Frenchman Denis Papin invented the first ship propelled by steam power in 1704, the first steam-driven warship was built by the American Robert Fulton in 1813. Called the *Demologos*, meaning the word of the people, by its designer, the vessel was officially named the US Steam Battery *Fulton*. In 1822 the Royal Navy first utilized steam power aboard the frigate HMS *Comet*. The French led the naval arms race of the 1850s with the launch of *Le Napoléon* in 1850, which was the very first purpose-built steam battleship in the world. This vessel was also one of the first to use the screw propeller. The British warship HMS *Agamemnon* followed in 1853. In 1855 came the side-wheelers *Mississippi* and *Missouri*, the US Navy's first oceangoing steam-driven capital ships.

Vertical-beam engine

The engines used for propelling the early paddle steamers were of the side-lever type, while those using screw propellers utilized vertical-beam engines, like the one shown here. In both systems the motion of the piston rod was transmitted to the connecting rod by a beam. A triple-expansion steam engine was introduced in 1881, which was more efficient than earlier models.

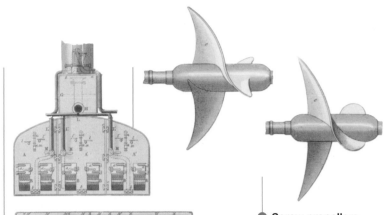

Martin boiler

Designed by the Chief Engineer of the US Navy, Daniel B. Martin, the vertical water-tube boiler was used in most American steam-propelled warships prior to the Civil War and by both sides during that conflict. These boilers were sometimes prone to explosion and could also cause terrible casualties if pierced by an enemy shell.

Screw propellers

The Bohemian engineer Josef Ressel designed and patented the first practicable screw propeller in 1827. In 1844 Swedish-born John Ericsson designed and developed the USS *Princeton*, the US Navy's first metal-hulled warship driven by screw propellers like those above.

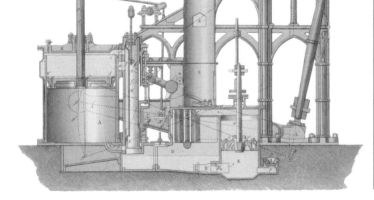

The Fulton

A catamaran-style hull with a centrally positioned paddle wheel, the *Fulton* was essentially a heavily armed and strongly built "mobile fort" for coastal defense. Launched in late October 1814, while the War of 1812 between the USA and Britain was in progress, she was completed shortly after Fulton's death in February 1815 and delivered to the US Navy in June 1816.

HMS Agamemnon

The Royal Navy commissioned steam-powered vessels such as HMS *Agamemnon* in greater numbers throughout the first half of the 19th century. At first these vessels incorporated side-wheel paddles, but by the 1830s they used screw propellers. Both types were first used extensively during the Crimean War of 1854–56.

Le Napoléon

Designed by the famous naval constructor Dupuy de Lôme, the 90-gun *Le Napoléon* was the first of a class of nine battleships built for the French Navy over a period of ten years. Still mainly dependent on their sails, steam power was intended for use only during battle and to allow ships to go to sea at will instead of being held in port by adverse winds.

Hand weapons

Missile weapons

Defenses
• mobile fort

Clothing

Warriors
• French Navy
• Royal Navy
• US Navy

Concepts & Tactics
• screw propeller
• steam power

Buildings & Transport
• metal-hulled warships
• side-wheelers
• steam-driven warships

Ironclads

The first clash

The age of the ironclad battleship began toward the end of the 1850s as a response to the development of rifled guns that used explosive shells capable of destroying wooden ships. Launched by the French navy in 1859, *La Gloire* had massive iron plates 4¾ inches (12 centimeters) thick sheathed over her wooden hull, which were capable of resisting shells of the most powerful guns of the time. The Royal Navy launched HMS *Warrior* in the following year. The first clash of ironclads occurred during the American Civil War in 1862. With limited resources, the Confederacy built a series of casemated ironclads, all of which were based on the original CSS *Virginia*. The Union Navy developed a semisubmersed Monitor-class ironclad with revolving gun turret. Both types of ironclads were unsuitable for service on the high seas.

HMS Warrior

Fully restored and berthed at Portsmouth, England, today, HMS *Warrior* was the largest and most heavily armored warship in the world when commissioned by the Royal Navy in 1861. Neither *Warrior* nor her sister ship *Black Prince* saw combat during their time of active service and within ten years were obsolete.

Battle of Hampton Roads, March 1862

Two vessels engaged each other in the four-hour Battle of Hampton Roads, but neither was seriously damaged. The *Virginia* had insufficient solid shot to inflict real damage, while the charges in the shells fired by the *Monitor* lacked the punch to penetrate the sloping armor of the *Virginia*.

The first true ironclad

The USS *Monitor* was the prototype for a series of ironclads built for the Union Navy between 1862 and 1865. Designed by John Ericsson, this revolutionary vessel carried two 11-inch (28-centimeter) Dahlgren guns in her revolving turret. Weighing 987 tons (895 metric tons), the deck of *Monitor* was mostly underwater, and she was capable of a maximum speed of only 7 knots.

Inside a Monitor gun turret

The interior of the turret of the Monitor *Passaic* shows her 11- and 15-inch (28- and 38-centimeter) Dahlgren smoothbore guns. The different size of ordnance was necessary, as the production of 15-inch guns could not initially meet the demand. The round shot in the foreground is in a hoisting sling ready to be loaded.

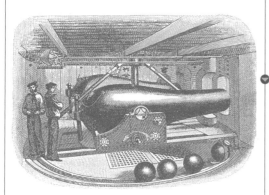

Monitor mania

The success of the original *Monitor* produced a Monitor mania in the Northern States during the Civil War, and the ship served as a prototype for numerous other vessels, including the twin-turreted *Puritan* and four- (later three-) turreted *Roanoke*. Developed in late 1864, neither of these vessels saw active service.

The Confederate ironclad Virginia

Converted from the hull of the steam frigate USS *Merrimac*—which was burnt and sunk when the Union Navy evacuated the Norfolk Navy Yard on April 20, 1861—the CSS *Virginia* was essentially a steam-powered floating gun platform with heavily armored sloping sides to deflect enemy shells.

The first ironclad battle

The *Virginia* attacked the wooden-hulled Union blockading fleet in Hampton Roads on March 9, 1862 and rammed and sank the USS *Cumberland* and grounded other vessels. The presence of the Confederate ironclad in Hampton Roads contributed to the delay and failure of the Union Peninsula Campaign to capture the Confederate capital of Richmond, Virginia.

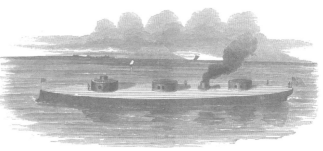

REVOLUTIONS IN
ARMS AND ARMOR

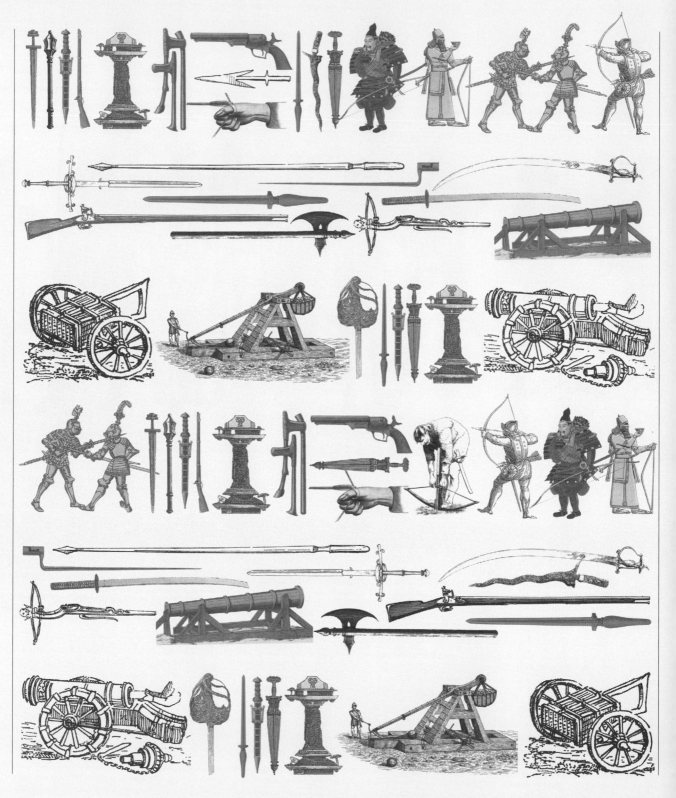

Weapons

The weapons race has challenged mankind's ingenuity, invention, and imagination since he first picked up a rock or a stick in anger, and weapons technology has been at the forefront of scientific exploration. There are conceptual leaps, such as, that from hitting someone with an object to the idea of throwing it at them, then the major leap to using mechanical means to make a throw go farther. Whether the first force-multiplier was a sling, or a blowpipe, or an *atlatl* doesn't matter. What is important is that man learned to exceed the reach of his throw while keeping himself out of harm's way.

With the invention of the bow things were taken to a whole new level, and it remained a significant weapon of war for thousands of years. The chariot-archers of Egypt and Assyria, the horse-archers from the steppes, and massed ranks of infantry bowmen in the European Middle Ages were so often decisive in battle.

Alchemists looking for the elixir of life first discovered gunpowder in 10th-century China. This explosive mixture of sulphur, carbon, and saltpeter changed the face of war for ever, although it did not immediately lead to the invention of the gun. From an early stage the Chinese used various explosive devices for war, including firework rockets attached to their arrows, but it wasn't until the 14th century that the gun was invented, and it took until the 16th century before it finally usurped the supremacy of the bow.

At closer quarters was the duel between cavalry and infantry. Cavalry attacked with lances and infantry repelled with pikes. At its peak the medieval lance evolved into a weapon of high impact. The horseman's breastplate was fitted with a hook-like bracket called an arrêt, or stop, and against this abutted a wooden flange attached to the lance. As such, man, seated in the high-backed saddle of his charger, formed a solid interlinked impact force with his horse and lance. One of the antidotes to this was the recruitment of massed professional infantry with long pikes.

However, in all war there comes the time when you have to close with the enemy in hand-to-hand combat. Clubs, maces, axes, and, of course, swords were of paramount importance. Swords, however, transcended the role of being mere weapons, and their iconic and symbolic prestige is enduring.

Swords

Hammered steel

Swords are capable of attack and defense in equal measure. As such, the blade must possess contrasting properties: the metal must be hard enough to take a sharp edge, while the core must be soft enough to not fracture on contact. Many early swords were made of bronze, which hardens by a factor of three when hammered. These were superseded by steel with the coming of the Iron Age *c.* 800 BCE. Steel is an alloy of iron and carbon, created by smelting with charcoal in a furnace. Heating and then controlling the speed of cooling changes the molecular structure of steel, which meant that steel blades could be made with an optimum construction of resilient, pliable cores and tough, hard edges. Swords were also strengthened and lightened with grooves, or fullers, and raised central ridges. The complex technology of sword manufacture ensured that they became high-status weapons and symbols of rank and prestige.

◗ Xiphos

A double-edged leaf-shaped blade used by Greek hoplites as a secondary weapon to the spear. Made of bronze, these blades were often strengthened with a central ridge.

◗ Khopesh

A characteristic early-Egyptian sword made from bronze. The cutting edge is on the outside of the curve, and the point lines up for a direct thrust with the arm. The hook at the base of the blade can be used to pull down an opponent's shield.

◗ Macahuitl

The earliest swords were made of wood. Some, like this Aztec sword, were inset with obsidian blades. The last ancient *macahuitl* was lost in a fire at the Armería Real, Madrid, in 1884.

◗ Kopis

The cutting edge is on the inside of the curve. Also known as the *machiara*, these swords were favored by Greek cavalry.

◗ Iron-Age sword

Typical of the early Iron Age, these Celtic swords were made from relatively soft steel, equivalent to wrought iron today.

Hand weapons
- Dark Age and medieval European swords
- *gladius hispaniensis*
- *khopesh*
- *kopis*
- *macahuitl*
- *xiphos*

Missile weapons

Defenses

Clothing

Warriors
- Greek hoplite
- medieval knight
- Roman legionary
- Roman centurion

Concepts & Tactics
- properties of steel

Buildings & Transport

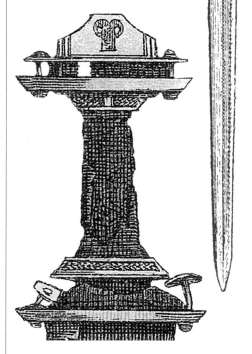

Anglo-Saxon sword, 5th–8th centuries
This image shows the hilt of an Anglo-Saxon-type sword. The blades were usually pattern-welded, when iron and steel rods were intertwined during the forging process, producing elaborate, highly prized patterns.

Arming sword, 12th–15th centuries
With its wheel pommel and simple cross guard, this single-handed sword is the classic weapon of the medieval knight.

War sword, 13th–14th centuries
From *c.* 1250 onward some swords were made larger than standard. These were called war or great swords.

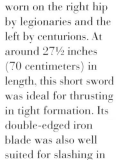

Gladius hispaniensis
The classic Roman sword, which was worn on the right hip by legionaries and the left by centurions. At around 27½ inches (70 centimeters) in length, this short sword was ideal for thrusting in tight formation. Its double-edged iron blade was also well suited for slashing in open combat.

Viking sword, 8th–11th centuries
At some stage during the 9th century, Viking smiths discovered how to forge long swords from a single billet of iron. After this, swords were manufactured in far greater numbers.

Swords

Cutting and thrusting

Medieval swords changed little from the sword of the Vikings until the second half of the 13th century, when there was a move toward increased diversity in design. Some swords were made in larger, outsize versions, while others were created in differing shapes. All were a response to continuing improvements in armor. Outside of Europe the sword developed in a range of national styles. The legendary steel of Japan was arguably matched by the wootz and Damascus steels of India and the Middle East. There has always been a debate about the relative merits of cut and thrust. Some swords were designed to be better for thrusting and others for cutting. From the early 16th century a new type of sword was created—the rapier. With its emphasis on the thrust it was designed for use in the civilian duel, but it also became a fashion item to be worn with everyday dress.

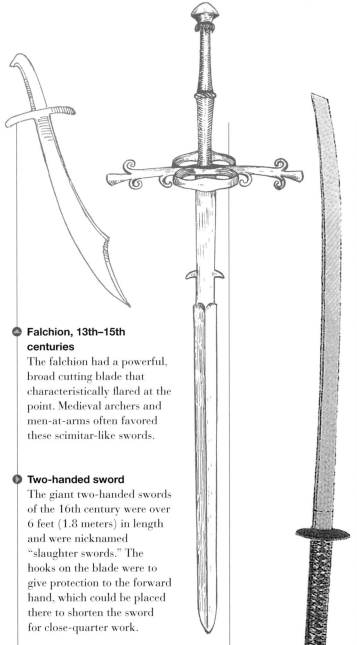

Falchion, 13th–15th centuries

The falchion had a powerful, broad cutting blade that characteristically flared at the point. Medieval archers and men-at-arms often favored these scimitar-like swords.

Two-handed sword

The giant two-handed swords of the 16th century were over 6 feet (1.8 meters) in length and were nicknamed "slaughter swords." The hooks on the blade were to give protection to the forward hand, which could be placed there to shorten the sword for close-quarter work.

Katana

This is the famed sword of the samurai. An elaborate forging process resulted in a blade with a soft, springy core wrapped with extremely hard steel, capable of taking the sharpest of edges.

Longsword, 14th–15th centuries

The extra-long grip of the longsword allowed for a powerful cutting action in a tight arc by moving both hands in opposite directions around the fulcrum of the grip.

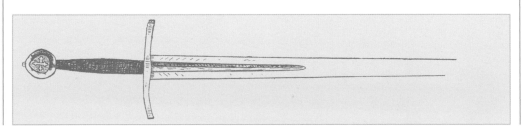

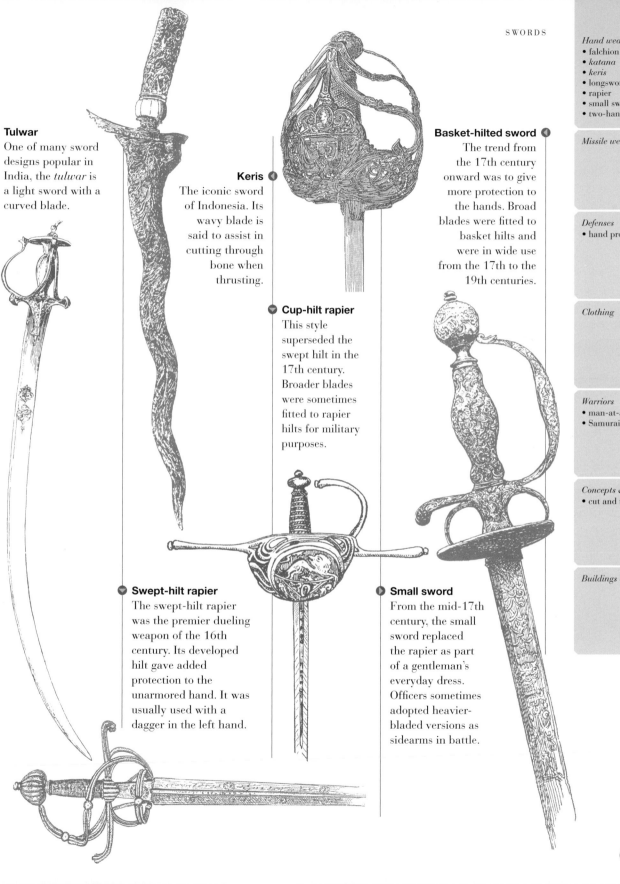

Tulwar
One of many sword designs popular in India, the *tulwar* is a light sword with a curved blade.

Keris
The iconic sword of Indonesia. Its wavy blade is said to assist in cutting through bone when thrusting.

Basket-hilted sword
The trend from the 17th century onward was to give more protection to the hands. Broad blades were fitted to basket hilts and were in wide use from the 17th to the 19th centuries.

Cup-hilt rapier
This style superseded the swept hilt in the 17th century. Broader blades were sometimes fitted to rapier hilts for military purposes.

Swept-hilt rapier
The swept-hilt rapier was the premier dueling weapon of the 16th century. Its developed hilt gave added protection to the unarmored hand. It was usually used with a dagger in the left hand.

Small sword
From the mid-17th century, the small sword replaced the rapier as part of a gentleman's everyday dress. Officers sometimes adopted heavier-bladed versions as sidearms in battle.

283

Weapons of Reach

Impact warfare

The pointed stick gave early man reach and allowed him to stay out of range of wild animals. Fitted with a head it became the spear and a basic weapon of warfare. Lighter spears were thrown, but heavier ones were used in hand-to-hand fighting, and thousands of spearsmen were employed in ancient armies. Early cavalry used spears both as a throwing weapon and as a lance. Until the 12th century it was extended on an outstretched arm, but in the early 1100s European knights started to lock their lances under the armpit in the couched position, rendering lance, man, and horse a single projectile unit and heralding a new form of impact warfare. Pole-arms proliferated during the Middle Ages. The pike dominated the battlefields of the ancient world as well as 16th- and 17th-century Europe, until the invention of the bayonet made it redundant. Weapons of reach had come full circle—the spear had been reinvented.

See also
The flintlock,
pages 186–7

Knight's lance

Lances, once embedded in the couched position, gradually became much heavier and thicker and swelled toward the counterbalancing butt. The hand grip, as in this 15th-century example (center), was shaped to soften the impact on the hand of striking a solid object.

Jousting lance

The three-pronged head of this lance (left) is called a coronel. It was designed to get maximum grip and purchase on an opponent's shield when jousting—the principal object of which was to shatter one's own lance. This one has a steel vamplate, or handguard, which was also a feature of some war lances.

Viking spear

The thrusting spear was highly regarded in Viking culture. It was the predominant battlefield weapon, ideally suited to fighting over the shield wall, where its reach was telling.

Norman cavalry spear

As shown on the Bayeux Tapestry, these spears were around 10 feet (3 meters) long. They could either be thrown or used as a lance. The transverse bar was to steady the spear-head on a stirrup and keep it away from the horse.

Persian double-headed lance

The heavy lance was not adopted in the East, where they continued a tradition of light horsemen using light lances, like this double-headed example from Persia.

Napoleonic lancer

Lances disappeared from the European battlefield from the mid-16th century to the late 18th but were reintroduced during the Napoleonic Wars. Light narrow-gauge lances were used with the advantage of reach on outstretched arms. They were not couched like the heavier medieval lances had been.

Poll-ax

This was the elite pole-arm of the medieval knight when fighting on foot. Poll is the medieval word for "head." The haft, at 5 feet (1.5 meters), was shorter than that on other pole-arms but could be used in combat both to block blows and to lever an opponent off balance.

Halberd

The halberd first evolved for use by Swiss foot soldiers facing cavalry attacks in the 14th century. It combined the advantages of the spear and the ax.

Bill

Developed from the agricultural bill, the military bill was adapted with a forward and back spike. It was a favored weapon of the common soldier in the Middle Ages.

Pike

Pikes ranged from 15¾ to 22 feet (4.8 to 6.7 meters) in length. They were used by the phalanxes of Philip of Macedon and by the armies of the English Civil War. A wall of pikes was impenetrable to cavalry. This example from the 15th century has metal strips called langets at the side to protect it from sword blows.

Spontoon

Also known as the half-pike, the spontoon was carried by officers of infantry from the late 17th to the early 19th centuries. It saw much service during the Revolutionary War in America.

Plug bayonet

Invented at some point in the 17th century, the bayonet converted a musket into a spear for close-quarter fighting. The first models plugged into the muzzle with the disadvantage that, once fitted, the gun could no longer be fired.

Socket bayonet

The socket bayonet fitted round the barrel of the musket, allowing it to remain operational as a firing weapon. It is thought to have been invented after the Battle of Killiekrankie in 1689.

Clubs, Maces, and Axes

Blows from a blunt instrument

Blunt trauma and broken bones are every bit as disabling as a sword cut or bullet wound. Hitting someone over the head with a blunt instrument is as basic as it gets, and this group of weapons begins with the elemental wooden club. Adding a stone or metal head to a haft turns a club into a mace, and such weapons have been used since the earliest times. However, maces reached their zenith in the age of plate armor. Its smooth glancing surfaces might turn a sword blade or an arrow, but a hefty strike with a blunt instrument could knock the man inside senseless or even kill him. Knights wore thickly padded garments beneath their armor to protect against such blows. Axes obviously have a terrifying ability to chop through flesh and bone, but they were also used against the armored man, utilizing the sharp edge of the blade to bite into the metal and transmit the force of the blow.

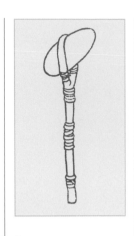

Stone mace
The tomahawk originally had a stone head. European settlers introduced the more familiar steel ax head. They were made in Sheffield, England, and then traded with the Native Americans.

Bearded ax
This common type of Saxon and Viking ax had a haft of around 19½ inches (50 centimeters) and was used single-handedly. The hanging blade could hook over and pull down an enemy's shield.

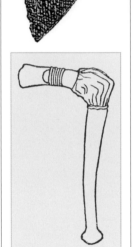

Palstave ax
This stone ax is primarily a tool, but it is thought that such tools would have been used as weapons of war during the Neolithic period.

Egyptian bronze axes
Axes and maces were the most common handheld weapons of the Egyptians during the Bronze Age, even though they had swords, spears, and other weapons.

Samoan club
This palm-wood club from Samoa is typical of the earliest types of concussive weapons.

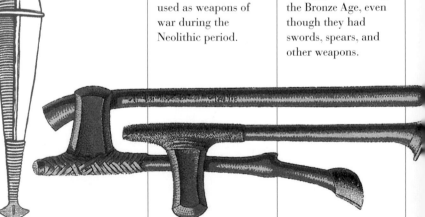

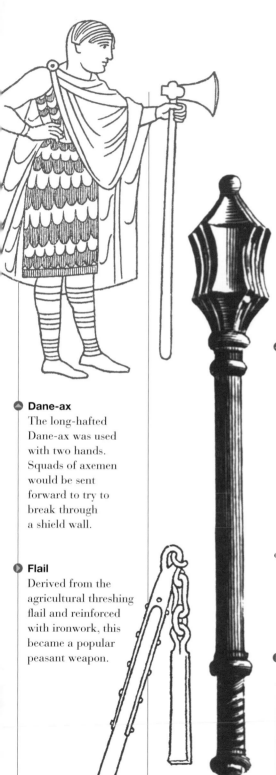

War hammer
Another horseman's favorite, the war hammer was designed to attack full plate armor.

Spiked mace
With the inception of plate armor, maces developed sharp spikes in order to gain purchase on glancing surfaces and transfer the shock to the man within.

Battle-ax
This type of ax was carried by mounted knights in the 14th and 15th centuries. The primary function of the ax blade was to gain purchase on the smooth surfaces of plate armor and transmit blunt trauma.

Flanged mace
A common type of 15th-century mace had flanges instead of spikes. This meant it could be hung from the saddle without troubling the horse.

Articulated mace
These weapons were popular with horsemen during the Middle Ages and were a combination of the mace and the flail.

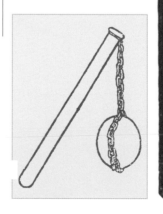

Dane-ax
The long-hafted Dane-ax was used with two hands. Squads of axemen would be sent forward to try to break through a shield wall.

Flail
Derived from the agricultural threshing flail and reinforced with ironwork, this became a popular peasant weapon.

Thrown Weapons

Early missiles

The earliest weapons were a thrown stick or stone—other primates are also known to pick up items and throw them at marauders—and simple rocks continued to be used right through the Middle Ages; for example, being thrown down from castle ramparts during a siege. The sling gave mechanical advantage to the thrower's arm, and stones could be launched with great accuracy and range. By the time of the Greeks, lead slingshot were being moulded to give consistency to the weight and shape of the missile. The most developed throwing spear was the Roman *pilum*. It had weight in its heavy wooden haft. The conical head was designed to pierce a shield and its shank was long enough to reach the man behind. Stuck in the shield the soft-iron shank would bend under the weight of the haft, rendering the shield useless.

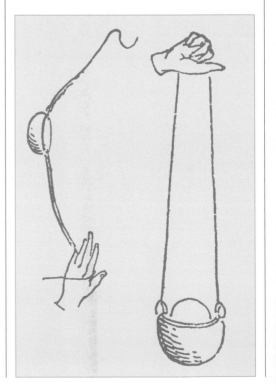

Fustibal
Staff slings (above left) were used at sieges on land. However, their main use was at sea, to throw earthenware pots of Greek fire on to enemy ships.

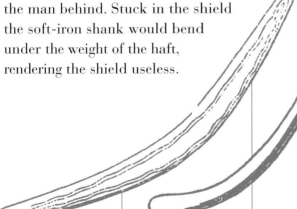

Boomerang
The Australian aboriginal boomerang appears in diverse forms, not all of which return. Used primarily in hunting, it can also be used in war.

Egyptian throw stick
Many of these survive in tombs. They had a more rounded cross-section than the boomerang and are shown in Egyptian art being used both for hunting and war.

Sling
Egyptians, Greeks, Romans, and other armies of the ancient world all relied heavily on slingers. They formed frontline skirmishers while the main army formed up.

Norman throwing mace

This scene from the Bayeux Tapestry depicts a throwing mace. They are believed to have been stones bound on to sticks.

Knobkerrie

Made of hard wood, this Zulu throwing stick could also be used as a mace.

Javelin

Short throwing spears, or javelins, were a mainstay of all armies up until the Middle Ages and were used both by infantry and cavalry.

Pilum

This is the throwing spear of the Roman legionary. A legionary carried two—one heavy and one light.

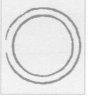

Chakram

The Sikh battle quoit had razor-sharp outer edges and was either thrown Frisbee-style or twirled around the index finger.

Hunga munga

African throwing knives appear in a variety of styles, but most have at least three blades of differing shape and size.

Francisca

Fitted with a short handle about a foot (30 centimeters) long, these throwing axes were usually used in pairs by Frankish and Saxon warriors. They were thrown at short range when closing with the enemy.

Hand grenade

Hand grenades were known in China as early as the 10th century. Basically small fused bombs, the grenade gained widespread use in Europe during the late 17th and 18th centuries and played an important role in the trench warfare of the First World War.

Bows

Deadly springs

The Holmegaard Bow, discovered in a peat bog in Denmark, is approximately nine thousand years old and is the oldest known surviving example of a bow. However, bows are likely to be significantly older than that, as arrowheads dating from twenty-five thousand years ago have been found in Africa. Different regions used different materials to make the bow, which is really just a large spring that can store and release energy. In temperate climes, where trees full of sap and springiness grew, bows were made of wood. In more arid conditions, where trees are either scarce or the wood is dry, composite materials were used. Horn, which resists compression, was bonded to sinew, which resists tension, and formed over a wooden core to make powerful bows. Bows were most effective on the battlefield when used at short range in massed volleys or with the hit-and-run tactics of chariot- and horse-archers.

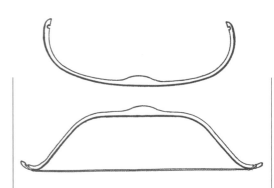

Turkish composite recurve bow
Made with horn and sinew laid on a wooden core, bows made from composite materials can be pre-stressed into recurved shapes, thus storing energy. Bows like this were the principal weapon of horse-archers.

Thumb ring
All cultures that used composite recurved bows also used a thumb ring. Most were of the shape shown here, although Chinese thumb rings were cylindrical.

Flat bow
With limbs of a flat cross section, such bows are known from the Neolithic period and were also favored by various tribal populations, including Native North Americans.

The angular bow
Used by the Egyptians, Hittites, and Assyrians, this was the chariot bow par excellence of the late Bronze Age. When unstrung it resembles a flattened W, when strung it forms a triangle, and when drawn it makes a perfect arc.

Thumb release
The base of the thumb ring hooks over the string and is then locked into position by bending the thumb and placing the index finger over it. When using a thumb ring the arrow sits on the right-hand side of the bow.

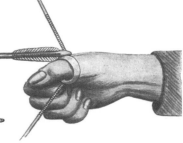

Chinese recurve bow
Many recurve bows—such as the Chinese, Tatar, Hunnic, and Persian—had extensions to the limbs called siyahs to accelerate the string return.

Japanese bow
Made of bamboo box section around a mulberry-wood core, then lacquered and bound with rattan, the Japanese bow was asymmetrical, with the bottom limb half the size of the upper. Bows were the principal weapon of mounted samurai.

English longbow
The best longbows were made from yew, but ash, elm, and other woods were also used. Although made from a single material, longbows could be slightly recurved by heating.

Arrowheads
(*1*) Barbed broadheads such as these were flesh-cutters and used primarily against cavalry. (*2*) Narrow, needlelike arrowheads were called bodkins. They were designed to punch through armor. (*3*) Incendiary arrows were used in sieges and naval warfare from at least the Roman period. During the Middle Ages they were made by filling a linen bag with gunpowder that had been made into a paste by soaking it in brandy. This was packed around the arrow and sealed with resin.

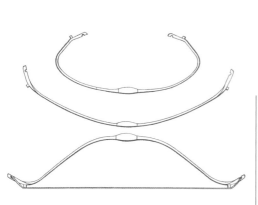

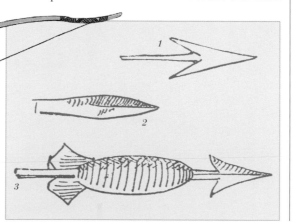

Hand weapons

Missile weapons
• angular bow
• composite bow
• flat bow
• Japanese bow
• longbow
• recurve bow

Defenses

Clothing

Warriors
• Assyrians
• Egyptians
• Hittites
• Native Americans
• Samurai

Concepts & Tactics
• hit-and-run

Buildings & Transport

Crossbows

The bow's power increases

The first crossbows had simple wooden prods, or bows, of up to 200 pounds (91 kilograms) draw weight. The string was hooked over a protruding peg, which was lowered when the trigger lever was operated. After the Crusades, Europeans discovered the power of the composite horn-and-sinew bow, and crossbows of much greater power were produced. Because of the increased tension on the peg and string, the rolling nut was developed. As crossbows became increasingly powerful they needed mechanical assistance to draw the string. As the mechanisms improved, so the power of the bows increased. During the 1600s advances in steel production saw high-tensile steel prods, producing the most powerful bows of all with draw weights of 1,500 pounds (680 kilograms) or more.

Belt and claw

The crossbowman places his foot in a stirrup at the front of the bow and hooks the string on to a claw attached to a belt. He can then use the power of his legs to span the bow.

Cord and pulley

In this system a cord was affixed to the butt of the crossbow at one end and to the man's belt at the other. A hook on the pulley attached to the string. It gave a power advantage of 2:1.

Wooden crossbow

This 19th-century drawing shows the bow with a rolling nut; more accurately, it should be a peg. Correctly, though, the man is spanning his hefty wooden crossbow by placing two feet on the bow part. With powerful bows the man would usually sit on the ground to do this.

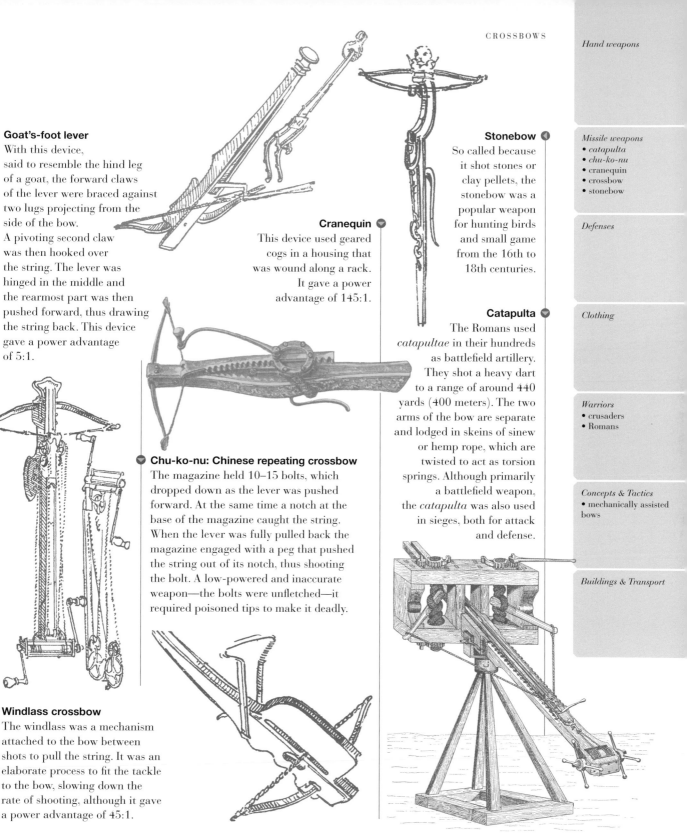

Goat's-foot lever

With this device,
said to resemble the hind leg
of a goat, the forward claws
of the lever were braced against
two lugs projecting from the
side of the bow.
A pivoting second claw
was then hooked over
the string. The lever was
hinged in the middle and
the rearmost part was then
pushed forward, thus drawing
the string back. This device
gave a power advantage
of 5:1.

Cranequin

This device used geared
cogs in a housing that
was wound along a rack.
It gave a power
advantage of 145:1.

Stonebow

So called because
it shot stones or
clay pellets, the
stonebow was a
popular weapon
for hunting birds
and small game
from the 16th to
18th centuries.

Catapulta

The Romans used
catapultae in their hundreds
as battlefield artillery.
They shot a heavy dart
to a range of around 440
yards (400 meters). The two
arms of the bow are separate
and lodged in skeins of sinew
or hemp rope, which are
twisted to act as torsion
springs. Although primarily
a battlefield weapon,
the *catapulta* was also used
in sieges, both for attack
and defense.

Chu-ko-nu: Chinese repeating crossbow

The magazine held 10–15 bolts, which
dropped down as the lever was pushed
forward. At the same time a notch at the
base of the magazine caught the string.
When the lever was fully pulled back the
magazine engaged with a peg that pushed
the string out of its notch, thus shooting
the bolt. A low-powered and inaccurate
weapon—the bolts were unfletched—it
required poisoned tips to make it deadly.

Windlass crossbow

The windlass was a mechanism
attached to the bow between
shots to pull the string. It was an
elaborate process to fit the tackle
to the bow, slowing down the
rate of shooting, although it gave
a power advantage of 45:1.

Siege Engines

Assault and battery

There were four main ways to besiege a castle or fortified town. One was to surround it and starve the occupants out, although this could take many months. A second was to undermine the walls by digging a sap or mine. When the mine passed under the wall it was braced with pit props, and a larger chamber created under the wall and supported with timber frames. A fire was laid to burn through the timbers and collapse the wall. The third was escalade, which meant going over the top of the walls with ladders and towers, an extremely hazardous undertaking. The fourth method was to batter down the walls with a battering ram or with great rock-flinging engines. These became so large that they had to be constructed on site. It was common to give these mighty engines a nickname. King Richard I called one of his "Bad Neighbor" and Edward I had one called "Warwolf."

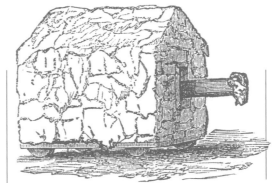

See also
Anatomy of a *ballista*, *pages 58–9*

Anatomy of an *onager*, *pages 62–3*

Siege engine technology, *pages 112–13*

Anatomy of a Trebuchet, *pages 114–15*

Battering ram

A heavy baulk of timber was suspended from the frame and swung on ropes. The wheeled ram was either pushed up to the wall or gateway by the men inside or a post was staked into the ground near its destination and the battering ram winched forward on ropes. It is covered with wet hides to prevent it being set alight with incendiary arrows or pots of Greek fire.

Mangonel

The mangonel was a much more powerful rock-hurling machine and of much greater size. Its throwing arm was wedged into massive skeins of twisted rope and was then winched back by levers.

Ballista

The Roman ballista worked on the same torsion principle as the *catapulta* (*see page 293*), with separate bow arms lodged into twisted skeins of rope. It shot rocks and stones as opposed to the darts of the *catapulta*.

Siege tower

Siege towers were built for escalade as a more defendable way of scaling the walls. Troops made their way up a series of ladders inside the tower and then streamed across a gangplank on to the enemy walls. The bottom tier was often equipped with a battering ram.

Counterweight trebuchet

The counterweight basket was filled with rocks, and the amount of ballast could be adjusted to alter range. Various means were used to lower the arm, including levers, winches, and pulleys. Some of the larger trebuchets were fitted with treadmills to operate the winding gear. An alternative to the counterweight was the traction trebuchet, which, instead of using a counterweight, employed dozens of men to pull simultaneously on ropes.

Counterweight trebuchet in action

In addition to the tremendous force of the counterweight moving the arm, there is a sling at the end, which effectively increases the length of the arm.

Siege crossbow

This image shows a giant siege crossbow that used stone shot, after a design by Leonardo da Vinci. The scale seems almost too fantastic, but certainly outsize crossbows were constructed for use in sieges.

Spring engine

Several medieval manuscripts portray engines like this, although there is no known account of their actual use.

Artillery

Technological advances

The first depiction of gunpowder artillery can be found in a 1327 manuscript written for Edward III. The gun was made of bronze and shaped like a vase with a short barrel. Within a few decades longer-barreled iron guns were being made. Staves of iron were laid around a wooden core and welded together. The wooden core was then burned out. To prevent the staves from splitting apart under pressure they were bound together by iron hoops. This was the same method as coopering a barrel, hence it became known as the barrel of a gun. The development of cast iron at the end of the 15th century allowed guns to be cast and then have the bore drilled out. It also paved the way for the introduction of iron shot; previously cannonballs were made from stone. Breech loading and rifling were two other major technical breakthroughs that improved the efficiency, power, and accuracy of artillery.

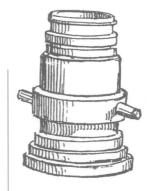

Mortar
A mortar is a short-barreled artillery piece designed to shoot large balls with a high trajectory. It was mainly used in sieges.

Ribauld
The ribauld or organ gun had multiple barrels. This 15th-century example has forty. Such pieces continued to be used until the 17th century.

Hoop-and-stave bombard
Bombard was the name given to early cannon. They had to be set up on a wooden frame and shot from a fixed position. The round shot was of stone—cast iron was not developed until the end of the 15th century.

Wheeled artillery
This 15th-century version of a bombard shows it mounted on a wheeled carriage and with a mechanism that allows it to be elevated.

Breech-pot cannon
The small vessel on the ground by this 15th-century gun is a breech pot. It was filled with black powder and then inserted at the breech end.

Hand weapons

Missile weapons
- bombard
- breech-loading cannon
- breech-pot cannon
- howitzer
- naval cannon
- rifled cannon

Defenses

Clothing

Warriors

Concepts & Tactics
- breech-loading
- rifling

Buildings & Transport

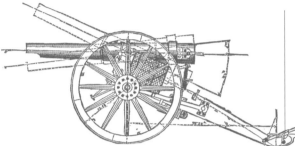

Breech-loading cannon

By the 16th century it was possible to have a fully breech-loading cannon. From this time on artillery played an ever-increasing role and was manufactured in a wide variety of sizes and calibers.

Howitzer

A howitzer was a large piece of artillery, part-mortar and part-cannon, capable of shooting with a parabolic trajectory. This example is from the 1840s, but such guns were known from the 18th century and used against field fortifications.

Rifled cannon

The American Civil War saw the extensive use of cannon with rifled barrels, which delivered increased power, range and accuracy. The Parrot 100-pounder had a range of 5 miles (8 kilometers), although there was no method of aiming over that distance.

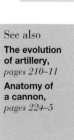

Naval cannon

Muzzle-loaded naval cannon had to be wheeled into the gun deck for loading and then the muzzle pushed out of the porthole for firing.

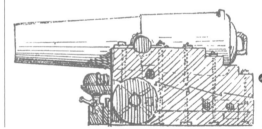

Different types of shot

(1) Case shot. Small balls were packed in a canister; when the shot was fired the balls spread in the manner of a shotgun blast. In the Middle Ages it was housed in a wooden casing and called lantern shot. (2) Chain shot. An anti-personnel shot that spun as it left the barrel. (3) Round shot. The standard shot for artillery, it was powerful against both fortifications and ship's hulls. (4) Bar shot. Antipersonnel shot that behaved in an identical way to chain shot.

See also
The evolution of artillery, *pages 210–11*
Anatomy of a cannon, *pages 224–5*

Handheld Firearms

From matchlock to Minié

By the end of the 14th century, iron tubes with a plug at one end and a touch-hole were being mounted on wooden stocks and used as handheld guns. They were muzzle-loading using loose powder and ball, ignited with a handheld match. It was an awkward procedure, but they were reasonably effective. Improvements came with the matchlock mechanism. A piece of burning matchcord was held in the jaws of a lever, which was lowered by a trigger lever. It meant the gun could be held with two hands and longer barrels became possible. The wheel-lock, flintlock, and percussion-lock all advanced the technology, but the biggest change came in the 19th century with the introduction of rifling and the Minié bullet, which allowed guns to be loaded quickly and fired over much greater distances.

Hackbut

Matchlock guns such as this, with a trigger lever, first appeared in the 15th century. Hackbut refers to the hook at the front, which sits over a rampart wall or a type of gunners' shield called a pavise, to steady the recoil.

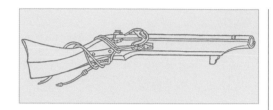

Arquebus

By the 16th century these matchlock guns were known as arquebuses. They had long barrels that gave added accuracy and range but which necessitated them being used with a rest.

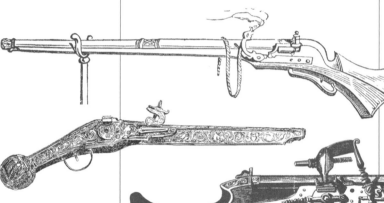

Wheel-lock pistol

This ingenious mechanism meant that a gun could be carried loaded and ready to fire, which made it ideal for cavalry. It led to the development of a compact version—the pistol—and 16th-century cavalry would often carry up to six loaded pistols in saddle holsters and the tops of their boots.

Close-up of wheel-lock mechanism

The wheel-lock was invented *c.* 1530. The serrated steel wheel was wound up by a clockwork mechanism and a piece of iron pyrites held against it by means of a lever. When the trigger was pulled, the priming-pan opened and the wheel revolved, generating a spark from the pyrites.

Pole-gun

The earliest type of hand-held firearms, like this pole-gun, remained in use well into the 15th century. The touchhole was ignited by a match or hot wire held in the hand not supporting the gun.

See also
Anatomy of a matchlock, *pages 158–9*

Anatomy of the flintlock, *pages 188–9*

The rifle-musket, *pages 216–17*

Anatomy of a repeating rifle and carbine, *pages 236–7*

Anatomy of a Colt revolver, *pages 240–1*

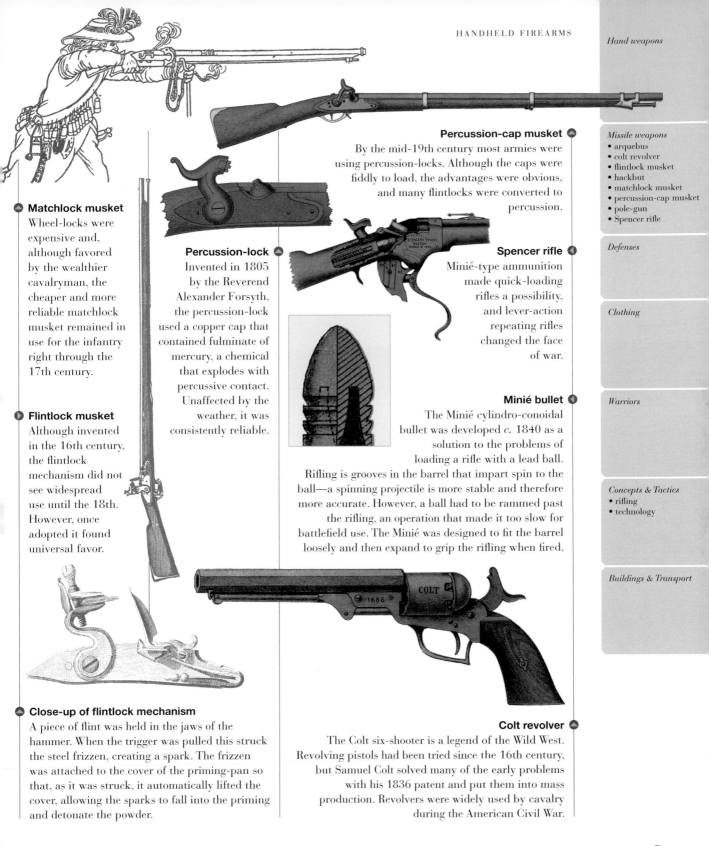

Matchlock musket
Wheel-locks were expensive and, although favored by the wealthier cavalryman, the cheaper and more reliable matchlock musket remained in use for the infantry right through the 17th century.

Flintlock musket
Although invented in the 16th century, the flintlock mechanism did not see widespread use until the 18th. However, once adopted it found universal favor.

Percussion-lock
Invented in 1805 by the Reverend Alexander Forsyth, the percussion-lock used a copper cap that contained fulminate of mercury, a chemical that explodes with percussive contact. Unaffected by the weather, it was consistently reliable.

Percussion-cap musket
By the mid-19th century most armies were using percussion-locks. Although the caps were fiddly to load, the advantages were obvious, and many flintlocks were converted to percussion.

Spencer rifle
Minié-type ammunition made quick-loading rifles a possibility, and lever-action repeating rifles changed the face of war.

Minié bullet
The Minié cylindro-conoidal bullet was developed *c.* 1840 as a solution to the problems of loading a rifle with a lead ball. Rifling is grooves in the barrel that impart spin to the ball—a spinning projectile is more stable and therefore more accurate. However, a ball had to be rammed past the rifling, an operation that made it too slow for battlefield use. The Minié was designed to fit the barrel loosely and then expand to grip the rifling when fired.

Close-up of flintlock mechanism
A piece of flint was held in the jaws of the hammer. When the trigger was pulled this struck the steel frizzen, creating a spark. The frizzen was attached to the cover of the priming-pan so that, as it was struck, it automatically lifted the cover, allowing the sparks to fall into the priming and detonate the powder.

Colt revolver
The Colt six-shooter is a legend of the Wild West. Revolving pistols had been tried since the 16th century, but Samuel Colt solved many of the early problems with his 1836 patent and put them into mass production. Revolvers were widely used by cavalry during the American Civil War.

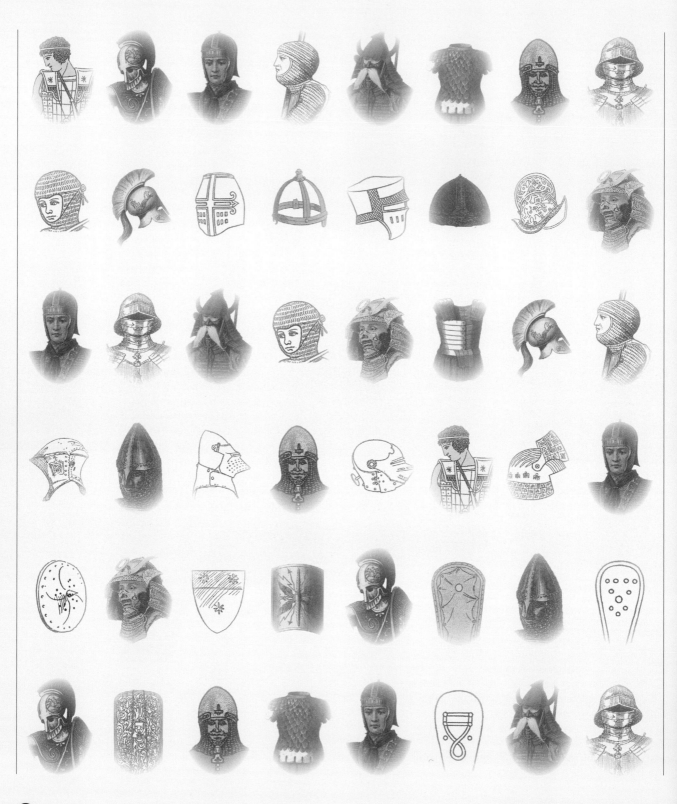

Armor

All armor is designed to provide protection against the weapons of its day; if it were not there would be no point in wearing it. So the answer to age-old questions, such as, whether plate armor could withstand the impact of an arrow is that it depends on the range from which it was shot, the type of head, the power of the bow, the angle at which it strikes the glancing surface of the armor, and, above all, the quality of the armor, something that varied a great deal. Medieval armorers perfected the art of hardening steel to a very high standard of proof, but such armor was only available to the wealthiest of patrons. Most men-at-arms had to make do with armor of a lower specification, which was adequate, and a soldier certainly was safer wearing it than not, but it might not withstand a direct strike at close range.

Wearing armor had its disadvantages. It was time-consuming to put on and there was additional weight to bear. But it was not as heavy as people might suppose—a man could run, ride, and fight in it—but it was none the less more tiring than not wearing it. It was also very hot because all armor required thick padding to be worn beneath the metal skin.

Different cultures took different views about how much to compromise mobility. The Greeks wore armor only on the thorax, head, and lower legs, while the Romans didn't protect the legs with armor at all, opting instead to carry very large shields. Helmets, the most important part of any armor, had three potential disadvantages. If the ears are covered, hearing is dulled, an effect exaggerated by the ambient noise of clanking armor. If the face is covered there is an inevitable impact on ventilation, and it was important to be able to breathe freely when fighting hard and bearing the weight and heat of armor. Most critically there is vision. In combat, peripheral vision was as important as seeing straight ahead, and any helm that offers any protection to the face will compromise that to some extent.

The solutions to these irreconcilable problems have been the quest of armorers through the ages. The choices they made were determined by climate, the materials and manufacturing techniques available, and the level of threat by the weapons of the day—and the results can tell us a great deal about the nature of warfare at any given time.

Body Armor

The science of protection

All body armor is a trade-off between providing protection and minimizing the debilitating effects of excess weight, heat, and restricted movement. Over time armorers have sought to solve these problems. Armor became a medium for artistic expression, its surfaces a canvas for artistic display, with fluting, etching, gilding, and other decorations—and the best armor indicated very high status. The metallic outer skin—mail or plate—was only part of an armor's defense, designed to deflect blows. It was the thickly padded arming clothes beneath that performed the crucial job of absorbing shock. It was the unique achievement of European armorers in the 15th century to fabricate plates of steel large enough to make full plate armor. All other cultures continued to use small plates joined together.

Roman lorica squamata
Another form of Roman armor had leaf-shaped scales of iron sewn on to a linen tunic. Scale armor like this, of bronze, had been in use since at least the time of Middle-Kingdom Egypt.

Hoplite armor
Hoplites remained lightly armored troops but wore a shaped bronze muscle-cuirass covering the thorax and bronze greaves for the lower legs, which could be especially vulnerable behind the shield.

Roman lorica hamata
Roman auxiliaries wore tunics of mail, which was a light and extremely flexible defense.

Roman lorica segmentata
This became the standard Roman legionary armor. It had flexible bands of plate and was both light and effective.

Greek linothorax
The *linothorax* was used during the Mycenaean and Classical periods to counteract the worst of fighting in the heat. It was made from multiple layers of linen glued together, and it gave surprisingly effective protection.

Hand weapons

Missile weapons

Defenses

Clothing
• brigandine
• *linothorax*
• mail armor
• plate armor
• Samurai armor

Warriors
• cuirassier
• hoplite
• knight
• Roman legionary
• Samurai

Concepts & Tactics
• artistic expression
• steel technology

Buildings & Transport

Mail armor
By the 13th century a knight could be covered from head to toe in mail.

Close-up of mail
Mail is a web of interlocked rings, each closed with a rivet. It should not be called chain mail, because a chain links single rings one on one.

Semi-plate, 14th century
From the mid-13th century mail was gradually augmented with plate defenses. These were visible externally on the joints. Additionally, a coat of plates—a poncho-type garment covering the thorax in large plates—was worn beneath the cloth surcoat.

Full plate, 15th-century German Gothic style
It was not until the second half of the 15th century, toward the end of the Middle Ages, that the "knight in shining armor" emerged. Improved steel manufacture produced armor of exceptional hardness. The armor was given additional strength by carefully worked shapes, which meant that the plates could be relatively thin.

Brigandine
Iron plates of around 1 square inch (6.5 square centimeters) were sewn on to fabric or leather to produce a flexible coat. Popular among light troops, it survived into the 16th century to be worn by the conquistadores.

17th-century cuirassier
Although armor was in major decline because of the increased use of more efficient firearms, three-quarter armors like this were in use by some heavy cavalry until the end of the 17th century.

Samurai armor
Samurai armor was made from small plates that were laced together with silk cords. The steel was lacquered to protect it from the damp climate. Full Japanese armor was only slightly lighter than its European counterpart.

Helmets

The warrior's crowning glory

The head needs protection more than any other part of the body, and this was addressed by wearing helms, which cover the whole head, or helmets, which came down no lower than the line of the ears. Most helms tended to be thicker over the crown than the sides because bearing too much weight on the head can cause its own problems. As with armor, it was essential for a helm to be well padded for it to be effective. At times when lance warfare or archery have been more prevalent, more face protection was evident, but this, in turn, was a trade-off against being able to breathe freely—vital when exerting yourself in combat—and being able to see clearly. Perfect protection always compromises something, and one of the biggest problems of wearing a helm was that it impaired hearing.

Spangenhelm
A popular form of European helmet from the 5th to 9th centuries, the spangenhelm had a metal framework into which leather or steel plates were fitted.

Nasal helm
The nasal bar gave good protection against slashing strokes across the face, while the conical crown defended against blows from swords or clubs by creating a glancing surface. The lower face was protected by padded mail.

Corinthian helm
The helm of the Greek hoplites, with its characteristic horsehair panache, was made from beaten bronze.

Full-face helm
Following the adoption of couched-lance techniques for mounted warfare at the end of the 11th century, full-face protection was developed for helms in the 12th century.

Great helm
By the 13th century the helm had become fuller and was often fastened to the chest and back by means of straps.

Cervelliere
This steel skullcap laced to the mail coif was worn underneath the great helm.

Hand weapons

Missile weapons

Defenses

Clothing
• armet
• cerveilliere
• combed morion
• Corinthian helm
• frogmouth helm
• full-face helm
• great helm
• kettle hat
• sallet
• Samurai helm
• spangenhelm

Warriors

Concepts & Tactics

Buildings & Transport

Houndskull Bascinet

This type of helm became popular in the 14th century and was a response to the increased use of battlefield archery. Vision is quite restricted as the sights sit some way forward of the eyes.

Frogmouth helm

This type of helm, with its angled vision and sturdy construction that sat on the shoulders, was used for jousting.

Sallet

The sallet (helm) and bevor (throat guard) was a two-piece head protection common with German armors of the 15th century. The visor could either be hinged, as here, or fixed. The word bevor stems from the French *baver*, to dribble.

Armet

This style of helm was more common with Italian armors of the 15th century. It gave extremely good face protection.

Kettle hat

A popular helmet for the infantry man-at-arms in the 15th century, this was especially well designed for those besieging a castle.

Combed morion

This was a style typical of the open-faced helm worn by conquistadores in the 16th century and pikemen in the 17th.

Samurai helm

The *kabuto* has a distinctively wide flare to the plates that protect the neck. It is adorned with elaborate clan crests and is often worn in conjunction with the *mempo*—a grotesque face mask—to strike terror into the enemy.

Shields

Protection and identity

From the earliest times shields were a symbol of personal identity and honor. There is the story of the Spartan mother who said to her son, "Either come back with your shield or on it," a reference to the custom of bearing a fallen warrior on his shield. It would have been a disgrace for him to lose it in battle. Apart from personal protection, a shield displayed the warrior's identity. It was a large surface suitable for decoration. In hero cultures, such as Sparta, individual warriors had their own emblems; in collective cultures —the Romans, for example—shield emblazons were of a uniform pattern identifying the legion. The most elaborate system of heraldry grew up in medieval Europe, partly as a response to the problems of identifying knights behind a full-face helm. Wood and leather have been the most common materials for constructing shields. Together they make a strong, lightweight composite that is good at resisting shock.

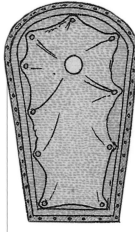

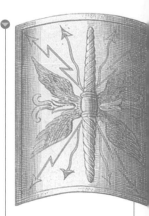

Hoplite shield ◉
Hoplon is a Greek word for shield, and so the Greek elite infantry became known as hoplites, or shield-bearers. Their shields were usually of wicker construction covered with hide. The *parablemata* was a leather apron that was sometimes attached to the bottom of the shield to offer added protection to the legs.

◉ **Egyptian shield**
Used widely by the massed ranks of Egyptian infantry, their shields were constructed by gluing and pegging wooden boards together and then covering them with animal hide.

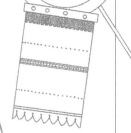

Scutum ◉
The classic shield of the Roman legionary had only a single handhold in the center. Shields were carried on the march and protected from the elements with a leather shield cover.

Saxon and Viking shields ◉
From the 7th to the 11th centuries, the principal battlefield tactic of the Anglo-Saxons and then the Vikings was to form a shield wall. They stood shoulder to shoulder and several ranks deep with interlocked shields. Their wooden shields were circular with an iron central boss.

⬤ Norman kite shield
Carried diagonally, the elongated tail of the kite shield offered some protection from missiles to a horse's flank when turning the animal in front of the enemy line.

⬤ Sword-and-buckler fighting, 13th century
Sword-and-buckler fighting was a popular martial art in its own right, especially among apprentices in London, who would gather at Smithfield for bouts. As they swaggered rowdily home, their bucklers hung over their hilts, they acquired the nickname swashbucklers.

Buckler ⬤
A buckler was a small metal hand shield. It was used to deflect blows with punching parries and also as an offensive fist. Widely used in the ancient world, it reached the height of its popularity during the later Middle Ages. Bucklers were in use as civilian weapons up until the end of the 16th century.

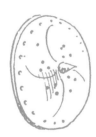

⬤ Heater shield
The Victorians gave this classic knight's shield its name, deriving it from the shape of the sole plate on a pressing iron, known as a heater. It was made of wood with a leather or linen facing.

⬤ Ecranche shield
Used for jousts and battle, the lance rests in the cutaway section and the concave shape minimizes the risk of lance strikes glancing up toward the face.

⬤ Pavise
Used by crossbowmen and, later, by handgunners, this large shield was propped on the ground and acted as a screen while they reloaded their weapons.

⬤ Targe
Although shields were largely redundant by 1500, the simple round shield—called a rondache, target, or targe—survived for some light troops. The targe was used well into the 18th century in Scotland.

Timeline 3000 BCE to 1865 CE

c. 3000 BCE

Invention of the wheeled vehicle in the form of an ox-cart.

Ox-Cart

2686–2181 BCE

The Old Kingdom in ancient Egypt: construction of the pyramids.

2040–1786 BCE

The Middle Kingdom in ancient Egypt: raids on neighboring territories using improved weaponry and tactics.

c.1650 BCE

Introduction of the horse-drawn chariot lends mobility to Bronze Age warfare.

c.1000 BCE

Appearance of the first disciplined infantry units, the first trained cavalry groups, and the first organized and effective siege trains, using Iron Age technology.

Assyrian royals and infantry

727 BCE

Death of Assyrian ruler Tiglath-Pileser III, who united Assyria and Babylonia to create the very first centralized empire which, within a further century, would include Egypt.

550 BCE

Cyrus overthrows the Median ruler of what is now Iran and founds the Achaemenid dynasty, rulers of the Persian empire.

264–241 BCE

First Punic War fought between Roman and Carthaginian navies: the Romans lost, despite having prepared a fleet of ships copied from an advanced Carthaginian model.

The Punic Wars

476 CE

End of the western Roman empire, which is followed by two centuries of Dark Ages.

793

Sack of the monastery of Lindisfarne (north-eastern England) by the Vikings.

800

Coronation of Charlemagne as "Roman Emperor" by the Pope. The culture may be feudal and involve military service, but Charlemagne also encourages learning from Latin texts, and the Carolingian Renaissance begins.

1066

The Norman conquest of England begins: William of Normandy invades, using a fleet of Viking longships of the smaller type called *snekkes*.

Snekkes

1227

Death of Genghis Khan, uniter of Mongol tribes into a powerful military force which initially relies on supreme horsemanship but later adapts instantly and successfully to methods of warfare learned from conquered peoples.

Genghis Khan

1240–1241

The Mongols invade Europe, bringing with them gunpowder technology they have encountered while occupying parts of China.

13th century

Typhoons described as *kamikaze* twice foil Mongol invasions of Japan.

1410

Defeat of the Teutonic Knights at the Battle of Tannenberg by a combined force of Polish and Lithuanian troops.

1453

Constantinople falls to the Ottoman Turks, heralding the end of the already fragmented Byzantine empire.

1480s

Height of the so-called Gothic style of knightly armor.

1490s

Formation of the Landsknechts light infantry units by Austrian Emperor Maximilian I, based on a Swiss model. Their organization and tactical discipline pave the way for modern armies.

Landsknechts

1525

Defeat of the French by the Spanish at the Battle of Pavia proves the increased importance of firearms and the diminished significance of chivalric knights.

1526

Babur, descendant of Tamerlane, rides into India from Afghanistan and founds the Mughal dynastic empire. His successors make great use of war elephants.

c.1530

Invention of the wheel-lock mechanism for generating a spark and so firing a musket.

Wheel-Lock Mechanism

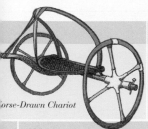

Horse-Drawn Chariot

1570–1069 BCE

The New Kingdom in ancient Egypt, in which population and culture are thoroughly militarized and the country enjoys a Golden Age of wealth and power.

Battle of Salamis

1275 BCE

Battle of Kadesh is fought between Egyptians and Hittites, both sides using a large number of charioteers.

c.1200 BCE

Supposed era of the Trojan War, described by Homer writing about four centuries later.

480 BCE

Battle of Salamis between a Greek fleet commanded by Themistocles and a Persian fleet under Xerxes I. Persian ships are lured close enough for Greek boarding parties to prove their superior hand-to-hand fighting techniques

334 BCE

Invasion of Persia by Alexander the Great, who triumphs partly because of a new style of warfare.

The Fall of Persia

240 BCE

Construction by Archias of Corinth of the *Syracusia*, probably the largest ship of ancient times, designed by Archimedes.

49 BCE

Last great Roman siege, at Massilia (now Marseilles, France), by Gaius Trebonius.

Siege at Massilia

1095

Pope Urban II calls for concerted action to recover the Holy Land from Muslim rule: the result is the First Crusade, and the capture of Jerusalem by the Crusaders four years later.

1187

Final capture of Jerusalem under siege by Saladin, commander of the Saracens, thus prompting the Third Crusade, in which King Richard the Lionheart is much involved.

Richard the Lionheart

1346

Mongols besiege the Genoese Black Sea trading port of Caffa, using their own dead as missiles catapulted over the walls. The siege is raised, but the Genoese return home carrying with them the Black Death.

Chinese Cannon

14th century

Cannon first appear in China, replacing gunpowder flame-throwers.

16th century

Considerable development in the design and structure of fortifications, beginning early in the century in Italy.

1511

Completion of the construction of Henry VIII's flagship the *Mary Rose*, one of the first ships able to fire a broadside using cannon mounted behind gunports.

1521

The Spanish rapidly overwhelm the Aztecs with their far superior military technology, despite being heavily outnumbered.

1577

Construction of the first "race-built" English galleon, the *Revenge*, at Deptford. Eleven years later, she becomes Sir Francis Drake's flagship against the Spanish Armada.

1603

Tokugawa Ieyasu is appointed shogun in Japan and sets up a government in Edo (Tokyo)—the role of the samurai becomes more political and less military.

1611

Accession of Gustavus Adolphus to the throne of Sweden, who immediately sets about introducing advanced developments in military tactics.

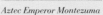

Aztec Emperor Montezuma

Timeline 3000 BCE to 1865 CE

1618

Beginning of the highly destructive Thirty Years War, initially a conflict of Christian religious denominational ideologies but increasingly a war over political and national interests.

The Thirty Years War

1630

Official dimensions of barrel length are established in England for the musket, the caliver, the arquebus and the carbine.

1632

Publication of the English translation of Ludovico Melzo's *Military Rules for the Cavalry*, which focuses particularly on the tactical deployment of troops on the field of battle. Publication the same year of the similar work, *Militarie Instructions for the Cavallrie*, by John Cruso.

1677

Grenades are formally added to the weaponry of the British Army.

1704–1709

Victories at Blenheim, Ramillies, and Malplaquet by the charismatic and supremely skillful tactician the Duke of Marlborough, fighting against the French in support of Austrian claims to the Spanish throne.

1730s

Development by the French of the 74 ship of the line, a type of cannon-carrying warship soon copied by all the major maritime powers.

Ship of the Line

1756–1763

The Seven Years War—a war involving major European nations that spread to their various colonies overseas, thus effectively something of a World War.

1775

Beginning of the American War of Independence, in which light infantry troops are increasingly important to the British forces. The British Legion is established, and combines light cavalry and infantry, uniformed in green.

Light Cavalry

1805

Admiral Lord Nelson's fleet defeats a larger, combined fleet of French and Spanish ships in the decisive Battle of Trafalgar, demonstrating the supremacy in seamanship and tactics of the Royal Navy.

1813

Launching of the first steam-driven warship, the *Fulton*, constructed for the United States Steam Battery by Robert Fulton. It was another nine years before the Royal Navy used steam power at sea.

The Age of Steam

1836

Samuel Colt patents his six-shooter Colt revolver.

Colt Revolver

Samuel Colt

1839

Beginning of the First Opium (Anglo-Chinese) War in which British military technology triumphs over antiquated Chinese weaponry and tactics.

1853

Approval by the British War Department of the Enfield rifled musket (the rifle) for use by troops in the immediately forthcoming Crimean War.

1854

The Charge of the Light Brigade during the Battle of Balaclava is a disaster caused as much by outdated tactics as by poor leadership.

1861

Commissioning of HMS *Warrior*, the largest and contemporarily the most heavily armored "ironclad" warship afloat.

HMS Warrior

1642

Beginning of the English Civil War for which continental methods and tactics of combat are hastily imported by both sides.

English Civil War

1645

Formation under Thomas, Baron Fairfax, of the New Model Army as a professional military unit on the Parliamentarian side. Nicknamed "Ironsides" by the Royalists, the New Model Army's first real test is the Battle of Naseby on June 14.

17th century

Siegecraft attains maximum efficiency during the second half of the century.

1736

Accession of Ch'ien Lung as Manchu Emperor of China, and subsequent expansion of the Ch'ing dynasty empire.

1740–1748

War of the Austrian Succession—a war involving major European nations which demonstrated that paid mercenaries (no matter how experienced) and domestic conscripts (no matter in what quantity) were by no means as effective as a fully-trained professional home-grown army like the Prussian army.

1746

Battle of Culloden, at which the (Jacobite) forces of Prince Charles Edward Stewart are partly through tactical errors and poor leadership defeated by the (Hanoverian) forces of George II under the command of his brother, the Duke of Cumberland.

1794

First use of aerial reconnaissance, using manned balloons, by the French during the Revolutionary Wars.

Reconnaissance Balloons

1803–1815

The Napoleonic Wars, in which Napoleon Bonaparte, with his mainly conscript armies and a constantly changing set of allies, fights against a far more traditional but equally inconsistent group of European opponents, and on an unprecedented scale.

The Napoleonic Wars

1815

Defeat of Napoleon at Waterloo. Cavalry charges previously used successfully in battle by Napoleon are on this occasion badly supported by the infantry.

1836

Publication in the USA of D. H. Mahan's *Complete Treatise on Field Fortification*, 25 years later to become the standard manual on the subject for both sides in the American Civil War.

1855

Adoption by the Army and Militia of the United States of Colonel Hardee's *Rifle and Light Infantry Tactics*, based on a French military manual.

1856

End of the Crimean War, during the three years of which technological advances include telegraphic communication, the construction of temporary railroads for conveying material, and medical treatment involving chloroform.

1857

Invention of the bell tent (also known as the Sibley tent) by Henry H. Sibley, a graduate of West Point Military Academy, New York.

1861

Introduction of the Springfield Rifle Musket, the range and accuracy of which necessitates hasty changes in standard close-order battlefield infantry formations.

The Crimean War

1861–1865

The American Civil War demonstrates that the contemporarily most useful deployment of cavalry is in long-distance raids behind enemy lines: 19 Confederate and 15 Union raids by cavalry parties are carried out to great effect.

1862

US inventor Dr Richard Gatling patents the original six-barreled Gatling gun.

Gatling Gun

1864

Signing by 12 nations of the first Geneva Convention on humane conditions of warfare.

Glossary

ARQUEBUS A 15th-/16th-century muzzle-loading matchlock gun, forerunner of the musket and rifle.

BASCINET An open-faced metal helmet of medieval European knights, to which a visor and neckplate were added later.

BASTION An arrow-shaped outward-facing projection of the wall of a castle or fort, providing a wide-angled defensive position.

BIREME A Phoenician, Greek, and Roman sailing galley otherwise propelled by two banks of oarsmen.

BODKIN An Anglo-Saxon dagger with a square cross-sectioned point, a form later applied to medieval iron arrowheads.

BOW-CHASER A cannon mounted in the bow of a sailing warship in order to fire at the rigging of a ship being chased and so slow it down.

BREECH-LOADING WEAPON A gun in which the bullet or shell is loaded at the firing end of the barrel (farthest from the target); not a muzzle-loading weapon.

BROWN BESS Nickname for any of a series of flintlock muskets used by the British army between the 1720s and the 1850s.

BUCKLER A small, generally circular forearm shield popular in northern Europe between 1100 and 1600.

CARABINIERS Originally, troops armed with the short musket known in English as a carbine; later, a light infantry company or a unit of cavalry (or of the mounted police).

CARBINE Originally a shorter-barreled musket; later, a short-barreled rifle or a long-barreled handgun.

CARRACK A high-sterned oceangoing three- or four-masted sailing ship of western Europe in the 15th and 16th centuries.

CASCABLE The rear end of a cannon, comprising the knob, the neck, and the decorative band or fillet.

CATAPHRACTS Heavily armored cavalry troops originally of the ancient Persian empire, then of the Roman and Byzantine empires.

CHAPEL-DE-FER A rounded, broad-brimmed medieval battle helmet used by combatants in Europe in the 13th to 16th centuries.

CHASSEUR A member of a regiment of French light infantry or light cavalry; an American Civil War trooper who wore a similar uniform.

COIF A chain-mail garment that left the face open but covered the whole head, the neck, and the shoulders.

CORVUS A wooden bridge or ladder set at the prow of Roman warships and used for boarding enemy vessels.

CRANEQUIN A 14th-century device for drawing tight the cord of a crossbow by turning the handle of a toothed ratchet pulley wheel.

CRENELLATION The classic shape of castle battlements by which the tops of the walls are cut by rectangular gaps (*embrasures*) separated by rectangular masonry-work (*merlons*).

CUIRASS The major part of a suit of armor that protects the chest; also, the part that additionally protects the back.

DESTRIER A medieval knight's war horse.

DRAGOON Originally, an infantry soldier able in an emergency to ride a horse; later, a member of a light cavalry regiment.

DRAKKAR Late Viking longships otherwise known as dragon ships.

FALCHION A heavy, single-edged, wide-bladed sword generally with a curve to the point, used in Europe from the 11th to the 16th centuries.

FAULDS The shortish skirt-like part of a suit of armor that provides protection for the hips and thighs.

FLINTLOCK MUSKET A muzzle-loading smoothbore musket that relied on the flintlock mechanism to ignite the powder in its flashpan. *See* frizzen.

FRAMEA A jabbing spear used by early Germanic warriors.

FRANCISCA A throwing ax used by early Germanic tribes, notably the Franks.

FRIZZEN A piece of steel on the flashpan lid over the flashpan of a flintlock musket, which when struck by the flint generates a spark that ignites the powder in the flashpan, which in turn ignites the main charge in the combustion chamber.

GABIONS Wickerwork cylinders that may be packed with earth and staked together as cover for artillery gunners and snipers.

GLADIUS HISPANICUS Shortish double-edged stabbing sword encountered by the Romans in Gaulish Spain and quickly adopted by them throughout the empire.

GOEDENDAG A heavy spear with a knobbed club between shaft and blade, used primarily in Flanders in the early 14th century.

GORGET A collar or neckplate in a suit of armor; part of a military uniform for the same body area.

HACKBUT Variant spelling of arquebus, closer to the original Dutch *hakebus*, "hook gun."

HALBERD An ax-headed pole spear with a reverse-thrusting spike.

HAUBERK A loose-sleeved mail jacket.

HOOP AND STAVE BOMBARD A large-caliber cannon made by forging straight lengths (staves) of iron in cylindrical form held together by hoops.

HOPLITES Men of the ancient Greek city-states when dressed and equipped for war.

HUSSARS Originally, irregular units of light cavalry in early 15th-century Hungary; similar units elsewhere in Europe and in North America from the 17th century.

KATANA Curved Japanese single-edged sword best known as a samurai sword.

KERIS Short dagger or knife, its blade often curved and its handle often raked, from Indonesia and nearby countries.

KHOPESH The so-called "sickle sword" of ancient Egypt.

KOPIS A forward-curving Greek cavalry sword for slashing down at infantry, about 3 feet (1 meter) in length.

LUNETTE A free-standing defensive barrier, rampart, or outwork, originally semicircular in shape.

MACAHUITL An Aztec wooden club in which multiple blades of obsidian (volcanic glass) were embedded.

MACHICOLATION An opening in the floor or ceiling of a room in a stronghold, through which boiling liquids and rocks might be rained upon attackers below.

MANIPLE A division of a Roman legion.

MANTLETS Portable solid sections of a barricade that could be set up together to defend against arrows or other missiles during the Middle Ages.

MATCHLOCK MUSKET A musket that incorporated a mechanical means of touching a lit match to the priming powder in the flashpan, which ignited the main charge in the breech of the barrel.

MINIÉ BALL A special form of expanding bullet that could be used in the muzzle-loading rifles that then became popular in the Crimean and American Civil Wars.

MORTAR A muzzle-loaded tube with baseplate and firing pin, which lobs special shells (mortar rounds) at low velocity and in high arcs.

MOTTE-AND-BAILEY CASTLE A castle introduced to Britain by the Normans in 1066, comprising a mound with a ditch around it (the motte) and a fortified settlement (the bailey) on top.

MUZZLE-LOADING WEAPON A gun in which the bullet or shell is loaded via the top of the barrel (nearest the target); not a breech-loading weapon.

ONAGER A late Roman mobile siege engine that made use of staff sling technology, not unlike a small trebuchet.

PALSTAVE AX A Bronze Age ax in which the metal ax head has molded neck flanges to fit it to the wooden haft.

PAVISE A large shield with a central vertical ridge on the outside. Used by medieval soldiers, especially archers and crossbowmen.

PELTAST An ancient Greek light infantryman who carried a wicker shield called a *pelte*.

PENTEKONTER An early Greek warship rowed by 25 oarsmen on each side.

PETRARY Any kind of medieval siege engine that hurled rocks—such as a mangonel or a trebuchet.

PILUM A heavy throwing spear much like a javelin with a pyramidal head, used by Roman legionaries.

POLEYNS Knee-protecting plates or structures in a suit of armor.

PRIMING PAN The flashpan of a musket in which the initial spark ignites the priming powder, which in turn ignites the main charge in the breech of the barrel.

QUARREL A square-headed bolt fired from a crossbow.

QUILLONS Two projections that form a basic hand guard on a sword.

QUINQUIREME A Greek and Roman sailing galley otherwise propelled by five banks of oarsmen.

REDAN A V-shaped outward-facing projection of the wall of a castle, fort, or lunette, providing a wide-angled defensive position.

RERE-BRACES The parts of a suit of armor that protect the upper arms.

REVETMENT A structure or projection on a wall intended to absorb the energy of incoming missiles and explosives.

RIBAULDQUIN An early 14th- and 15th-century multibarreled gun that fired a simultaneous volley of iron shot. Also called an organ gun.

RONDEL A long, slim, medieval dagger with a rounded handle or pommel. Also, any rounded defensive piece of a suit of armor.

SABATONS Parts of a suit of armor intended to cover and protect the feet.

SAPPING Digging a trench or tunnel to attack or undermine the defenses of a besieged stronghold.

SCUTUM The semi-cylindrical shield used by Roman legions.

SEAX/SCRAMASAX Large cutting knife worn by men in central, northern, and western Europe (notably Saxons and Franks) during the Dark Ages.

SNAPHAUNCE LOCK An early form of the flintlock musket firing mechanism without a specific steel flashpan lid. *See* frizzen.

SNEKKE The smallest and most common longship of the Viking fleet.

SPENCER RIFLE A manually operated lever-action repeating rifle adopted by the Union Army during the American Civil War.

TRIREME A Phoenician, Greek, and Roman sailing galley otherwise propelled by three banks of oarsmen.

TRUNNION One of a pair of rests on which a gun can be pivoted.

Bibliography

Barber, R and Barker, J, *Tournaments: Jousts, Chivalry and Pageants in the Middle Ages*, The Boydell Press, Woodbridge, 1989

Blackmore, H L, *Guns and Rifles of the World*, London, 1965

Blair, C, *European Armor c.1066 – c.1700*, Batsford, London, 1979

Brown, R A (ed.), *Castles: a History and Guide*, Blandford, Poole, 1980

Capwell, T, *The Real Fighting Stuff*, Glasgow Museums, 2007

Casson, L, *The Ancient Mariners: Seafarers and Seafighters of the Mediterranean in Ancient Times* (second edition), Princeton University Press, 1991

Chandler, D, *The Art of War in the Age of Marlborough*, London, 1976

Chandler, D, *The Campaigns of Napoleon*, London, 1967

Chase, K, *Firearms: A Global History to 1700*, University of Cambridge Press, 2003

Chenevix Trench, C, *A History of Marksmanship*, Follett, 1972

Connolly, P, *Greece and Rome at War*, Macdonald, 1981

Cruso, J, *Militarie Instructions for the Cavallerie*, Cambridge 1632; reprinted Kineton, 1972, with commentary by Brig. P Young

Davis, Maj. G B et al, *The Official Military Atlas of the Civil War*, Government Printing Office, Washington, 1891–1895

Dawson, D, *Origins of Western Warfare*, Westview, 1996

Dawson, D, *The First Armies*, Cassell, 2001

Drews, R, *The End of the Bronze Age*, Princeton, 1995

Drews, R, *Early Riders: The Beginnings of Mounted Warfare*, Taylor and Francis, 2004

Duffy, C, *Fire and Stone: the Science of Fortress Warfare 1660–1860*, Newton Abbot, 1975

Duffy, C, *Frederick the Great: A Military Life*, London, 1985

Duffy, C, *The Army of Frederick the Great*, Newton Abbot, 1974

Duffy, C, *The Army of Maria Theresa*, Doncaster, 1990

Duffy, C, *The Military Experience in the Age of Reason*, London, 1987

Edge, D, and Paddock, J M, *Arms and Armour of the Medieval Knight*, Bison Books, London, 1991

Edgerton, R, *Death or Glory: The Legacy of the Crimean War*, Westview, Boulder, Colorado, 1999

Ferrell, J, *The Dr Leo S Figiel Collection of Mogul Arms*, Butterfield & Butterfield, San Francisco, 1998.

Ferrill, A, *The Origins of War: From the Stone Age to Alexander the Great*, Perseus, 1997

Field, R, *American Civil War Fortifications (2): Land and field fortifications*, Osprey Publishing, 2005

France, J, *Western Warfare in the Age of the Crusades 1000–1300*, Cornell Press, Ithaca New York, 1999

Gabriel, R A, *Genghis Khan's Greatest General: Subotai the Valiant*, Praeger, 2004

Gernet, J, *A History of Chinese Civilization*, University of Cambridge Press, 1985

Gillingham, J, *Richard the Lionheart*, Weidenfeld & Nicolson, London, 1989

Glover, M, *Warfare in the Age of Bonaparte*, London, 1980

Goldsworthy, A, *The Complete Roman Army*, Thames & Hudson, 2003

Goldsworthy, A, *Roman Warfare*, HarperCollins, 2005

Griffith, P, *The Art of War in Revolutionary France*, London, 1998

Grose, G, *Military Antiquities Respecting a History of the English Army, with a Treatise on Ancient Armor and Weapons*, London, 1801

Guilmartin Jr., J F, *Gunpowder and Galleons: Changing Technology and Mediterrean Warfare at Sea in the Sixteenth Century* (revised edition), The United States Naval Institute, Annapolis, Maryland, 2003

Hamilton, E P, *The French Army in America and... The Musket Drill of 1755*, Ottowa, 1967

Hanson, V, *The Western Way of War*, California, 1989

Hardee's Rifle and Light Infantry Tactics, J. O. Kane, Publisher, 126 Nassau Street, New York, 1862

Hardy, R and Strickland, M, *The Great Warbow*, The History Press, 2005

Hartog, L de, *Genghis Khan*, IB Tauris, London, 1999

Haythornthwaite, P J, *The English Civil War 1642–1651: An Illustrated Military History*, Poole, 1983

Haythornthwaite, P J, *Napoleonic Weapons and Warfare: Napoleonic Cavalry*, London, 2001, and *Napoleonic Infantry*, London, 2001

Hooper, N and Bennett, M, *Cambridge Atlas of Warfare: The Middle Ages 768–1492*, Cambridge University Press, 1996

Hughes, Maj. Gen. B P, *Firepower:Weapons Effectiveness in the Battlefield 1630–1850*, London, 1974

Hughes, Maj. Gen. B P, *Open Fire: Artillery Tactics from Marlborough to Wellington*, Chichester, 1983

Johnson, R U (ed.) et al, *Battles and Leaders of the Civil War*, four volumes, Thomas Yoseloff, New York, 1956

Keen, M, *Chivalry*, Yale University Press, New Haven and London, 1984

Kemp, A, *Weapons and Equipment of the Marlborough Wars*, Poole, 1980

Knight, I, *The Anatomy of the Zulu Army*, Greenhill, London, 1995

Lane-Poole, S, *Saladin and the Fall of Jerusalem*, Greenhill, London, 2002

Lavery, B, *Nelson's Navy: The Ships, Men, and Organization, 1793–1815*, The United States Naval Institute, Annapolis, Maryland, 1989

Murphey, R, *Ottoman Warfare 1500–1700*, UCL Press, London, 1999

Nafziger, G F, *Imperial Bayonets: Tactics of the Napoleonic Battery, Battalion and Brigade as found in Contemporary Regulations*, London and Mechanicsburg, 1996

Newark, T, *Warlords*, Arms and Armour Press, London, 1996

Nicolle, D, *Medieval Warfare Source Book, Volume 1 and 2*, Arms and Armour Press, London, 1995, 1996

Nordhoff, C, *Man-of-War Life*, The United States Naval Institute, Annapolis, Maryland, 1985

Norman, A V B, and Pottinger D, *English Weapons and Warfare 449–1669*, Dorset Press, New York, 1966

Nosworthy, B, *Battle Tactics of Napoleon and his Enemies*, London, 1995

Oakeshott, E, *The Archaeology of Weapons*, Lutterworth Press, 1960

Parker, G, *The Military Revolution*, University of Cambridge Press, 1996

Paterson, W F, *A Guide to the Crossbow*, Society of Archer-Antiquaries, 1990

Peterson, H L, *Arms and Armor in Colonial America 1526–1783*, Dover Publications, 2000

Peterson, H L, *The Book of the Gun*, Hamlyn, 1968

Robinson, F, *Islamic World*, University of Cambridge Press, 1996

Rose, S, *Medieval Naval Warfare, 1000–1500*, Routledge, New York, 2002

Rothenberg, G E, *The Art of War in the Age of Napoleon*, London, 1977

Rules for the Management and Cleaning of the Rifle Musket, Model 1863 for the Use of Soldiers, Government Printing Office, Washington, 1863

Sinclaire, C, *Samurai*, Salamander, London, 2001

Sprague, M, *Norse Warfare: Unconventional Battle Strategies of the Ancient Viking*, Hippocrene Books Inc., New York, 2007

Stone, G C, *A Glossary of the Construction, Decoration, and Use of Arms and Armor*, New York, 1961

Taylor, C, *The American Indian*, Salamander, London, 2002

Todd, F P, *American Military Equipage, 1851–1872, Volumes I & II*, The Company of Military Historians, Providence, Rhode Island, 1974–77

Tucker, S, *Arming the Fleet: U.S. Navy Ordnance in the Muzzle-Loading Era*, The United States Naval Institute, Annapolis, Maryland, 1989

Turnbull, S, *Samurai: The Warrior Tradition*, Arms and Armour Press, London, 1996

Turnbull, S, *The Samurai Sourcebook*, Weidenfeld & Nicolson, 2000

Turner, J, *Pallas Armata: Military Essays...*, London 1683, reprinted New York, 1968

Vale, M G A, *War and Chivalry: Warfare and Aristocratic Culture in England, France, and Burgundy at the end of the Middle Ages*, University of Georgia Press, 1981

Wagner, E, *Cut and Thrust Weapons*, London, 1967

Wagner, E, *European Weapons and Warfare 1618–48*, London, 1979

Warry, J, *Warfare in the Classical World*, Oklahoma, 1995

Windham, W, *A Plan of Discipline composed of the use of the Militia of the County of Norfolk*, London, 1759, reprinted Ottowa, 1969

"W.T.", *The Compleat Gunner*, London 1672, reprinted Wakefield, 1971

Index

Index

Acknowledgments

Consultant editor

TIM NEWARK is widely published in the field of military history, with publications including *Highlander* (2010), *The Fighting Irish* (2012), and *Camouflage* (2007). Former editor of *Military Illustrated*, he has served as a historical consultant to the Royal Mail, in addition to writing multiple television documentary series including Heroes & Weapons of WW2.
Contribution: The Wider World, Anatomy of a Phalanx, Anatomy of a Roman Siege.

Contributors

MATTHEW BENNETT is a senior lecturer at the Royal Military Academy, Sandhurst, UK. He has written many academic articles on chivalric and crusader warfare, and his publications include *The Cambridge Atlas of Warfare: The Middle Ages 768–1487*.
Contribution: Medieval Warfare.

DR DOYNE DAWSON studied ancient history at Princeton and military history at West Point. He is Professor of International Affairs at Sejong University, Seoul, Korea, and has written key works on the origins of warfare.
Contribution: The Ancient Way of War, Rome and Her Enemies, The Dark Ages, Viking Invaders.

RON FIELD was awarded a Fulbright Scholarship in 1982 and was associate editor of the Confederate Historical Society of Great Britain from 1983 to 1992. He was elected a Fellow of the Company of Military Historians, based in Washington, DC, in 2005, and his publications on the American Civil War are highly regarded.
Contribution: The Harbinger of the Modern Battlefield, War at Sea.

PHILIP HAYTHORNTHWAITE is an internationally respected author and historical consultant specializing in the military history, uniforms, and equipment of the 18th and 19th centuries. The Napoleonic Period is his main area of research, and he has published over 40 military titles.
Contribution: The Firearms Revolution, The Flintlock at War.

MIKE LOADES is a military historian and historical weapons expert best known for his appearances in dozens of television documentaries. He is author of *Swords and Swordsmen* (2010), *The Longbow* (2013), and *The Composite Bow* (2016).
Contribution: Revolutions in Arms and Armor, Introduction.

All illustrations have been reproduced from the following, except where noted below:

Boutell, Charles, *Arms and Armour in Antiquity and the Middle Ages*, London, Reeves & Turner, 1874

Burton, Sir Thomas, F, *The Book of the Sword*, London, Chatto & Windus, 1884 (Modern edition published by Dover Publications, New York, 1987)

Clark, Geo T, *Medieval Military Architecture Vol 1 and 2*, London, Wyman & Sons, 1884

Colomb, Vice Admiral P H, *Naval Warfare*, London, W H Allen & Co, 1899

Demmin, Auguste, *An Illustrated History of Arms and Armour from the Earliest Period to the Present Time*, London, George Bell & Sons, 1877

Du Chaillu, Paul B, *The Viking Age Vol 1 and 2*, New York, Charles Scribner's Sons, 1890

Farrow, Edward S, *Farrow's Military Encyclopaedia Vol 1 to 3*, New York, 1885

Fox, Frank, *The Story of the British Navy*, London, Adam & Charles Black, 1913

Grant, James, *British Battles On Land And Sea Vol 1 to 3*, Cassell Petter & Galpin, 1897

Heck, J G, *Iconographic Encyclopaedia of Science, Literature & Art*, New York, Rudolphe Garrigue, 1851

Hottenroth, Friedrich, *Le Costume Chez Les Peuples Anciens et Modernes*, Paris, Armand Guérinet, 1890

Hottenroth, Friedrich, *Trachten, Haus-, Feld-und Kriegsgeräthschaften der Völker alter und neuer Zeit*, Stuttgart, Verlag von Gustav Weise, 1884

Hugo, Herman, *De Militia Equestri Antiqua Et Nova... Libri Quinque*, B. Moreti, 1630

Payne-Gallwey, Sir Ralph, *A Summary of the History, Construction and Effects in Warfare of the Projectile-Throwing Engines of the Ancients: With a Treatise on the Structure, Power and Management of Turkish and Other Oriental Bows of Mediaeval and Later Times*, Longmans, Green & Co, London, 1907

Payne-Gallwey, Sir Ralph, *The Crossbow*, 1903 (Modern edition published by Dover Publications, New York, 1995)

Racinet, Albert, *Le Costume Historique*, Paris, Librairie de Firmin-Didot et cie, 1888

Rules for the Management and Cleaning of the Rifle Musket Model 1863

Schmidt, Rodolphe, *Les Armes A Feu Portatives, leur Origine et leur Developpement Historique et Technique*, Paris, 1877